NETWORKS, ROUTERS AN
FUNCTION, PERFORMANCE

TRANSPUTER AND OCCAM* ENGINEERING SERIES

Editors
M. Jane, J. Hulskamp, P. Welch, D. Stiles and T.L. Kunii

Volume 32

Previously published in this series:

A. Allen (Ed.), Transputer Systems – Ongoing Research (WoTUG-15)
J. Edwards (Ed.), Occam and the Transputer – Current Developments (WoTUG-14)
P. Welch, D. Stiles, T.L. Kunii and A. Bakkers (Eds.), Transputing '91
H.S.M. Zedan (Ed.), Real-Time Systems with Transputers (OUG-13)
S.J. Turner (Ed.), Tools and Techniques for Transputer Applications (OUG-12)
J. Wexler (Ed.), Developing Transputer Applications (OUG-11)
A. Bakkers (Ed.), Applying Transputer Based Parallel Machines (OUG-10)
C. Askew (Ed.), Occam and the Transputer – Research and Applications (OUG-9)
J. Kerridge (Ed.), Developments Using Occam (OUG-8)
T. Muntéan (Ed.), Parallel Programming of Transputer Based Machines (OUG-7)
G.L. Reijns and J. Luo (Eds.), Transputing in Numerical and Neural Network Applications
H. Webber (Ed.), Image Processing and Transputers
L. Annell and M. Törngren (Eds.), Nordic Transputer Applications
A.M. Veronis and Y. Paker (Eds.), Transputer Research and Applications 5 (NATUG-5)
D.L. Fielding (Ed.), Transputer Research and Applications 4 (NATUG-4)
A.S. Wagner (Ed.), Transputer Research and Applications 3 (NATUG 3)
J.A. Board, Jr. (Ed.), Transputer Research and Applications 2 (NATUG 2)
G.S. Stiles (Ed.), Transputer Research and Applications 1 (NATUG 1)
M.R. Jane, R.J. Fawcett, T.P. Mawby (Eds.), Transputer Applications – Progress and Prospects
M. Valero, E. Oñate, M. Jane, J.L. Larriba and B. Suárez (Eds.), Parallel Computing and Transputer Applications
T.S. Durrani, J.J. Soraghan, W.A. Sandham and S.M. Forbes (Eds.), Applications of Transputers 3
D.J. Pritchard and C.J. Scott (Eds.), Applications of Transputers 2
L. Freeman and C. Phillips (Eds.), Applications of Transputers 1
J. Hulskamp and D. Jones (Eds.), Transputers and Parallel Applications (ATOUG-5)
J. Hulskamp, T. Bossomaier and T. Hintz (Eds.), The Transputer in Australasia 2 (ATOUG-4)
T. Bossomaier, T. Hintz and J. Hulskamp (Eds.), The Transputer in Australasia (ATOUG-3)
S. Noguchi and H. Umeo (Eds.), Transputer/Occam Japan 4
T.L. Kunii and D. May (Eds.), Transputer/Occam Japan 3 (OUGJ-3)
H. Neishlos (Ed.), Parallel Processing: Technology and Applications

ISSN: 0925-4986

inmos®

Networks, Routers and Transputers:

Function, Performance, and Applications

Edited by: M.D. May
P.W. Thompson
P.H. Welch

SGS-THOMSON MICROELECTRONICS
INMOS is a member of the SGS–THOMSON Microelectronics Group

IOS Press

1993

Amsterdam • Oxford • Washington • Tokyo

ISBN 90 5199 129 0

Publisher:

IOS Press
Van Diemenstraat 94
1013 CN Amsterdam
Netherlands

Distributor in the USA and Canada:

IOS Press, Inc.
P.O. Box 10558
Burke, VA 22009-0558
USA

Distributor in the UK and Ireland:

IOS Press/Lavis Marketing
73 Lime Walk
Headington
Oxford OX3 7AD
England

Distributor in Japan:

Kaigai Publications, Ltd.
21 Kanda Tsukasa-Cho 2-Chome
Chiyoda-Ka
Tokyo 101
Japan

Printed in Great Britain by Bell and Bain Ltd., Glasgow

Preface

High speed networks are an essential part of public and private telephone and computer communications systems. An important new development is the use of networks within electronic systems to form the connections between boards, chips and even the subsystems of a chip. This trend will continue over the 1990s, with networks becoming the preferred technology for system interconnection.

Two important technological advances have fuelled the development of interconnection networks. First, it has proved possible to design high–speed links able to operate reliably between the terminal pins of VLSI chips. Second, high levels of component integration permit the construction of VLSI routers which dynamically route messages via their links. These same two advances have allowed the development of embedded VLSI computers to provide functions such as network management and data conversion.

Networks built from VLSI routers have important properties for system designers. They can provide high data throughput and low delay; they are scalable up to very large numbers of terminals; and they can support communication on all of their terminals at the same time. In addition, the network links require only a small number of connection points on chips and circuit boards. The most complex routing problems are moved to the place where they can be done most easily and economically – within the VLSI routers.

The first half of this book brings together a collection of topics in the construction of communication networks. The first chapters are concerned with the technologies for network construction. They cover the design of networks in terms of standard links and VLSI routing chips, together with those aspects of the transputer which are directly relevant to its use for embedded network computing functions. Two chapters cover performance modelling of links and networks, showing the factors which must be taken into consideration in network design.

The second half of the book brings together a collection of topics in the application of communication networks. These include the design of interconnection networks for high–performance parallel computers, and the design of parallel database systems. The final chapters discuss the construction of large–scale networks which meet the emerging ATM protocol standards for public and private communications systems.

The 1990s will see the progressive integration of computing and communications: networks will connect computers; computers will be embedded within networks; networks will be embedded within computers. Thus this book is intended for all those involved in the design of the next generation of computing and communications systems.

February 1993

Credits

This book has been assembled from a number of sources. The authors of the chapters are as follows:

Chapter 1	M.D. May and P.W. Thompson
Chapter 2	M.D. May, R.M. Shepherd and P.W. Thompson
Chapter 3	M. Simpson and P.W. Thompson
Chapter 4	H. Gurney and C.P.H. Walker
Chapter 5	J.M. Wilson
Chapter 6	C. Barnaby, V.A. Griffiths and P.W. Thompson
Chapter 7	C. Barnaby and M.D. May
Chapter 8	C. Barnaby, M.D. May and D.A. Nicole
Chapter 9	J.M. Kerridge
Chapter 10	C. Barnaby and N. Richards
Chapter 11	C.J. Adams, J.W. Burren, J.M. Kerridge, P.F. Linnington, N. Richards and P.H. Welch
Appendix A	C.P.H. Walker
Appendix B	C.P.H. Walker
Appendix C	R. Francis
Appendix D	R. Francis

The editors would also like to thank all those who assisted with the preparation of the manuscript, particularly Alan Pinder and Glenn Hill of the INMOS documentation group, who provided vital support for the use of the document preparation system.

Work on this subject has been supported under various ESPRIT projects, in particular 'Parallel Universal Message-passing Architecture' (PUMA, P2701), and more recently also under the 'General Purpose MIMD' (P5404) project. The assistance of the EC is gratefully acknowledged.

Contents

1 Transputers and Routers: Components for Concurrent Machines

1.1 Introduction

This chapter describes an architecture for concurrent machines constructed from two types of component: 'transputers' and 'routers'. In subsequent chapters we consider the details of these two components, and show the architecture can be adapted to include other types of component.

A transputer is a complete microcomputer integrated in a single VLSI chip. Each transputer has a number of communication links, allowing transputers to be interconnected to form concurrent processing systems. The transputer instruction set contains instructions to send and receive messages through these links, minimizing delays in inter-transputer communication. Transputers can be directly connected to form specialised networks, or can be interconnected via routing chips. Routing chips are VLSI building blocks for interconnection networks: they can support system-wide message routing at high throughput and low delay.

1.2 Transputers

VLSI technology enables a complete computer to be constructed on a single silicon chip. The INMOS T800 transputer [1], integrates a central processor, a floating point unit, four kilobytes of static random access memory plus an interface for external memory, and a communications system onto a chip about 1 square centimetre in area.

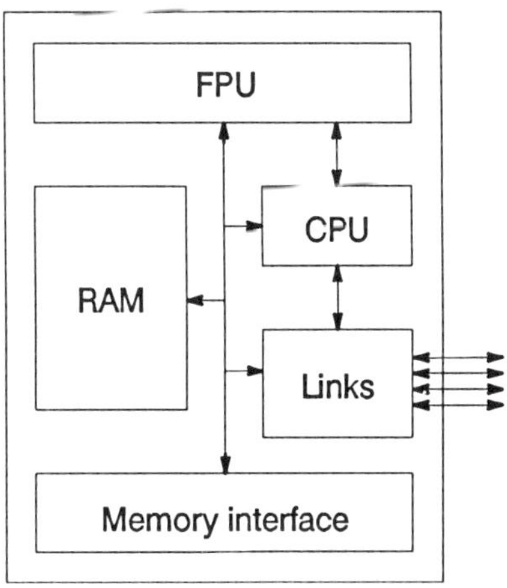

T800 Transputer

As a microcomputer, the transputer is unusual in that it has the ability to communicate with other transputers via its communication links; this enables transputers to be connected together to construct multiprocessor systems to tackle specific problems. The transputer is also unusual in that it has the ability to execute many software processes, sharing its time between them automatically, to create new processes rapidly, and to perform communication between processes within a transputer and between processes in different transputers. All of these capabilities are integrated into the hardware of the transputer, and are very efficient. This is discussed in more detail in chapter 2.

The use of transputers for parallel programming has been greatly simplified by the development of the occam programming language [2]. The occam language allows an application to be expressed as a collection of concurrent processes which communicate via channels. Each channel is a point-to-point connection between two processes; one process always inputs from the channel and the other always outputs to it. Communication is synchronised; the first process ready to communicate waits until the second is also ready, then the data is copied from the outputting processes to the inputting process and both processes continue.

Each transputer has a process scheduler which allows it to share its time between a number of processes. Communication between processes on the same transputer is performed using the local memory; communication between processes on different transputers is performed using a link between the two transputers. Consequently, a program can be executed either by a single transputer or by a collection of transputers connected in a network. Three different ways of using transputers to execute the component processes of a typical program are shown below.

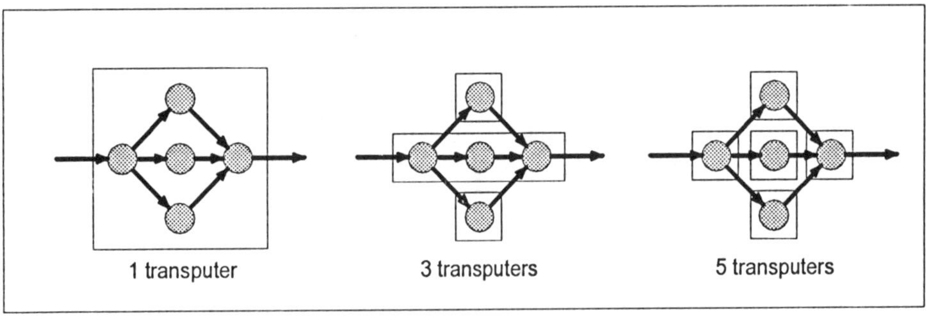

Figure 1.1 Allocations of processes to processors

Figure 1.1 shows the same collection of processes executed on three different specialised networks. In the first network, which is a single transputer, each communication channel connecting two processes is implemented using the local memory of the transputer. In the other examples some or all of the channels are implemented by physical links between different transputers.

Transputers have also been used to construct a number of general purpose computers, which all consist of an array of transputers connected together in a network. In some machines the network can be configured by software, for example by connecting the links via a programmable crossbar switch. Many applications have been successfully ported to these machines and have demonstrated efficient parallel processing.

One of the problems with existing general purpose transputer machines is the need to carefully match algorithms to the interconnection networks of specific machines, which results in a lack of software portability. It has become clear that a standard architecture is needed for these general purpose message-passing machines. An attractive candidate is a collection of transputers connected by a high throughput, low delay communication network supporting communication channels between processes anywhere in the network.

1.3 Routers

There are many parallel algorithms in which the number of communication channels between processes on different transputers is much greater than the number of physical links available to connect the transputers. In some of these algorithms, a process executed on one transputer must communicate with processes on a large number of other transputers. These requirements for system-wide communication between processes can be met by:

- new transputers including hardware to multiplex many 'virtual links' along a single physical link (see chapter 2)
- new VLSI message-routing chips (routers) which can be used to construct efficient communication networks

This new communications architecture allows communication channels to be established between any two processes, regardless of where they are physically located in the system. This simplifies programming because processes can be allocated to transputers to optimize performance after the program has been written. For general purpose message-passing computers, a further benefit is that processes can be allocated to transputers by a compiler, which effectively removes configuration details from the program, thereby enhancing portability.

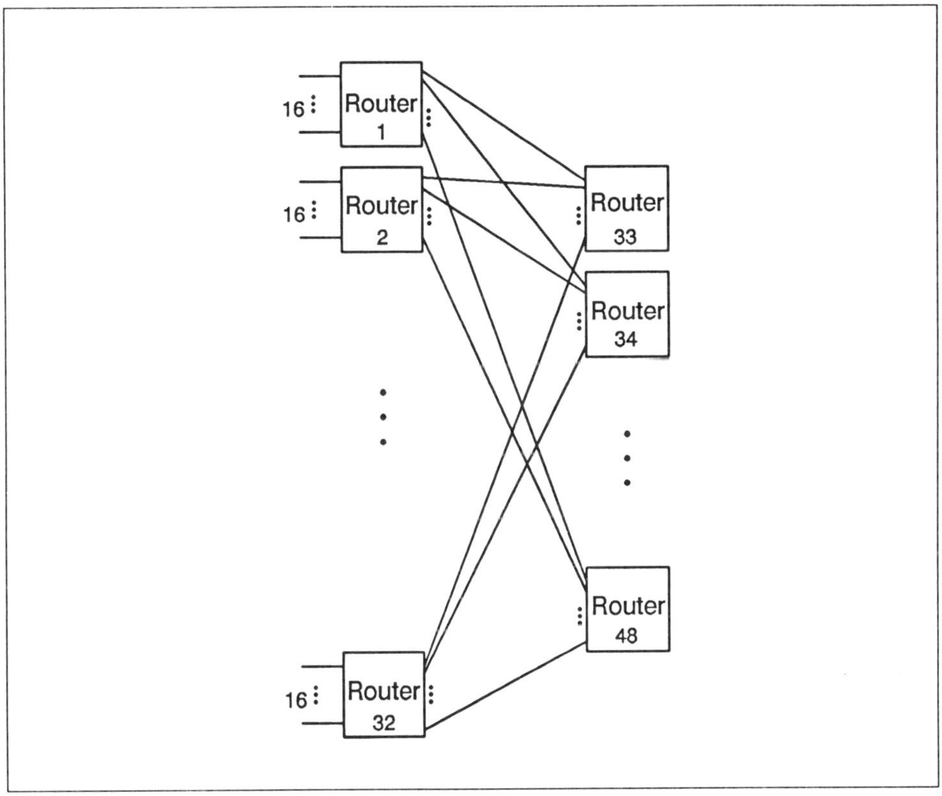

Figure 1.2 Network constructed from routers

The use of two separate chips, one to perform computing (the transputer) and one to perform communication (the router) has several practical advantages:

- Transputers can be directly connected without routers in systems which do not require message routing, so avoiding the silicon cost and routing delays.
- It allows routers to have many links (e.g.32) which in turn allows large networks to be constructed from a small number of routers, minimizing the delay through the network. For example, 48 such routers can connect 512 terminals with only 3 routing delays, as in figure 1.2.

- It avoids the need for messages to flow through the transputer, reducing the total throughput of the chip interface. This reduces the pin count, power consumption and package costs of the transputer.
- It supports scalable architectures in which communication throughput must be balanced with processing throughput. In such architectures, it is known that overall communication capacity must grow faster than the total number of processors - a larger machine must have proportionately more routers.

Since the new architecture allows all the virtual links of a transputer to pass through a single physical link, system-wide communication can be provided by connecting each transputer to a routing network via a single link. The provision of several links on transputers allows each transputer to be connected to several different networks. Examples of the use of this technique are:

- The use of two (or more) identical networks in parallel to increase throughput and fault–tolerance
- The use of a main network and an (independent) monitoring and debugging network
- The use of a main network and an independent network for input and output (or for access to discs)

Another technique for increasing the communications throughput is to construct the network using two (or more) links in parallel for each connection. An example of a 2-dimensional network of this kind is shown in figure 1.4.

In some cases, it is convenient to construct a network from routers and attach transputers to its terminal links. An example is the multi-stage network shown in figure 1.2. An alternative is to construct a network such as a hypercube or an array from a number of nodes, each node consisting of one or more transputers and a router as shown in figure 1.4.

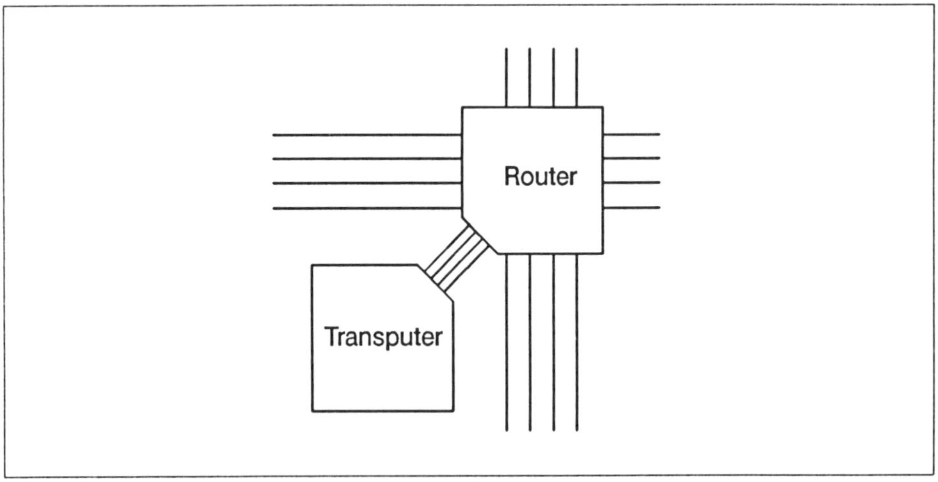

Figure 1.3 Node combining a transputer and a router

Operation of Routers

Each router has a number of communication links and operates as follows:

- It uses the header of each packet arriving on each link to determine the link to be used to output the packet;
- It arbitrates between two (or more) packets which must both be output through the same link, and causes them to be output one after another;

- It starts to output each packet as early as possible (immediately after the output link is determined, provided that the output link is not already in use for another packet).

The overall throughput of the router is determined by the number of links which can be operating concurrently. An important benefit of employing serial links for packet routing is that it is simple to implement a full crossbar switch in VLSI, even for a large number of links. Use of a full crossbar allows packets to be passing through all of the links at the same time.

The ability to start outputting a packet whilst it is still being input can significantly reduce delay, especially in networks which are lightly loaded. This technique is known as *wormhole routing.* In wormhole routing, the delay through the switch can be minimized by keeping headers short and by using fast, simple, hardware to determine the link to be used for output.

The use of simple routing hardware allows this capability to be provided for every link in the router. This avoids the need to share it between many links which would increase delay in the event of several packets arriving at once. Equally, it is desirable to avoid the need for the large number of packet buffers commonly provided in some packet routing systems (in which each packet is input to a buffer before output starts). The use of small buffers together with simple routing hardware allows a single VLSI chip to provide efficient routing between a large number of links.

The simple communications architecture allows a wide variety of implementations:

- CMOS VLSI can be used to construct routers with a large number of links;
- It is straightforward to combine transputers and small routers on a single chip;
- It is possible to construct routers in ECL or Gallium Arsenide technology to support extremely high speed implementations of the link.

For some purposes, it may be useful to combine a router together with each transputer in a single chip (or a single package). One example is the construction of a two dimensional array of simple transputers for image processing (for this application, no off-chip memory is needed, and most communication is local). The architecture of the routing system makes such a combination possible, as in figure 1.4.

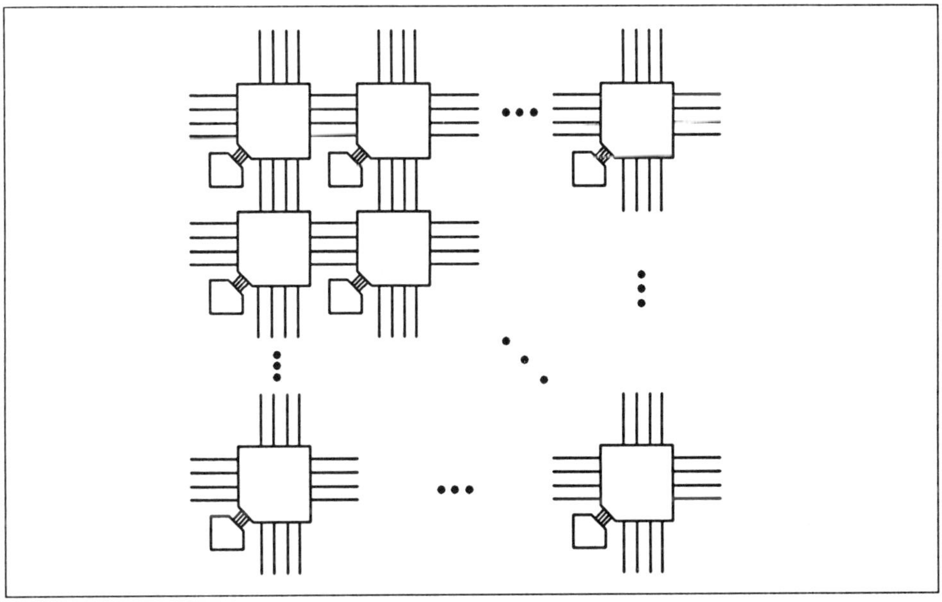

Figure 1.4 Two dimensional array of nodes

1.4 Message Routing

1.4.1 Avoiding Deadlock

The purpose of a communications network is to support efficient and reliable communication between processes. Consequently, an essential property of a communications network is that it should not deadlock, i.e. arrive in a state where further progress is impossible. However, deadlock can occur in most networks unless the routing algorithm is designed to prevent it. For example, consider the square of four nodes shown in figure 1.5. Suppose that every node attempts to send a packet to the opposite corner at the same time, and that the routing algorithm routes packets in a clockwise direction. Then each link will become 'busy' sending a packet to the adjacent corner and the network will deadlock.

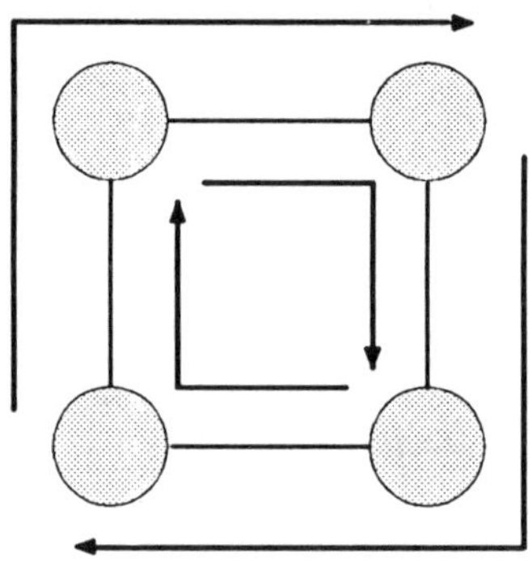

Figure 1.5 Deadlock in a simple network

It is important to understand that deadlock is a property of the network topology and the routing algorithm used; it can also arise with buffered packet routing. In the above example, a single packet buffer at each node is sufficient to remove the deadlock but, in general, the number of packet buffers needed to eliminate deadlock depends on the network topology, the routing algorithm and the applications program. This is clearly not a satisfactory basis for a general purpose routing system.

All of the above problems can be avoided by choosing networks for which deadlock-free wormhole routing algorithms exist. In such networks, buffers are employed only to smooth the flow of data through the network and to reduce congestion; often a buffer of size much less than the length of a packet is sufficient for this purpose. Most important of all, the buffering needed is not dependent on the network size or the applications program. It is possible to construct a single universal router which can be used for networks of arbitrary size and for programs of arbitrary complexity. An essential property of such a router is that, like a transputer, it can communicate on all of its links concurrently.

It turns out that many regular networks constructed from such routers have deadlock free routing algorithms. Important examples are trees, hypercubes and grids.

A deadlock free routing algorithm for Trees

A tree consists of a collection of nodes with a single external link from the root. Assume that two trees[1] T_1 with root link r_1 and T_2 with root link r_2 are both deadlock free; they will always perform internal communication without deadlock, and will accept and transmit packets along the root link without deadlock.

A new tree is formed by connecting the root links r_1 and r_2 to a new root node R; a further link r on this node is the root link of the newly constructed tree T.

Any packet arriving at R along r_1 is routed either to r_2 or to r. If it is routed to r_2, it will be consumed by T_2, because T_2 is deadlock free. If it is routed to r, it will eventually be consumed by the environment. By symmetry, packets arriving along r_1 will also be consumed. A packet arriving along r will be routed to either T_1 or T_2; in either case it will be consumed because both T_1 and T_2 are deadlock free.

It remains to show that a tree with only one node is deadlock free; this is true because the node can send and receive packets concurrently along its single (root) link.

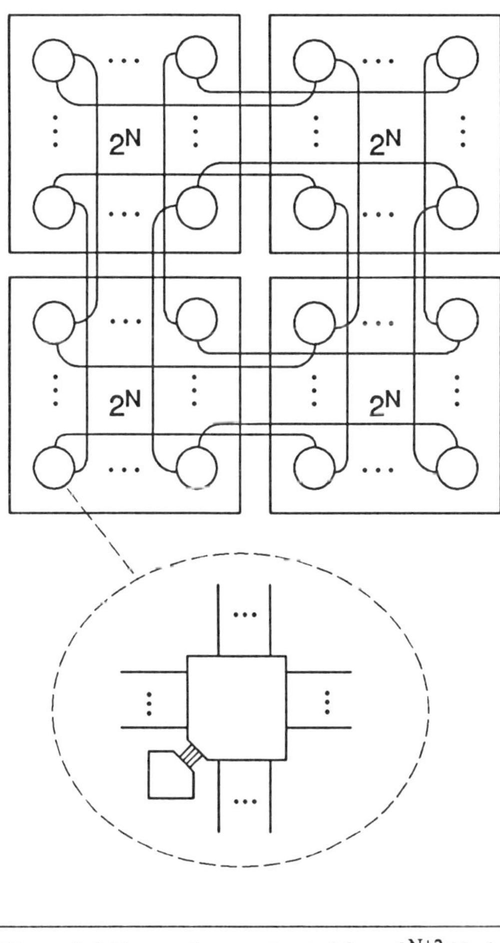

Figure 1.6 Hypercube constructed from 2^{N+2} Nodes

1. Note that this construction can easily be generalized from binary to n-ary trees.

A deadlock free routing algorithm for Hypercubes

To avoid deadlock in a hypercube, each packet is successively routed through the dimensions, starting from the highest.

A simple inductive argument can be used to show that this routing algorithm is free of deadlocks. Suppose that the order-N hypercube is deadlock free. Combine two such order-N hypercubes H_1 and H_2 to form an order-(N+1) hypercube by linking corresponding nodes of H_1 and H_2. Any packet originating at a node $\boldsymbol{n}$ in H_1 and destined for a node in H_2 will first travel along the link joining $\boldsymbol{n}$ to the corresponding node in H_2; from this node it will be delivered by routing within H_2 and this is deadlock free by assumption. Similarly, any packet originating at a node $\boldsymbol{n}$ in H_2 and destined for a node in H_1 will first travel along the link joining $\boldsymbol{n}$ to the corresponding node in H_1; from this node it will be delivered by routing within H_1 and this is deadlock free by assumption. An important property of the node is that it is able to send and receive along a link at the same time; this is needed to ensure that a packet can flow from node h_1 in H_1 to the corresponding node h_2 in H_2 at the same time as a packet flows into h_1 from h_2.

It remains to show that the order-0 hypercube is deadlock free (which it is, being just a single node)!

The effect of the routing algorithm can easily be understood in terms of the example shown in figure 1.5 above, which shows a 2–cube. Instead of routing all packets in a clockwise direction, the deadlock-free algorithm routes two of the packets anti-clockwise. Since the links are bi–directional this allows all of the packets to be routed without deadlock, as illustrated in figure 1.7.

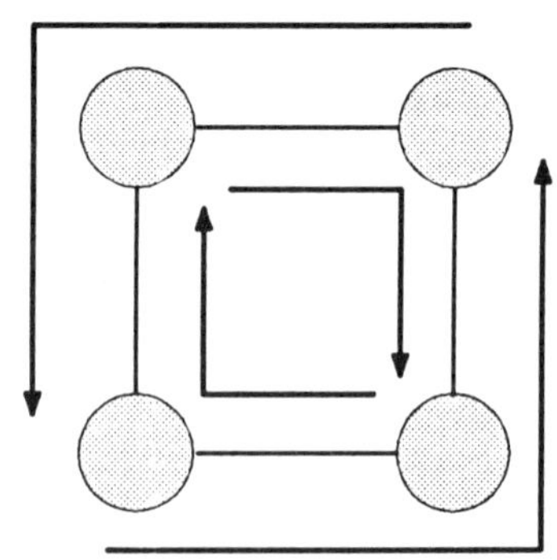

Figure 1.7 Avoiding deadlock in a simple network

The fact that the hypercube is symmetrical means that the order of sequencing through the dimensions does not matter; it is important only that every packet is sequenced in the same order.

A deadlock free routing algorithm for Arrays

The technique of routing a packet by systematically sequencing through the dimensions can be applied to any processor array. In fact, any rectangular processor array - whatever its size and dimension - is deadlock free! To prove this it is first necessary to establish that a line of processing nodes (a one-dimensional array) is deadlock free; this is guaranteed if a packet generated at a node takes the shortest path to its destination node.

A simple inductive argument similar to that used for the hypercube can now be used to establish that this routing algorithm is deadlock free.

1.5 Addressing

Every packet must carry with it the address of its destination; this might be the address of a transputer, or the address of one of a number of virtual channels forming input channels to a transputer. As a packet arrives at a router, the destination address must be inspected before the outgoing link can be determined; the delay through the router is therefore proportional to the address length. Further, the address must itself be transmitted through the network and therefore consumes network bandwidth.

It is therefore important that this address be as short as possible, both to optimize network latency and network bandwidth. However, it is also important that the destination link can be derived from the address quickly and with minimal hardware. An addressing system which meets both of these requirements is *interval labelling.*

1.5.1 Interval Labelling

An *interval labelling scheme* [6] assigns a distinct label to each transputer in a network. For simplicity, the labels for an N transputer network can be numbers in the range $[0,1,\ldots,N-1]$. At each router in the network, each output link has one or more associated *intervals*, where an interval is a set of consecutive labels. The intervals associated with the links on a router are non-overlapping and every label will occur in exactly one interval.

As a packet arrives at a router, the address is examined to determine which interval contains a matching label; the packet is then forwarded along the associated output link.

The interval labelling scheme requires minimal hardware; at most a pair of comparators for each of the outgoing links. It is also very fast, since the output link can be determined, once the address has been input, after only a single comparison delay provided all the comparisons are done concurrently.

There remains the question of how to assign labels to an arbitrary network. The following examples give labelings for networks constructed from nodes as shown in figure 1.3. Intervals are represented with the notation $[a,b)$, which means the set of labels greater than or equal to a and less than b; note however that the comparisons are performed modulo the total number of labels, and intervals are permitted to 'wrap around' through zero.

Trees can be labelled

The transputers in a binary tree[2] with N nodes are labelled as follows. Suppose there are L nodes to the left of the root node. Then the transputers to the left of the root are numbered $0,\ldots,L-1$; the transputer of the root node is labelled L; the transputers to the right are labelled $L+1,\ldots,N-1$,

Any node n in the tree is itself the root node of a subtree S with nodes $s_l,\ldots,s_h$. The interval associated with the left link of n is $[s_l,\ldots,n)$; that associated with the right link is $[n+1,\ldots,s_h+1)$; that associated with the root link is $[s_h+1,\ldots,s_l)$. The interval $[s_h+1,\ldots,s_l)$ consists of all of the labels in the tree apart from those in S; numerically it consists of the two intervals $[s_h+1,\ldots,N+1)$ and $[0,\ldots,s_l)$. An example is shown in figure 1.8. This shows the labels assigned to each node, and the intervals assigned to the links of two of the nodes.

2. This construction can easily be generalized from binary to general trees, as illustrated in figure 1.8.

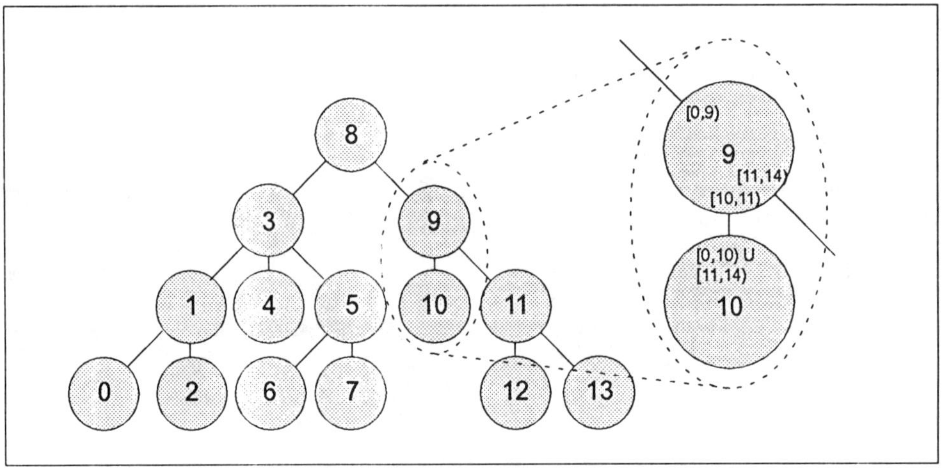

Figure 1.8 A Tree with Interval Labelling

Hypercubes can be labelled

The labelling of the hypercube follows the construction given for the deadlock free routing algorithm. In combining the two order-n hypercubes H_1 and H_2, the transputers in H_1 are labelled $0, \ldots, 2^n - 1$ and those in H_2 are labelled $2^n, \ldots, 2^{n+1} - 1$. The link from each node h_1 in H_1 to the corresponding node h_2 in H_2 is labelled with the interval $[2^n, \ldots, 2^{n+1})$ at h_1, and with $[0, \ldots, 2^n)$ at h_2. This inductively constructs a hypercube together with the deadlock-free routing algorithm described above.

Arrays can be labelled

The labelling for an array follows the construction of the deadlock free routing algorithm. An n-dimensional array is composed of m arrays of dimension $n-1$, with m corresponding nodes (one from each $n-1$ dimensional array) joined to form a line. If each of the $n-1$ dimensional arrays has p nodes, the nodes in the $n-1$ dimensional arrays are numbered $0, \ldots, p-1; p, \ldots, 2p-1; \ldots; (m-1)p, \ldots, mp-1$. On every line the link joining the ith node to the $(i+1)^{th}$ node is labelled $[ip, \ldots, mp)$ and the link to the $(i-1)^{th}$ node is labelled $[0, \ldots, (i-1)p)$. This inductively labels an array to route packets according to the deadlock free algorithm described above. An example is shown in figure 1.9. This shows the labels assigned to each node, and the intervals assigned to the links of one of the nodes.

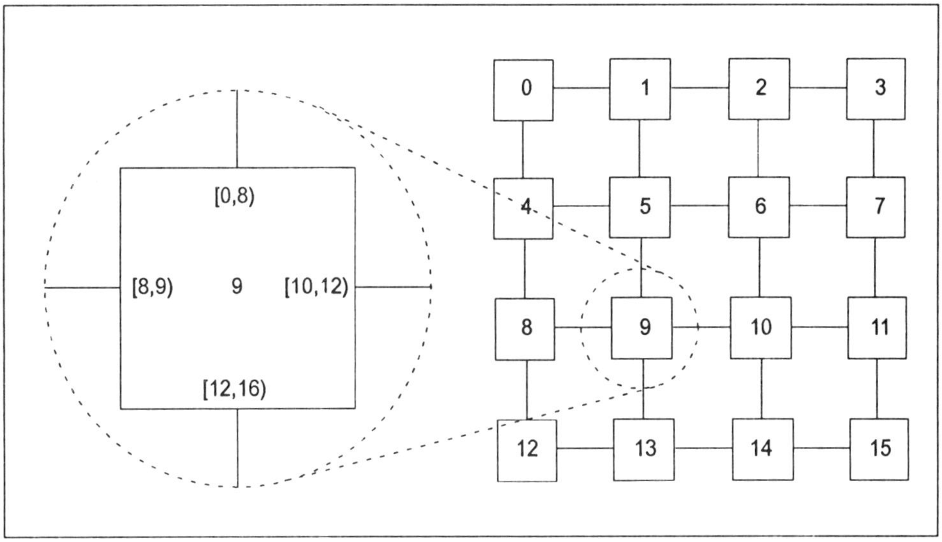

Figure 1.9 An Array with Interval Labelling

Labelling arbitrary networks

The above labelings provide optimal routing, so that each packet takes one of the shortest paths to its destination. It can easily be shown [6] that any network can be labelled so as to provide deadlock free routing; it is only necessary to construct a spanning tree and label it as described above. This may produce a non-optimal routing which cannot exploit all of the links present in the network as a whole. Optimal labelings are known for all of the networks shown below:

trees
hypercubes
arrays
multi-stage networks
butterfly networks
rings[3]

In high performance embedded applications (or in reconfigurable computers) specialised networks are often used to minimize interconnect costs or to avoid the need for message routing. In these systems, a non-optimal labelling can be used to provide low-speed system-wide communications such as would be needed for system configuration and monitoring.

1.5.2 Header Deletion

The main disadvantages of the interval labelling system are that it does not permit arbitrary routes through a network, and it does not allow a message to be routed through a series of networks. These problems can be overcome by a simple extension: *header deletion*. Any link of a router can be set to delete the header of every packet which passes out through it; the result is that the data immediately following becomes the new header as the packet enters the next node.

Header deletion can be used to minimize delays in the routing network. To do this, an initial header is used to route the packet to a destination transputer; this header is deleted as it leaves the final router and enters the transputer. A second header is then used to identify the virtual link within

3. Note that the optimal labelling of a ring requires that one of the connections be duplicated in order to avoid deadlock.

the destination transputer. As the number of transputers is normally much less than the number of virtual links, the initial header can be short, minimizing the delay through each router.

Another important use of header deletion is in the construction of hierarchical networks. In the 2-dimensional array of figure 1.4, each transputer could be replaced with a local network of transputers as shown in figure 1.10. Headers are deleted as packets leave or enter a local network. A single header can be used to route a packet within a local network, whilst three headers are needed to route a packet via the 2-dimensional array.

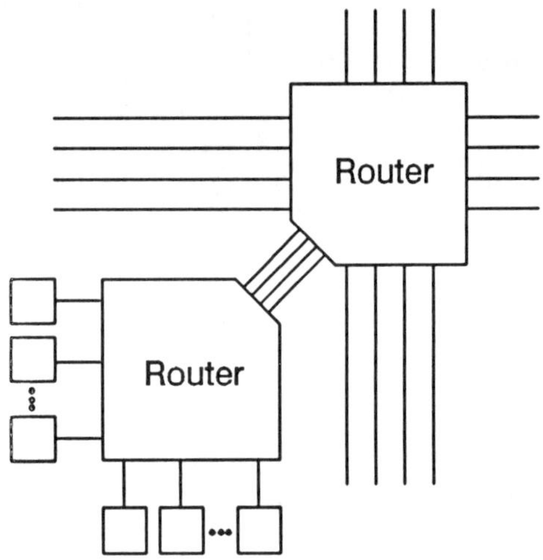

Figure 1.10 Local network of transputers and a router

1.6 Universal Routing

The routing algorithms described so far provide efficient deadlock free communications and allow a wide range of networks to be constructed from a standard router. Packets are delivered at high speed and with low latency provided that there are no collisions between packets travelling through the same link.

Unfortunately, for general purpose concurrent computers, this may not be enough. In any sparse communication network, some communication patterns cannot be realized without collisions. Such collisions within the network can reduce system performance drastically. For example, some parallel algorithms require that all messages from one phase of a computation are delivered before the next phase starts; the late arrival of a single message delays *all* of the processors. In the absence of any bound on message latency it is difficult - and in many cases impossible - to design efficient concurrent programs. The problem of constructing general purpose concurrent computers therefore depends on the answer to the following question:

Is it possible to design a *universal* routing system: a realizable network and a routing algorithm which can implement all communication patterns with bounded message latency?

In fact, a universal routing system allowing the construction of scalable general purpose parallel computers was discovered by Valiant in 1980 [3]. This meets two important requirements:

- The throughput of the network increases proportionately with the number of nodes.

- The delay through the network increases only slowly with the number of nodes (proportional to *log(p)* for *p* nodes).

Notice that the aim is to maximize capacity and minimize delay under heavy load conditions - a *parallel* communications network is a vital component of a parallel computer. This is not the same as, for example, minimizing delay through an otherwise empty network.

A p-node hypercube has a delay of proportional to *log*(p) (written O(*log*(p))) if there are no collisions between packets. This is an unreasonable assumption, however, as all of the transputers will be communicating via the network simultaneously. An important case of communication is that of performing a *permutation* in which every transputer simultaneously transmits a message and no two messages head for the same destination. Valiant's proof [4] demonstrates constructively that permutation routing is possible in a time proportional to *log*(p) on a sparse p-node network even at high communication load.

To eliminate the network hot-spots which commonly arise when packets from many different sources collide at a link in a sparse network, two phase routing is employed. Every packet is first dispatched to a randomly chosen intermediate destination; from the intermediate destination it continues to its final destination. This is a distributed algorithm - it does not require any central co-ordination - so it is straightforward to implement and scales easily. Randomization does not, in fact, strictly guarantee a delivery time which is O(*log*(p)) - but it gives it a sufficiently high probability to achieve the universality result. The processors will occasionally be held up for a late message, but not often enough to noticeably affect performance. Simulated results of universal routing are presented in chapter 7.

1.6.1 Randomizing Headers

How is the two-phase algorithm implemented? As a packet enters a randomizing network, it must be supplied with a new, random, header; this header will be used to route the packet to a router which will serve as the intermediate destination. Any input link of a router can be set to *randomize* packets as they arrive. Whenever a packet starts to arrive along such a link, the link first generates a random number and behaves as if this number were the packet header. The remainder of the packet follows the newly supplied random header through the network until the header reaches the intermediate (random) destination.

At this point, the first (randomizing) phase of the routing is complete and the random header is removed to allow the header to progress to its final destination in the second (destination) phase. The removal of the random header is performed by a *portal* in each router which recognizes the random header associated with the router. The portal deletes the random header with the result that the original header is at the front of the packet, as it was when the packet first entered the network. This header is now used to route the packet to its final destination.

Unfortunately, performing routing in two phases in the same network makes the paths of the packets more complicated. The result is that deadlock can now occur.

1.6.2 Avoiding Deadlock

A simple way to avoid deadlock is to ensure that the two phases of the packet transmission use completely separate links. The node numbers are partitioned into two halves: one half contains the numbers used for the randomizing phase. The numbers in the other half are used for the destination phase. Similarly the links are partitioned into two sets: one set is used in the randomizing phase and the other set in the destination phase.

Effectively this scheme provides two separate networks, one for the randomizing phase, and one for the destination phase, with only one set of routers. The combination of the two networks will be deadlock free if both of the networks are deadlock free. The simplest arrangement is to make the randomizing network have the same structure as the destination network - and to make both employ one of the known deadlock free routing algorithms.

Universal routing can be applied to a wide variety of networks including hypercubes and arrays [5].

1.7 Conclusions

Concurrent machines can be constructed from two components: transputers and routers. Transputers can be connected via their links to form dedicated processing systems in which communication takes place only between directly connected transputers. They can also be connected via routers allowing system-wide communication.

The provision of system-wide inter-process communication simplifies the design and programming of concurrent machines. It allows processes to be allocated to transputers after a program is written in order to optimize performance or minimize cost. It ensures that programs will be portable between different machines, although their performance will vary depending on the capabilities of the specific communications network used.

The communications architecture allows a wide variety of implementations. VLSI routers can provide routing between a large number of links, minimizing network delays. Very fast routers with fewer links can be constructed using high-speed technology. Transputers and routers can be combined on VLSI chips to provide network nodes.

Transputers and routers can be used to build machines in which a balance is maintained between communication throughput and processing throughput. Universal routing can be used to achieve bounded communication delay, and fast process scheduling within the transputers allows this communication delay to be hidden by a small amount of excess parallelism. An immediate possibility is the development of a standard architecture for *scalable general purpose* concurrent computers, as discussed in chapter 8.

References

[1] M. Homewood, D. May, D. Shepherd, *The IMS T800 Transputer* IEEE Micro **7** no. 5, October 1987

[2] INMOS Limited, *occam2 reference manual*, Prentice Hall 1988

[3] L.G. Valiant, *A scheme for fast parallel communication* SIAM J. on Computing **11** (1982) pp. 350–361

[4] L.G. Valiant, *General Purpose Parallel Architectures*, TR–07–89, Aiken Computation Laboratory, Harvard University

[5] L.G. Valiant, G.J. Brebner, *Universal Schemes for Parallel Communication* ACM STOC (1981) pp. 263–277

[6] J. van Leeuwen, R.B. Tan *Interval Routing* The Computer Journal **30** no. 4 pp. 298–307 1987

2 The T9000 Communications Architecture

2.1 Introduction

This chapter describes the communications capabilities implemented in the IMS T9000 transputer, and supported by the IMS C104 packet router, which is discussed in chapter 3. The T9000 retains the point-to-point synchronised message passing model implemented in first generation of transputers but extends it in two significant ways. The most important innovation of the T9000 is the virtualization of external communication. This allows any number of *virtual* links to be established over a single hardware link between two directly connected T9000s, and for virtual links to be established between T9000s connected by a routing network constructed from C104 routers. A second important innovation is the introduction of a many-one communication mechanism, the resource. This provides, amongst other things, an efficient distributed implementation of servers.

2.2 The IMS T9000

The IMS T9000 is a second–generation transputer; it has a superscalar processor, a hardware scheduler, 16K bytes of on-chip cache memory, and an autonomous communications processor.

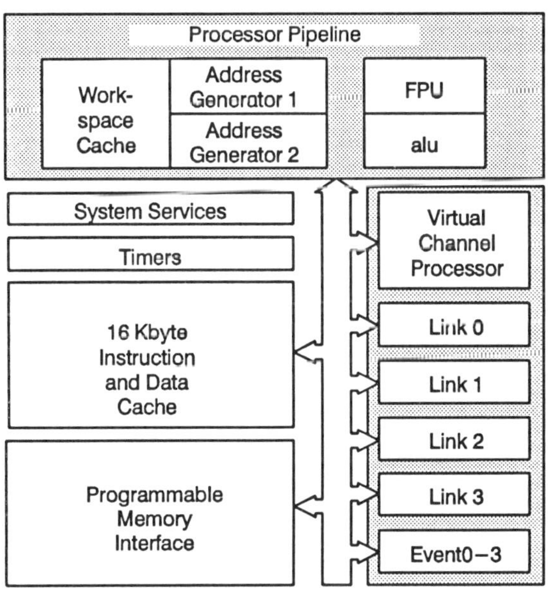

Figure 2.1 The IMS T9000 Transputer

The T9000's scheduler allows the creation and execution of any number of concurrent processes. The processes communicate by passing messages over point-to-point *channels*. Channels are unidirectional, and message passing is synchronised and unbuffered; the sending process must wait until the receiving process is ready, and the receiving process must wait until the sending process is ready. Once both processes are ready the message can be copied directly from one process to the other. The use of this type of message passing removes the need for message queues and message buffers in the implementation, and prevents accidental loss of data due to variations in the order in which processes happen to be executed. The T9000's scheduler also provides each process with its own timer, and the means for a process to deschedule until its timer reaches a specified alarm time.

The T9000's processor and scheduler implement communication between processes executing on the same processor. The T9000's communication system allows processes executing on different transputers to communicate in the same manner as processes on the same transputer. The communication system has four link interfaces, each of which may be directly connected to a link interface of another transputer, or may be connected via a network of routing devices to other transputers. Messages are passed over these links by the autonomous communications processor, the *virtual channel processor* (VCP).

2.3 Instruction set basics and processes

2.3.1 Sequential processes

The T9000 has a small set of registers which support the execution of sequential processes:

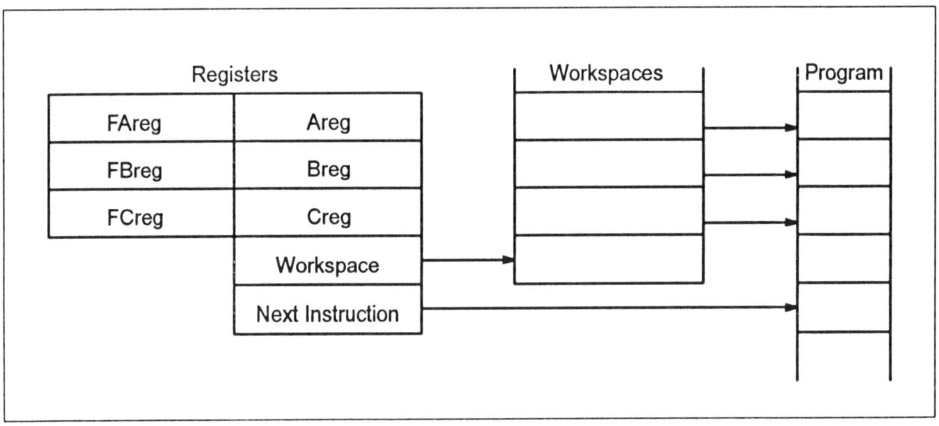

Figure 2.2 IMS T9000 Registers

The workspace pointer (Wptr) points to the workspace of the currently executing process. This workspace, which is typically organized as a falling stack, contains the local variables and temporaries of the process. When a process is not executing, for example while it is waiting for a communication, its workspace also contains other information, such as the process' instruction pointer.

The instruction pointer (Iptr) points at the next instruction to be executed by the current process.

The Areg, Breg and Creg are organized as stack. The stack is used for the evaluation of integer and address calculations, and as the operands of more complex instructions, such as the communication instructions. The FAreg, FBreg and FCreg form another stack, used for floating point arithmetic.

2.3.2 Concurrent processes

The T9000 provides efficient support of concurrency and communication. It has a hardware scheduler which enables any number of processes to be executed together, sharing the processor time. This removes the need for a software kernel.

At any time, a concurrent process may be:

active	being executed on a list waiting for execution
inactive	ready to input ready to output waiting until a specified time waiting for a semaphore

The T9000's scheduler operates in such a way that inactive processes do not consume any processor time.

The active processes waiting to be executed are held on a list. This is a linked list of process workspaces, implemented using two registers, one of which points to the first process on the list, the other to the last.

In figure 2.3, S is executing, and P, Q and R are active, awaiting execution.

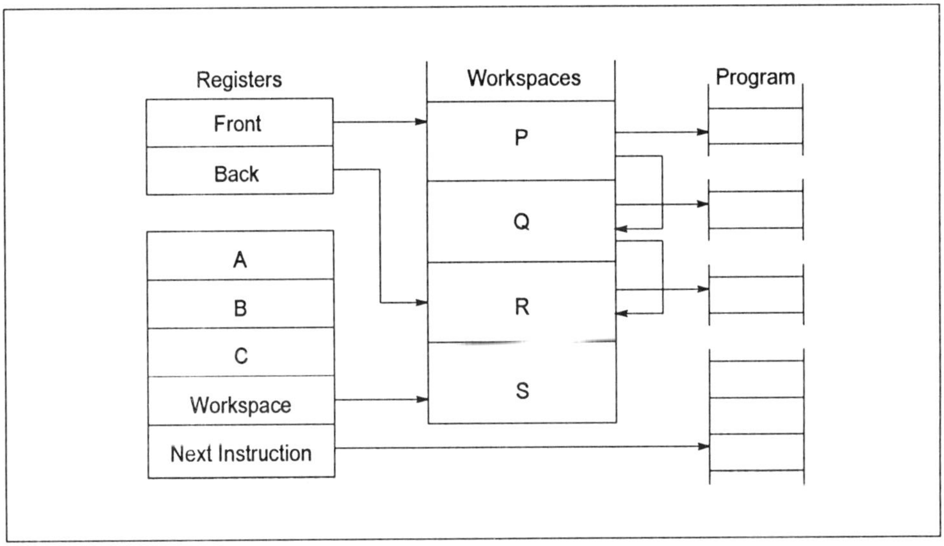

Figure 2.3 Active processes

The T9000 provides a number of instructions to support the process model. These include *start process*, and *end process*. The *start process* instruction creates a new concurrent process by adding a new workspace to the end of the scheduling list, enabling the new concurrent process to be executed together with the ones already being executed. The *end process* instruction allows a number of concurrent processes to join together, so that a successor process is executed when, and only when, all of its predecessors have terminated with an *end process* instruction.

Priority scheduling

The T9000 scheduler is actually more complex than described above. It provides two scheduling queues, one for each of two priorities. Whenever a process of high priority (priority 0) is able to proceed, it will do so in preference to a low priority (priority 1) process. If a high priority process becomes active whilst a low priority process is executing, the high priority process preempts the low priority process.

To identify a process entirely, it is necessary to identify both the process' workspace and its priority. These can be encoded in a single word by or-ing the priority of the process into the bottom bit of the workspace address; the resulting value is known as the *process id*.

2.4 Implementation of Communications

The T9000 provides a number of instructions which implement communication over channels. These instructions use the address of the channel to determine whether the channel is internal or is a virtual channel. This means that the same instruction sequence can be used, allowing a process to be written and compiled without knowledge of where its channels are connected.

Since channels are distinct objects from the processes which communicate over them, they serve to hide the internal structure of such processes from each other. A process which interacts with others only via channels thus has a very clean and simple interface, which facilitates the application of structured programming principles.

Before a channel can be used it must be allocated and initialized. The details depend on whether the channel is to connect two processes on the same transputer, or two processes on different transputers.

2.4.1 Variable length input and output

The *variable input message (vin)*, *variable output message (vout)* and *load count* instructions provide the basic message passing mechanism of the T9000. They convey a message and its length, from an sending process to an receiving process. The receiver specifies the maximum length of message that it is prepared to receive, and the sender the actual length of the message to be sent. If the actual length is longer than the receiver is prepared to receive than an error is signalled.

A sending process performs an output by loading the evaluation stack with a pointer to the message, the length of the message and the address of the channel. It then executes a *vout* instruction. A receiving process performs an input by loading the evaluation stack with a pointer to the variable, the maximum length of message and the address of the channel. It then executes a *vin* instruction followed by a *load count* instruction. The *load count* instruction either loads the length of the message received onto the evaluation stack, or signals an error, if the length specified by the sender was too long.

2.4.2 Internal channel communication

A channel between two processes on the same transputer is implemented by a single word of memory. Before the channel is used it must be initialized to the special value `NotProcess` (=80000000_{16}) which cannot be the address of the workspace of any process.

At any time, an internal channel (a single word in memory) either holds the identity of a process, or holds the special value `NotProcess`, which indicates that the channel is empty. The channel is initialized to `NotProcess` before it is used.

When a message is passed using the channel, the identity of the first process to become ready is stored in the channel, and the processor starts to execute the next process from the scheduling list. When the second process to use the channel becomes ready, the message is copied, the waiting process is added to the scheduling list, and the channel is reset to its initial state. It does not matter whether the receiving or the sending process becomes ready first.

In figure 2.4, a process *P* is about to execute an output instruction on an 'empty' channel *C*. The evaluation stack holds a pointer to a message, the address of channel *C* and a count of the number of bytes in the message.

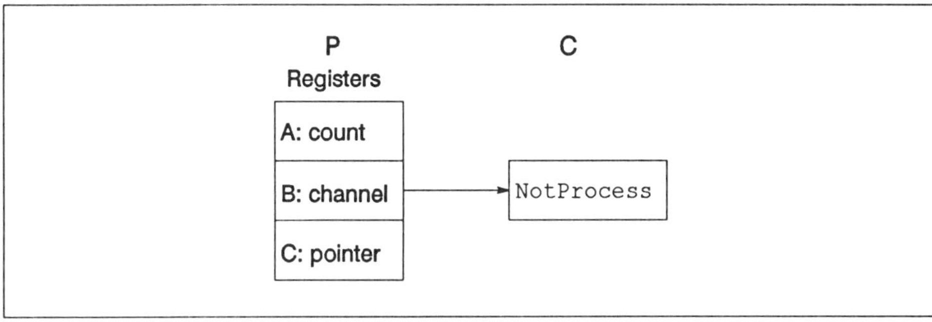

Figure 2.4 Output to empty channel

After executing the variable output instruction, the channel *C* holds the address of the workspace of *P*, and the address and length of the message to be transferred are stored in the workspace, as shown in figure 2.5. *P* is descheduled, and the processor starts to execute the next process from the scheduling list.

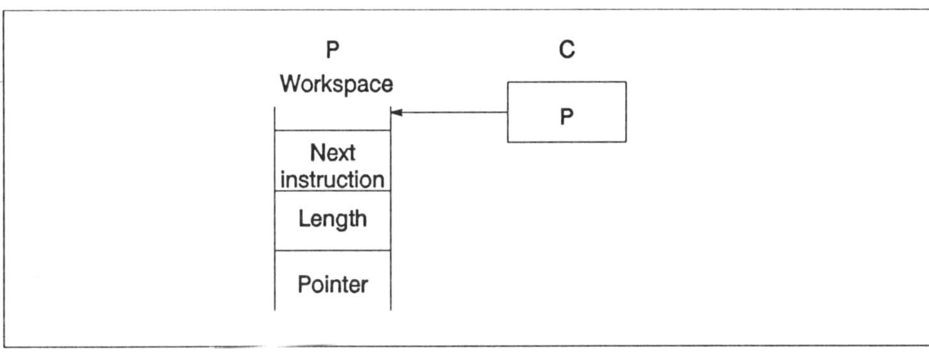

Figure 2.5 Outputting Process Descheduled

The channel *C* and the process *P* remain in this state until a second process, *Q* executes a variable input instruction on the channel, as shown in figure 2.6.

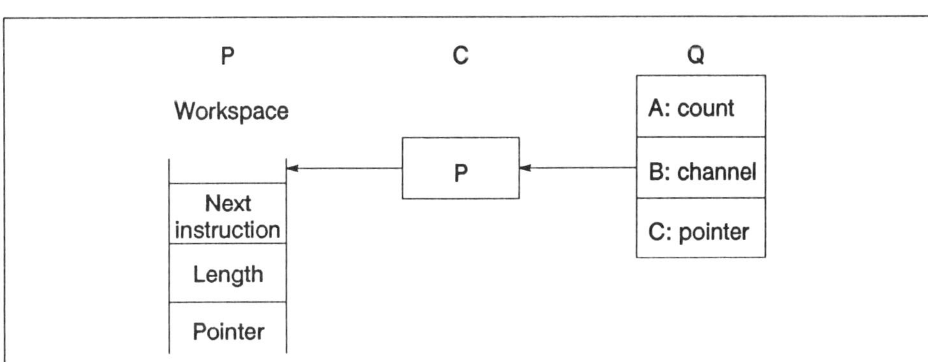

Figure 2.6 Input on a Ready Channel

Since the channel is not empty, the message is copied and the waiting process *P* is added to the scheduling list. The channel *C* is reset to its initial 'empty' state, as shown in figure 2.7. The length of the message (as specified by *P*) is recorded in the workspace of *Q* so that it can be put onto the stack by the *load count* instruction.

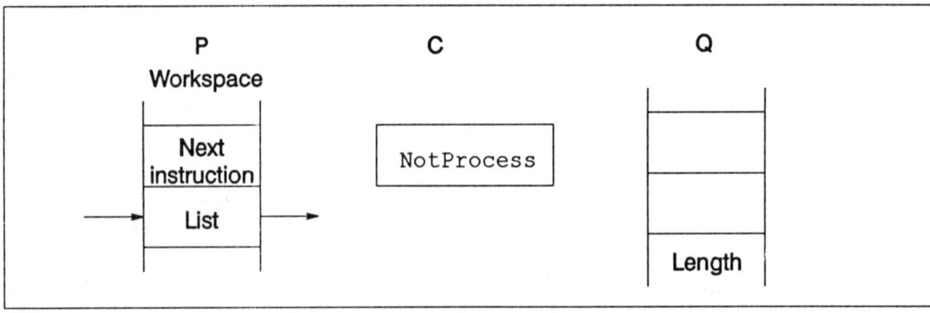

Figure 2.7 Communication completed, output ready first

If *P* is the receiving process and *Q* the sending one, the same set of pictures apply, except that the final state is as shown in figure 2.8.

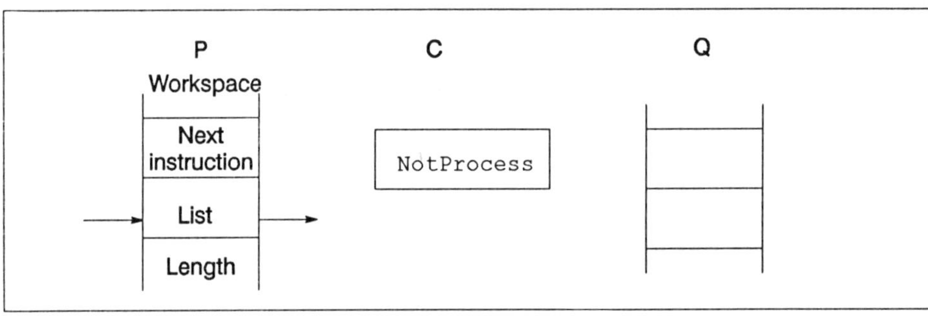

Figure 2.8 Communication completed, input ready first

2.4.3 External channel communication

The synchronised message passing of the transputer requires that data be copied from the sending process to the receiving process, and that the sending process continue execution only after the receiving process has input the data. Where the processes communicating reside on different transputers, it is necessary to transfer the data from one transputer to the other, and to signal in the other direction that an input has occurred. Thus the connection between the processes must convey information in both directions.

Virtual links

In the first–generation transputers, each point-to-point physical link between transputers provides two communication channels, one in each direction. In the new transputers, each physical link provides an *arbitrary* number of point-to-point *virtual links*. Each virtual link provides two channels, one in each direction. Hardware within the transputer multiplexes virtual links onto the physical links. At any moment, each physical link has an associated list of virtual links waiting to use it.

Each virtual link is represented by a pair of *virtual link control blocks* (VLCBs), one on each transputer. When a process executes an input or output instruction to send or receive a message on a virtual link, the process is descheduled and its identity is stored in the control block. At the same time the control block is used to determine the physical link to be used for the communication, and is added to the associated list of waiting virtual links. An example of how the lists might look at one moment is illustrated in figure 2.9.

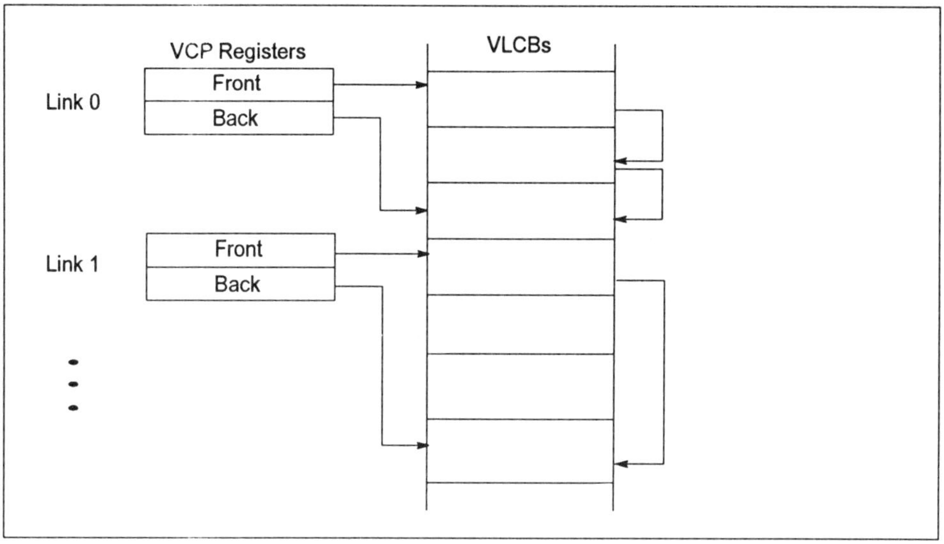

Figure 2.9 Queues of VLCBs

Message–passing Protocol

When an output is performed, the message is transmitted as a sequence of packets, each of which is restricted in length to a maximum of 32 data bytes. There are several reasons for this which are explained below. Each packet of the message starts with a *header*, which is used to route the packet to an receiving process on a remote transputer. The header also identifies the control block of the virtual link used by the remote receiving process. Thus a virtual link is established by setting up a control block in each of two transputers such that the header in each control block is set to cause packets to address the other control block.

Each packet of a message is transferred directly from the sending process to the physical link and is transferred directly from the physical link to the receiving process, provided that a process is waiting when the packet arrives. An acknowledgement packet is dispatched back along the virtual link as soon as each packet starts to arrive (thus transmission of acknowledge packets can overlap transmission of message packets). At the outputting end of the virtual link, the process will be rescheduled after the last acknowledgement packet has been received.

When the first packet of a message starts to arrive on a virtual link, it is possible that no process is waiting to input the message. In this case, it is essential that the packet is stored temporarily so that communication via other virtual links sharing the same physical link is not delayed. A single packet buffer associated with each virtual link control block is sufficient for this purpose, since the outputter will not send any further packets until an acknowledgement packet is received.

The splitting of messages into packets of limited size, each of which is acknowledged before the next is sent, has several important consequences:

- It prevents any single virtual link from hogging a physical link
- It prevents a single virtual link from hogging a path through a network
- It provides flow-control of message communication and provides the end-to-end synchronization needed for synchronised process communication
- It requires only a small buffer to be used to avoid blocking in the case that a message arrives before a process is ready to receive it

Each VLCB must be initialized with the address of the packet buffer for the input channel, the header to be used for outgoing packets, and which physical link is to be used by the virtual link.

The implementation of message–passing

When a message is passed via a virtual channel the processor of the T9000 delegates the job of transferring the message to the VCP and deschedules the process. Once a message has been transferred the VCP causes the waiting process to be rescheduled. This allows the processor to continue the execution of other processes whilst the external message transfer takes place.

In figure 2.10 processes *P* and *Q*, executed by different transputers, communicate using a virtual channel *C* implemented by a link connecting two transputers. *P* outputs, and *Q* inputs; note that the protocol used by the VCP ensures that it does not matter which of *P* and *Q* becomes ready first.

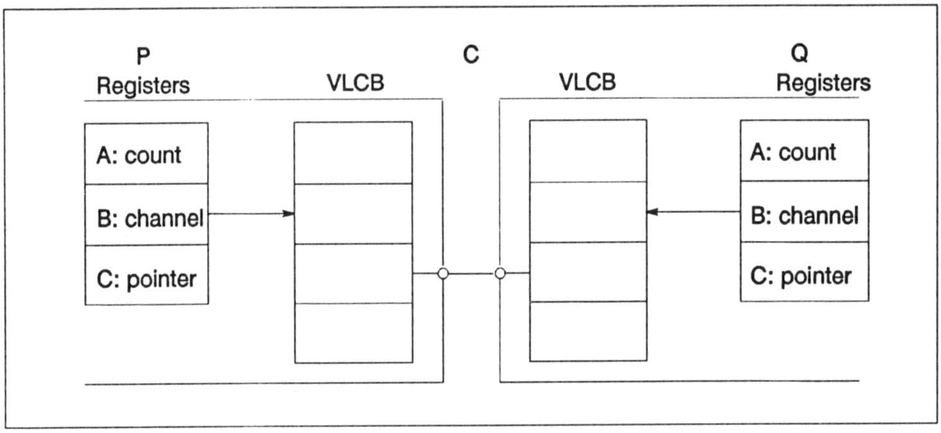

Figure 2.10 Communication between transputers

The VCP, on being told to output a message, stores the pointer, count and process id into the VLCB, and causes the first packet of the message to be sent. The VCP maintains queues of VLCBs for packets to be sent on each link, so the sending of a packet is in two parts; firstly adding the VLCB to the corresponding queue, and then subsequently taking the VLCB from the front of the queue and sending a packet, with the header provided by the VLCB. The queues of VLCBs are illustrated in figure 2.9.

Subsequently, on receipt of an acknowledge packet for this virtual channel, the VCP sends the next packet of the message. This continues until all packets have been sent. When the final acknowledge is received, the VCP reads the process id from the VLCB and causes the waiting process to be scheduled.

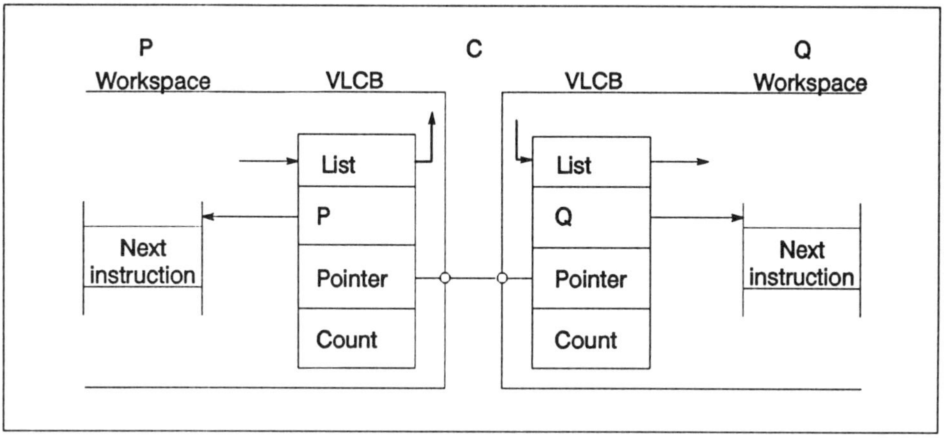

Figure 2.11 Communication in Progress

The receiving transputer's response to the first packet will depend upon whether a corresponding *variable input message* instruction has yet been executed. The VCP can determine this from the state of the VLCB associated with the virtual channel on which the packet has arrived. If an input instruction has not yet been executed, then the VCP stores the packet into the packet buffer provided by the VLCB, and an acknowledgement will subsequently be generated once an input instruction is executed.

When a process executes a *variable length input* instruction, the processor passes the process identifier, the virtual channel address, the pointer, and the maximum length, to the VCP and deschedules the process. The VCP, on being told to input a message, stores the pointer, maximum length and process id into the VLCB and records that an input has been requested. The VCP then examines the VLCB to determine whether a data packet has already arrived. If the data packet has already arrived, it will now be handled; otherwise data packets are handled as they arrive.

When a data packet is handled, the VCP acknowledges the packet by adding the VLCB to a queue for the sending of acknowledge packets. (Acknowledge packets are sent in just the same way as data packets, but use a separate set of queues.) The VCP then stores the data into the memory locations specified by the input instruction, provided that the total amount of data that has been received is not greater than the maximum amount specified. If more data than this is received then all data in excess of the maximum allowed is discarded. When a final data packet is received, the VCP reschedules the receiving process, having first recorded the amount of data received[4] into the process' workspace. This value will be used by a subsequent *load count* instruction.

The message is thus copied through the link, by means of the VLCBs at either end being alternately queued to send data and acknowledge packets respectively, as illustrated in figure 2.11. After all this is done the processes *P* and *Q* are returned to the corresponding scheduling lists as shown in figure 2.12.

4. If too much data is received, a special error value (= $FFFFFFFF_{16}$) is recorded instead.

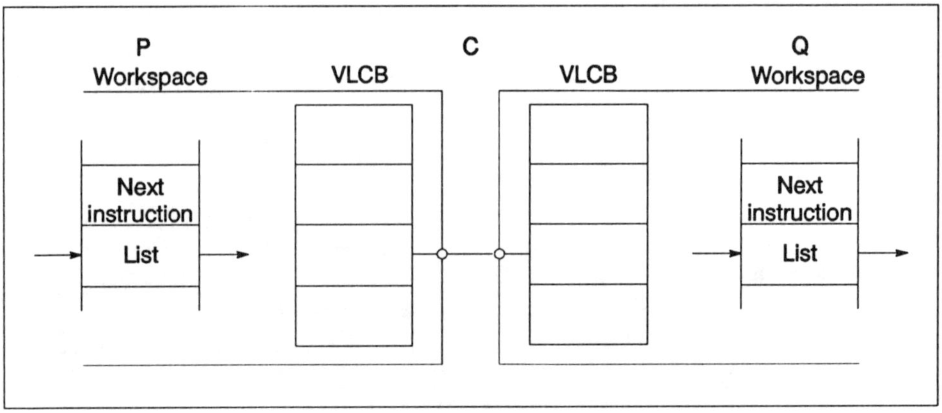

Figure 2.12 Communication completed

2.4.4 Known length communication

In many cases both the sender and receiver of a message know the precise length of the message to be transferred in advance. In this case it is possible to optimize the operation of message passing and the T9000 provides a number of instructions which do this. The most important of these are *input message* and *output message*[5].

These instructions are like *vin* and *vout* except that both the receiver and the sender specify the actual length of message to be passed. There is no need for an instruction which corresponds to *load count* in this case.

The operation of known length internal communication is similar to variable length communication. However, the first process to synchronize does not need to store the length, since the same length will be specified by the second process.

The operation of known length external communication is identical to the variable length case, except for the omission of the *load count* instruction.

2.5 Alternative input

In a system, it is sometimes necessary for a process to be able to input from any one of several other concurrent processes. For example, consider a process which is implementing a bounded buffer between two other processes, one of which (a peripheral of some kind) outputs data to the buffer along a channel, the other (the "consumer") requests data from the buffer along another channel, and receives it via a third, as illustrated in figure 2.13. The behavior of the buffer process is determined not only by its internal state, but also by whether the other processes wish to add or to take data from the buffer.

The alternative construct is a means to select between one of a number of guarded processes, each comprising a guard and an associated process; the guard is typically an input[6]. The alternative selects a guarded process whose guard is ready. If a particular guarded process is selected then both the guard and the associated process are executed. Guards may also have a boolean part which force the guard to be disregarded if the boolean is `FALSE`.

5. Note that this is the only form of communication supported by the first–generation transputers.

6. In principle, outputs could equally well be used as guards; however the implementation becomes considerably more complex if both inputs and outputs are allowed as guards. Thus in the T9000 output guards are not allowed.

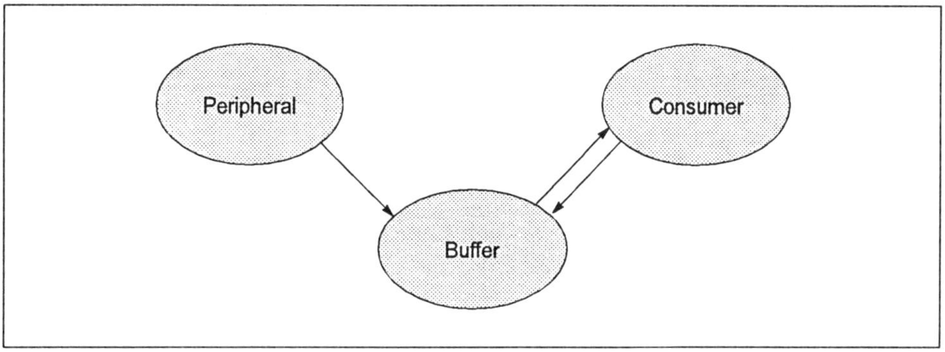

Figure 2.13 Buffer process

The T9000's implementation of alternative separates the selection of a guarded process from its execution. This means that the only new mechanism needed is one to support selection.

The idea behind the selection mechanism is that for each guard, the channel is examined to see if it is ready. If, when all the channels have been examined, no ready channel has been found, the process deschedules until at least one is ready. The process then re–examines the channels and chooses the first one that it finds ready. The key to the mechanism is therefore, the means by which a process can deschedule until one of several channels becomes ready.

The first aspect of this mechanism is that channels can be *enabled* and *disabled.* A channel is enabled (by the process performing the alternative) by executing an *enable channel* instruction. One effect of this instruction is that if the channel subsequently has an output performed on it, the output will signal the process performing alternative that the channel has become ready. An enabled channel is disabled by the process performing alternative executing a *disable channel* instruction, which reverses the effect of an *enable channel* instruction.

The second aspect of the mechanism is the use of a special workspace location by the process performing alternative. This location serves a number of purposes. Firstly, in the case of a straightforward input it is used to hold the pointer to the location to store the message, as discussed previously; consequently it is referred to as the "pointer location". Secondly, whilst an alternative is being performed, it contains one of the special values `Enabling` (= `NotProcess` + 1), `Waiting` (= `NotProcess` + 2), or `Ready` (= `NotProcess` + 3). As no process which is performing a normal input could be descheduled with one of these values in its pointer location (processes being forbidden to input messages to these addresses), the value in the location distinguishes a process performing alternative from an inputting process. Thirdly, it is used to record whether any channel which has been examined is ready. Finally, it is also used to record whether a process performing alternative is active or descheduled.

The implementation of alternative can now be explained.

Alternative start

The first thing that a process does to perform an alternative is to execute an *alternative start* instruction. This sets the pointer location of the workspace to the value `Enabling`, indicating that an alternative is in progress, that no guard has yet been seen to be ready, and that the process performing alternative is active.

Enable channel

The process performing alternative then executes an *enable channel* instruction for every channel guard. This instruction determines whether the channel is ready, and, if it is not ready, the instruction enables it. If, on the other hand, the channel is ready the instruction sets the value in the pointer location to `Ready`.

For an internal channel, the processor determines whether a channel is ready by examining the channel word. If it contains the identity of another process, then that process has performed an output on the channel, and so the channel is ready. Otherwise, the channel is empty, and so is enabled by writing inti it the process id of the process performing alternative.

For a virtual channel, the processor uses the VCP to enable the channel. The VCP examines the VLCB of the channel; if the packet buffer already contains the first packet of a message then the channel is ready. Otherwise, the VCP records in the VLCB that the channel has been enabled.

Alternative wait

Once a process has enabled all the channels from which it wishes to make a selection, it executes an *alternative wait* instruction. This first writes the value `-1` to location 0 of the workspace, in preparation for the selection process. Then, if the pointer location still contains the value `Enabling`, indicating that no guard is yet ready, the instruction writes the value `Waiting` into the pointer location, indicating that the process performing alternative is not active, and deschedules the process. Otherwise, the pointer location contains `Ready`, indicating that at least one guard is ready, so the process continues to make its selection.

If a process deschedules on execution of an *alternative wait* instruction, it will be scheduled when one of the guards becomes ready. The process will then proceed to make its selection.

Output on an enabled channel

When an output occurs on an internal channel which contains a process id, the sending process distinguishes between a channel which is ready for input and a channel which is ready for alternative input by examining the pointer location of the waiting process. If this word contains one of the special values `Enabling`, `Waiting`, or `Ready` then the channel is in use by a process performing an alternative. In this case the sending process will store information into its own workspace and deschedule as if the inputter were not ready, and may also perform some other actions, depending on the value in the pointer word of the receiving process:

- If the value is `Enabling` then the output instruction changes the value to `Ready`, indicating that an enabled channel is ready.
- If the value is `Waiting`, and hence the process performing alternative is descheduled, then the output instruction changes the value to `Ready`, and schedules the process performing alternative.
- If the value is `Ready`, the output instruction performs no additional action.

When an output occurs on an enabled *virtual* channel, the VCP of the outputting transputer will send the first packet of the message as usual; indeed, the sending transputer has no indication that the channel has been enabled. When the first packet arrives on an enabled virtual channel, the VCP places the packet in the packet buffer, and records that a packet has arrived as is normal for for a channel on which no input has been performed. The VCP also informs the scheduler that an enabled channel has become ready. The scheduler will then examine the pointer word of the process which enabled the channel and performs the same actions as an output instruction executed by a local process, as described above.

Once an output has been performed on an enabled channel two conditions are true; firstly, that the process performing alternative is active (either because it has not descheduled, or because a channel which has become ready has scheduled it); and secondly, the pointer word of the process performing alternative has the value `Ready`. These two, together with the condition for descheduling when an *alternative wait* instruction is executed, ensure that a process executes the instruction following an *alternative wait* instruction if, and only if, at least one guard is ready.

Disable channel

The process performing alternative selects a guarded process by executing a *disable channel* instruction for each guard and then executing an *alternative end* instruction. In addition to the channel address, the *disable channel* instruction takes a code offset as a parameter. This is the offset from the *alternative end* instruction to the code for the guard. If the *disable channel* instruction finds that a channel is ready, then workspace 0 is examined; if it contains a value other than `-1` then a selection has already been made, so no further action is taken. If it contains `-1` then this is the first ready channel to be disabled and the code offset associated with this channel is written into workspace 0.

The operation of *disable channel* depends on whether the channel is internal or is a virtual channel.

For an internal channel, the channel word is examined. If it contains the identity of the process performing alternative, an output has not been performed, the channel is not ready, and the instruction resets the channel word to `NotProcess`. If the channel contains the identity of a sending process, then the channel is ready and may be selected.

For a virtual channel, the processor uses the VCP to disable the channel. The VCP examines the VLCB of the channel; if it contains the first packet of a message then the channel is ready. Otherwise, the VCP removes the information that the channel is enabled from the VLCB.

Alternative end

When all the guards have been disabled, one will have been selected, because guards are not disabled until at least one is ready, and the first ready guard that is disabled will be selected. The process performing alternative jumps to the code corresponding to the selected guard by executing the *alternative end* instruction. This instruction reads the code offset from workspace 0, and adds it to the instruction pointer. In this way the guarded process corresponding to the selected channel is caused to be executed.

A note about boolean guards

In the above, the fact that the guarded processes can have boolean guards has been overlooked. In fact, the *enable channel* and *disable channel* instructions take an additional parameter which is the boolean guard. If the guard is `FALSE` (= 0) they perform no action.

2.5.1 Extensions of alternative

Prioritized and fair alternatives

The T9000's alternative mechanism actually implements a prioritized alternative, the guards being prioritized in the order in which they are disabled. This can be directly useful; for example, consider a bounded buffer where we wish to prioritize receiving data from the peripheral over supplying it to a consumer. This can easily be achieved by always disabling the channel to the consumer process[7] first, so that if both the peripheral and the consumer happen to be ready, the alternative end instruction will always find the offset to the code which interacts with the peripheral.

The prioritized alternative which is actually provided can also be used to implement fair alternatives. For example, if we wish to ensure that the bounded buffer on average favours neither the

7. Since the implementation only provides for input guards, it is necessary to use two channels between the buffer and the consumer process, so that the consumer can perform an *output* to the buffer to indicate its readiness to receive an item.

peripheral nor the consumer, then this can be achieved by always disabling first the channel which was not selected on the previous iteration of the buffer control loop.

Other guards

In addition to inputs from channels, alternatives allows two other types of guard which may be used in addition to, or instead of channel guards.

The first is a `SKIP` guard, which is always ready. This guard is useful in conjunction with boolean guards, and is supported by the *enable skip* and *disable skip* instructions.

The second is a timer guard, which can be used for implementing timeouts, or for arranging for several different time related operations to be scheduled by a single process. The implementation of timer guards is built upon the implementation described above. However, some extra mechanisms are needed, and this necessitates the use of the *timer alternative start* and *timer alternative wait* instructions, rather than *alternative start* and *alternative wait,* for any alternative which contains timer guards. Timer guards are supported by the *enable timer* and *disable timer* instructions.

2.6 Shared channels and Resources

2.6.1 Alternative

The alternative mechanism is very general. It allows a choice to be made between channels, `SKIP`s and timers; each guard of an alternative may contain a boolean part; and the choice between guards is prioritized. Furthermore, there is complete freedom about how the channels are used both within and outside the alternative. It is this generality that necessitates the enabling and disabling of all the guards every time an alternative is executed, a consequence of which is that the cost of an alternative is proportional to the number of guards. This cost is incurred every time a selection is made.

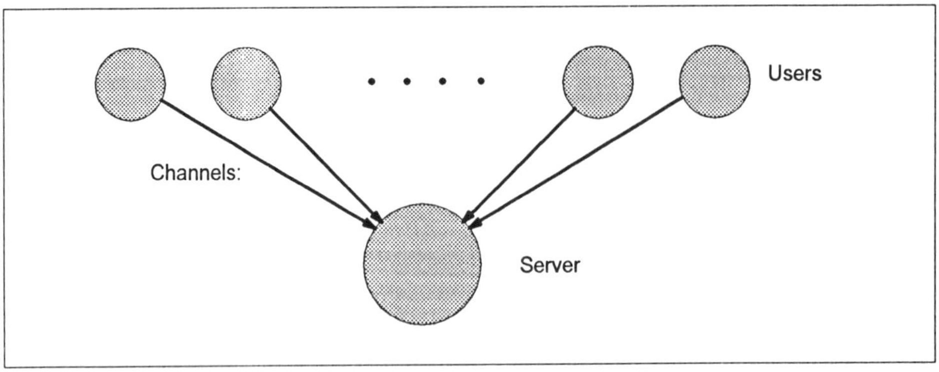

Figure 2.14 Server and users

2.6.2 Servers

One common use of an alternative is to implement a server, or to provide access to a resource. For example figure 2.14 illustrates the notion of a simple server which offers a service to N users, each connected to the server by one of an array of channels.

As the provision of the service may involve further interaction with the user, it is necessary for the code which provides the service to be passed its identity. In this case, the index of the channel in the array identifies the user.

In addition to the potentially large cost of the alternative, there is another potential drawback to this implementation of a server; this is, that the server must know the identity of all the channels connecting to users, since it has to enable and disable them in order to select one. A user cannot use a resource that does not know about the channel along which it communicates. A further difficulty is that fairness between the users is complicated to implement.

The T9000 provides a communication mechanism called a "resource" which overcomes both of these these problems . A resource may be thought of as a shared channel which connects a number of "user" processes to a "server" process.

2.6.3 Sharing a channel by a semaphore

Before describing the T9000's resource mechanism and its use, we will first consider another mechanism that might be used.

Using an efficient semaphore mechanism (which the T9000 does provide), we could implement resources by means of a single communication channel, whose use was shared by means of a semaphore. The resulting system would comprise a channel, used to synchronize with the server, and a queue of processes waiting to use the server, belonging to the semaphore. Whilst this mechanism would work, it has two drawbacks:

- It is not a distributed mechanism – it would work only on a single transputer.
- It no longer allows channels to be used as an abstraction. Rather than merely communicating via a channel, a user would have to first claim the semaphore.

The resource mechanism overcomes both of these problems.

2.6.4 Resources

A resource connects a number of user processes to a single server process. The resource comprises a number of *resource channels*, one for each user, and a *resource data structure* (RDS). A user process communicates with the server by outputting on its resource channel, exactly as if it were an ordinary channel. The server selects a resource channel by executing a a *grant* instruction with the address of the RDS. Once a user process has output on a resource channel, the grant will deliver the *identifier* of the chosen resource channel to the server. The server can then input from the chosen resource channel. Thus the operation of a resource is like that of an alternative, in that the functions of selection and communication are separated.

The identifier associated with a resource channel is a single word value which is delivered to the server on completion of a grant. This is the only information delivered to the server to identify the chosen resource channel, and hence, the user. Although it might seem as though the server should receive the address of the chosen resource channel, this is not always adequate. For example, in the server shown in figure 2.14 above, the service–providing code may need the index of the channel rather than the channel itself, so that it can use this index in an array of reply channels. On the other hand, if the channel address is what is wanted, then the identifier can be set to be the channel address.

Resource data structure

The resource data structure contains one word used to synchronize the server process with a user process, and a pair of words used to implement a queue. Unlike a channel shared by a semaphore, the queue is not a queue of waiting processes, but a queue of resource channels, each of which has been output to by a user process.

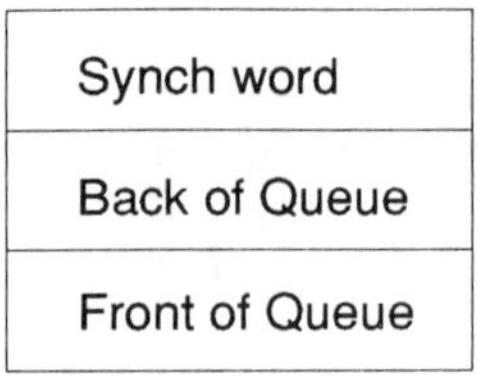

Figure 2.15 Resource Data Structure (RDS)

An RDS is initialized by setting both the synchronization word and the front pointer to `NotProcess`.

Resource channels

A resource channel is a channel together with an a pair of words. In the case of a virtual resource channel, the extra pair of words are associated with the VLCB of the receiving (resource) side. The address of a resource channel does not distinguish it from an ordinary channel, and a resource channel which is not currently part of a resource may be used used just like an ordinary channel, in which case the pair of words is not used.

Resource instructions

In addition to the output instructions mentioned previously, there are three instructions provided to implement the resource mechanism. These are:

- *mark resource channel*
- *grant*
- *unmark resource channel*

The operation of *mark resource channel*

The resource mechanism allows resource channels to be made part of a resource ("marked") by either the server or by the user[8]. A server may mark a resource channel irrespective of when the user outputs on the channel; a user must mark a resource channel prior to outputting on the channel.

A resource channel is marked as being part of a resource by the execution of a *mark resource channel* instruction. This instruction takes three parameters; a pointer to the resource channel, the identifier, and a pointer to the RDS. There are two possibilities: either the channel is empty, or an output has already occurred.

If the channel is empty, then the identifier and the pointer to the RDS are stored in the extra words associated with the channel. For an internal channel, the special value `ResChan` (= `NotProcess` + 2) is written into the channel word to indicate that it is part of a resource; for an external channel the VCP records this in the VLCB. This is illustrated in figure 2.16.

8. A user located on a different transputer from the server must arrange for a process local to the server to do this. This is discussed in section 2.7.3.

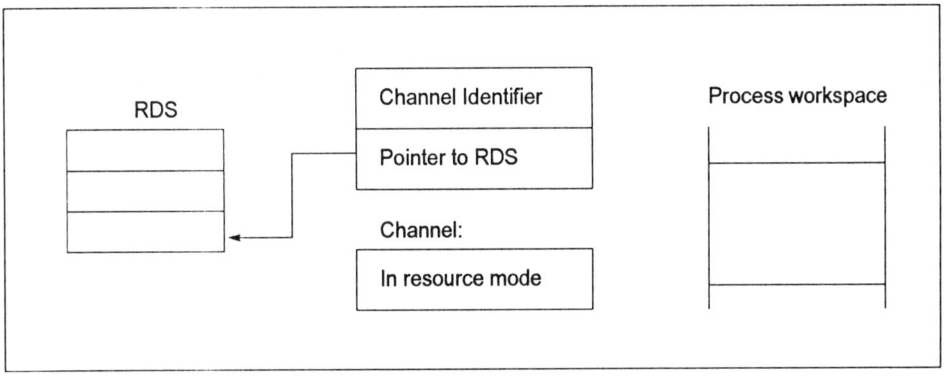

Figure 2.16 Channel after *mark resource channel* but before *output*

If an output has already been executed on the channel, then the *mark resource channel* instruction must be being executed by the server. In this case the channel will be queued on the RDS, using the first of the pair of words to form a linked list, with the second extra word containing the identifier. This is illustrated in figure 2.19.

The operation of *grant*

A server process grants use of a resource by loading the evaluation stack with a pointer to the resource data structure and a pointer to a location which is to receive the identifier of the granted resource channel, and then executing a *grant* instruction.

If there is a resource channel on the queue, it is dequeued and its identifier is written into the location provided for it. The server then continues and can input from the (now unmarked) resource channel.

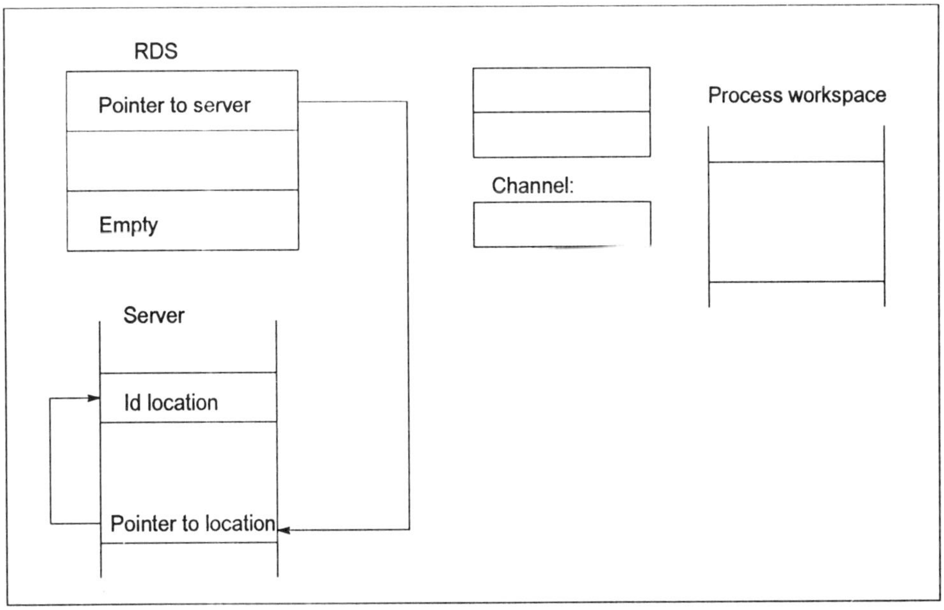

Figure 2.17 RDS and Server after *grant*

If there is no resource channel on the queue, then there is no user process waiting for the resource. In this case the instruction writes the process id of the server into the synchronization word of the RDS, writes the address to where the identifier will be written into the workspace of the server and deschedules it. This is illustrated in figure 2.17. The server will be rescheduled when a user outputs to the resource. Thus the resource mechanism also provides non–busy waiting, just like alternative.

Note that once a resource channel is granted to a resource it becomes unmarked. It must be re–marked before it can be used as part of the resource again. In the meantime it can be used as a normal channel.

The operation of *output*

An output performed on a unmarked resource channel is indistinguishable from an output on an ordinary channel, as illustrated in figure 2.18.

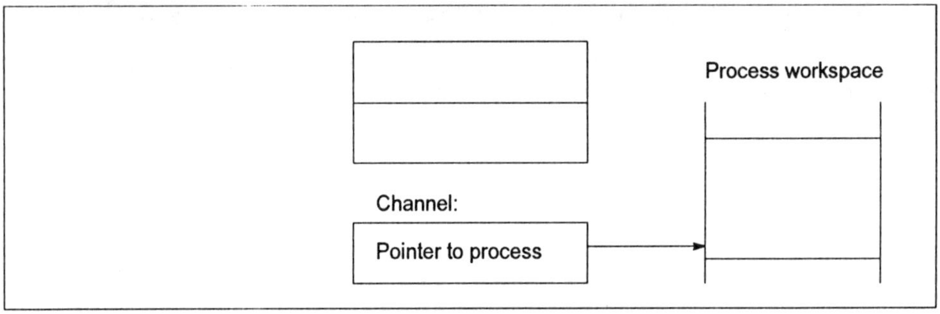

Figure 2.18 Channel after *output* only

When an output is performed on a marked internal channel, the output instruction reads the channel word in the normal way. On discovering that it contains the special value `ResChan`, indicating that it is a marked resource channel, the instruction reads the pointer to the RDS from one of the extra words of the resource channel and examines the RDS.

If there is no server present in the RDS, the output instruction queues the resource channel onto the RDS, as shown in figure 2.19. If there is a server present, then the instruction grants the channel to the server; the channel word is set to the process id of the sending process, the resource channel's identifier is written into the address specified in the pointer location of the server's workspace, and the server is rescheduled, as shown in figure 2.20.

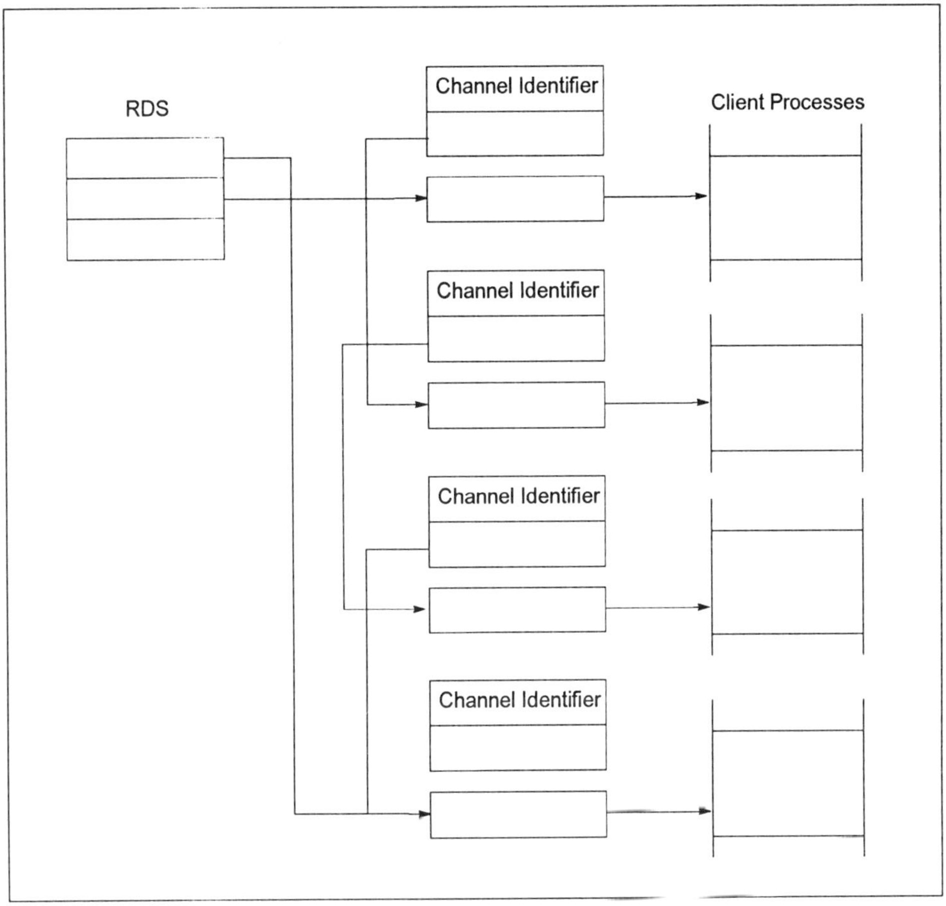

Figure 2.19 Four resource channels after *mark resource channel* and *output*

When an output is performed on a marked virtual resource channel the first packet is transmitted in the normal way. Indeed, there is no indication at the output end of the virtual channel that the channel is a resource channel. When the packet arrives at the receiving transputer, the VCP will notice that the packet has arrived on a marked resource channel, and cause the associated RDS to be examined by the scheduler. If there is no process id of a server present in the RDS, then the scheduler queues the resource channel on the RDS as shown in figure 2.19. If there is a process id in the RDS, then the channel is unmarked and granted to the server. The scheduler reads the pointer to where the server wishes the identifier to be stored from the server's pointer location, stores the identifier there, and reschedules the server as shown in figure 2.20.

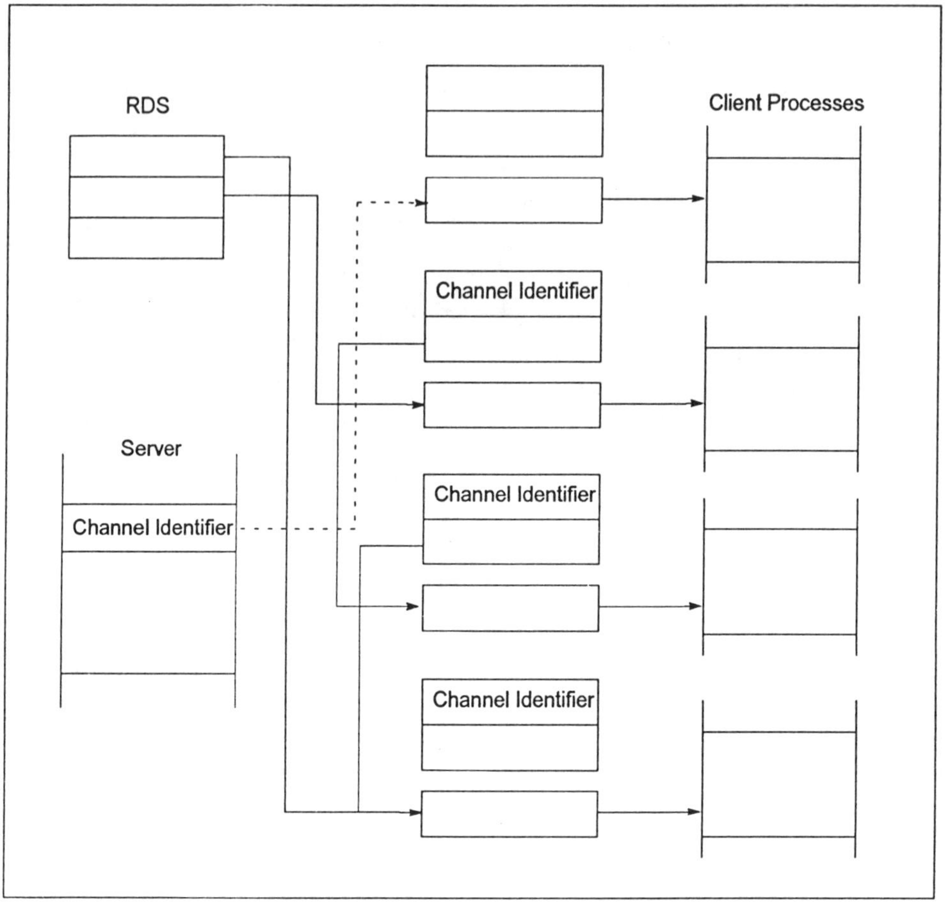

Figure 2.20 RDS with queued resource channels and server after *grant*

Note that in both the internal and external case the resource channel is then in the same state as a channel after an output has been performed and before the corresponding input has been performed, as shown in figure 2.18.

2.7 Use of resources

The T9000's resource channel mechanism can be used in several ways, three of which we now discuss.

2.7.1 Resources as a replacement for alternative; Omniscient servers

Consider the server example shown in figure 2.14, in which a set of users request some service from a server by communicating on an array of channels. We assume that the central server process repeatedly chooses a user which has requested it, provides some service for a time, and then chooses another user. If no user requires the service, the server will wait non–busily.

Although this can be implemented directly using the T9000's alternative mechanism, the cost may be too high if there are a large number of users, and the time taken to perform the service is small. However, if this is so, we can implement the above server using a resource.

The server process first creates and initializes a resource data structure, and then marks all of the resource channels in the array as being part of that resource. The identifier of each resource channel is set to the index of that channel in the array. The server then repeatedly selects a user by performing *grant*, inputs from the chosen user and provides the service. The granting of the chosen channel enables it to be used as an ordinary channel, and so the server has to re-mark the channel to include it in the resource when the server has completed this iteration. Finally, if and when the server terminates, the channels may have to be placed in a state where they can be used again as ordinary channels. This is done by means of the *unmark resource channel* instruction.

In order that the new code works correctly, the channels must have been allocated as resource channels. This can be achieved either by allocating all channels as resource channels, or by allocating only those channels used in resources as resource channels, in order to optimize memory usage.

This implementation has a one-off set up and take down cost, proportional to the number of users, and a *constant* per-iteration cost which is *independent* of the number of users. The users (sending processes) cannot distinguish between this implementation and one using alternative – or indeed one in which every user is provided with its own server, which simply performs input!

The use of resources instead of alternative is efficient only where a number of constraints are obeyed. Boolean guards and explicitly prioritized selection must be avoided, and the server process must interact with only the selected user, and not with any other users.

2.7.2 Resources in alternatives

Although the above has been suggestive that resources are some sort of a replacement for alternatives, they are in fact complementary. Resources may be used as guards in alternatives by means of the *enable grant* and *disable grant* instructions.

The use of resources in this way is very natural. For example, consider a bounded buffer process, with several providers of data and several users thereof, as illustrated in figure 2.21.

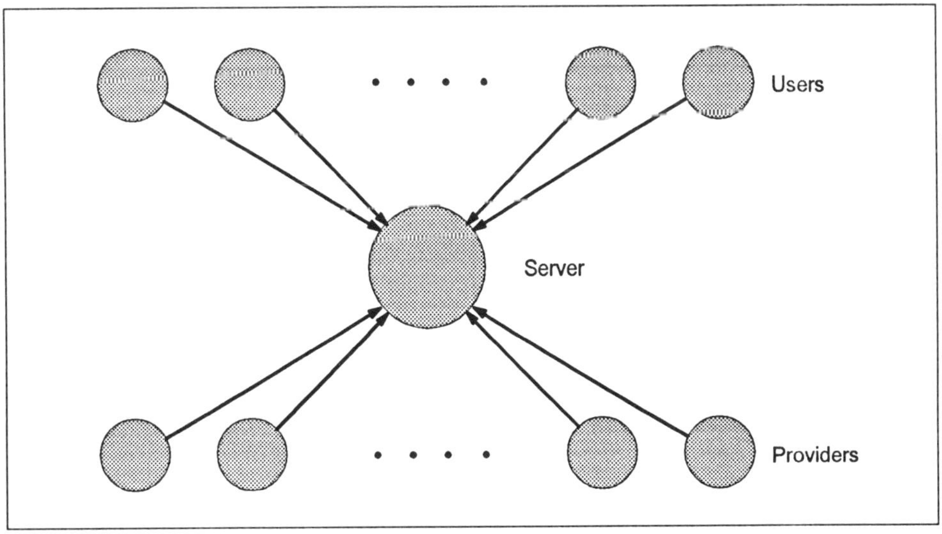

Figure 2.21 Server with users and inputs

This can be implemented using two resources, one for the users and one for the providers. The server can use an alternative to select between the users as a group and the providers as a group, and then within each branch of the alternative it can make a further selection by the resource mechanism as already described. This ensures that the server will wait (non–busily) until either a user or a provider is ready to communicate. When there are many inputs and users waiting, the server can prioritize either users or providers within the alternative as previously explained.

2.7.3 Ignorant servers

We have seen how to use resources instead of alternatives. In that case, the server knows through which channels its users communicate, and how many users there are, but the users are unable to distinguish the resource from an alternative. We now consider how resources can be used when the server and the users know only the location of the RDS. In this case the resource channels can be generated dynamically as needed.

We start by explaining how to do this where the users are located on the same transputer as the server, and then we explain how to do this where the users and server may be located on different transputers.

Local server and users

In this case the user knows that it is going to use a resource channel and knows the RDS of the resource. The user allocates three words of memory for use as a resource channel, initializes the channel part to `NotProcess`, and executes a *mark resource channel* instruction which specifies the RDS of the resource and gives the address of the channel itself as the identifier of the channel. The user then performs an output on the channel. The server, when it grants this resource channel, will be delivered the address of the channel, and can then input from the user. In practice, it will probably be necessary for the resource to be able to output to the user, as well as the user outputting to the resource. A channel can be established in the reverse direction according to some convention known both to user and server.

Distributed servers and user

The distributed case is more complex because the user cannot initialize and mark a resource channel by itself. Firstly, as the user and server are located on different transputers, a *virtual* resource channel must be used. It must first be allocated, then both ends of the virtual link must be initialized. Once this has been done something must mark the input side of the virtual channel; this something must be executed on the same transputer as the server, not on the same transputer as the user!

However, if we assume the existence of a distributed kernel, capable of allocating, initializing and marking virtual channels, the distributed case becomes straightforward. Firstly, the user asks the kernel to initialize and mark a virtual channel connected to the server[9]. The kernel then cooperates with the kernel on the server's machine to initialize the virtual channel, and then the local kernel waits for the remote kernel to mark the virtual channel. The local kernel then informs the user process of which virtual channel to use, and the user process proceeds to output on that channel.

2.8 Conclusion

The T9000 transputer and C104 router provide the mechanisms necessary for the construction of large concurrent distributed systems. The T9000 provides a process and communication model, based around synchronised message passing over unidirectional point-to-point channels including an efficient and non-busy implementation of message passing, alternative and resources.

The communication system of the T9000 enables channels to be established between processes executing on different transputers, and for the same communication model to be maintained whether processes are located on a single transputer, or on a number of transputers.

9. The kernel can appear as a local server to the user.

When two T9000 transputers are directly connected, many virtual channels are provided in each direction between processes on the two transputers. If C104 routers are used, a network may be built which allows processes distributed over any number of transputers to communicate. The scheduling and communication mechanisms of the T9000 provide efficient support for a wide variety of operating system kernel functions and concurrent programming constructs.

3 DS-Links and C104 Routers

3.1 Introduction

Millions of serial communication links have been shipped as an integral part of the transputer family of microprocessor devices. This 'OS-Link', as it is known, provides a physical point–to–point connection between two processes running in separate processors. It is full–duplex, and has an exceptionally low implementation cost and an excellent record for reliability. Indeed, the OS-Link has been used in almost all sectors of the computer, telecommunications and electronics markets. Many of these links have been used without transputers, or with a transputer simply serving as an intelligent DMA controller. However, they are now a mature technology, and by today's standards their speed of 20 Mbits/s is relatively low.

Since the introduction of the OS-Link, a new type of serial interconnect has evolved, known as the DS-Link. A major feature of the DS-Link is that it provides a physical connection over which any number of software (or 'virtual') channels may be multiplexed; these can either be between two directly connected devices, or can be between any number of different devices, if the links are connected via (packet) routing switches. Other features include detection and location of the most likely errors, and a transmission speed of 100 Mbits/s, with 200 Mbits/s planned and further enhancement possible.

Although DS-Links have been designed for processor to processor communication, they are equally appropriate for processor to memory communication and specialized applications such as disk drives, disk arrays, or communication systems.

3.2 Using links between devices

DS-Links provide point–to–point communication between devices. Each connected pair of DS-Links implements a full–duplex, asynchronous, flow–controlled connection operating at a programmable speed of up to 100 MBits/s or more. Point to point links have many advantages over bus based communications in a system with many devices:

- There is no contention for the communication mechanism, regardless of the number of devices in the system.
- There is no capacitive load penalty as more devices are added to the system.
- The communications bandwidth does not saturate as more communicating devices are added to the system. Rather, the larger the number of devices, the greater the total communications bandwidth of the system.
- Removing the bus as a single point of failure improves the fault–tolerance of the system.

For small systems, a number of DS-Links on each device can provide complete connection between a few devices. By using additional message routing devices, networks of any size and topology can be built with complete connection between all devices.

3.3 Levels of link protocol

As with most communications systems, the links can be described at a number of levels with a hierarchy of protocols. The lowest level of electrical signals is considered in detail in chapter 4.

3.3.1 Bit level protocol

To achieve the speed required, a new, simple link standard has been produced. DS-Links have four wires for each link, a data and 'strobe' line for each direction. The data line carries the actual signal, and the strobe line changes state each time the next bit has the same value as the previous one[10]. By this means each DS pair carries an encoded clock, in a way which allows a full bit–time of skew–tolerance between the two wires. Figure 3.1 shows the form of signals on the data and strobe wires. All signals are TTL compatible.

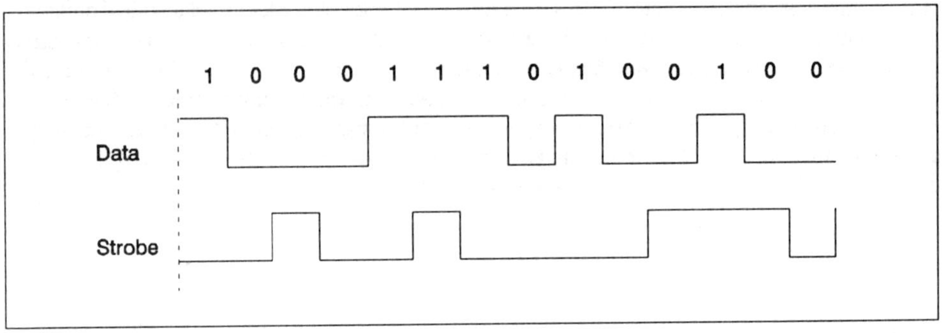

Figure 3.1 Link data format

Since the data–strobe system carries a clock, the links are asynchronous; the receiving device synchronizes to the incoming data. This means that DS-Links 'autobaud'; the only restriction on the transmission rate is that it does not exceed the maximum speed of the receiver. It also simplifies clock distribution within a system, since the exact phase or frequency of the clock on a pair of communicating devices is not critical.

3.3.2 Token level protocol

In order to provide efficient support for higher level protocols, it is useful to be able to encode "tokens" which may contain a data byte or control information (in other standards these might be referred to as "characters" or "symbols" – note that they have no relation to the "token" of a token–ring network). Each token has a parity bit plus a control bit which is used to distinguish between data and control tokens. In addition to the parity and control bits, data tokens contain 8 bits of data and control tokens have two bits to indicate the token type (e.g. 'end of message'). This is illustrated in figure 3.2.

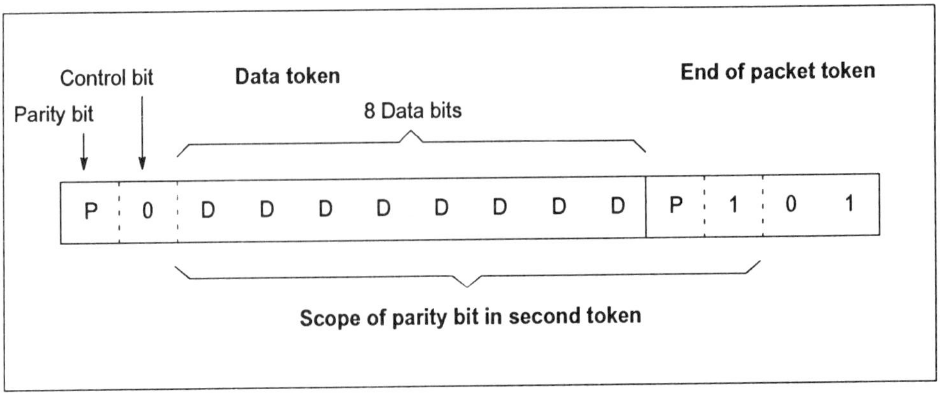

Figure 3.2 Token level protocol

10. NB: This does not correspond with the usual meaning of 'strobe', which would be a signal which indicates *every* time that another signal is valid.

The parity bit in any token covers the parity of the data/control flag in the same token, and the data or control bits in the previous token, as shown in figure 3.2. This allows an error in any single bit of a token, including the token type flag, to be detected even though the tokens are not all the same length. **Odd** parity checking is used. To ensure the immediate detection of errors null tokens are sent in the absence of other tokens. The coding of the control tokens is shown in table 3.1, in which P indicates the position of the parity bit in the token.

Table 3.1 Control token codings

Flow control token	FCT	P100
End of packet	EOP	P101
End of message	EOM	P110
Escape token	ESC	P111
Null token	NUL	ESC P100

Note that the token level of the protocol is independent of details of the higher levels, such as the amount of data contained in a packet, or the particular interpretations of packets of different types.

Token level flow control

Token level flow control (i.e. control of the flow of tokens between devices) is performed in each link module, and the additional tokens used are not visible to the higher–level packet protocol. The token–level flow control mechanism prevents a sender from overrunning the input buffer of a receiving link. Each receiving link input contains a buffer for at least 8 tokens (more buffering than this is in fact provided). Whenever the link input has sufficient buffering available for a further 8 tokens, a flow control token (FCT) is transmitted on the associated link output, and this FCT gives the sender permission to transmit a further 8 tokens. Once the sender has transmitted a further 8 tokens it waits until it receives another FCT before transmitting any more tokens. The provision of more than 8 tokens of buffering on each link input ensures that in practice the next FCT is received before the previous batch of 8 tokens has been fully transmitted, so the token level flow control does not restrict the maximum bandwidth of the link. This is analyzed in detail in chapter 6.

Token level flow control greatly simplifies the higher levels of the protocol, since it prevents data from being lost due to buffer overflow and so removes the need for re–transmission unless errors occur. To the user of the system, the net result is that a connected pair of DS-Links function as a pair of fully handshaken FIFOs, one in each direction.

Note that the link module regulates the flow of data items without regard to the higher level objects that they may constitute. At any instant the data items buffered by a link module may form part or all of one or more consecutive higher–level objects. FCTs do not belong to such objects and are not buffered.

3.3.3 Packet level protocol

In order to transfer data from one device to another, it is sent as one or more packets (in some other serial standards these might be called "frames" or "cells"). This allows a number of simultaneous data transfers to be interleaved on the same link. It also allows data to be routed by packet switches such as the IMS C104 (described later).

Every packet has a header defining the destination address followed by zero or more data bytes and, finally, a 'terminator' token, which may be either an 'end of packet' or an 'end of message' token. See figure 3.3. This simple protocol supports data transfers of any length, even when (for reasons of smooth system performance) the maximum packet size is restricted; the receiving device knows when each packet and message ends without needing to keep track of the number of bytes received.

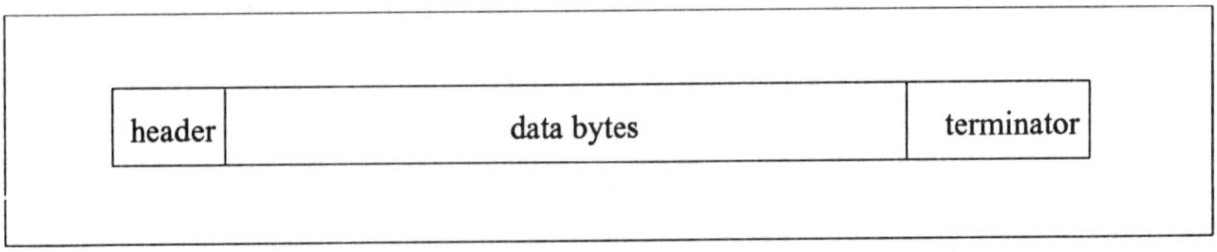

Figure 3.3 Packet format

3.3.4 Higher level protocols

A variety of higher level protocols can be layered on top of this basic system. DS-Link packets can be used as a transport mechanism for protocols defined by other standards such as ATM, SCI and FibreChannel. They also provide very efficient support for synchronised channel communication, as described below.

3.4 Channel communication

A model of communication which can be implemented very efficiently by DS-Links is based on the ideas of communicating sequential processes. The notion of 'process' is very general, and applies equally to pieces of hardware and pieces of software. Each process can be regarded as a "black box" with internal state, which can communicate with other processes using communication channels. Each channel is a point–to–point connection between two processes. One process always inputs from the channel and the other always outputs to it. Communication is synchronized: the first process ready to communicate waits until the second is also ready, then the data is copied from the outputting process to the inputting process and both processes continue. Because a channel is external to the processes which use it, it provides a connection between them which hides their location and internal structure from each other. This means that the interface of a process can be separated from its internal structure (which may involve sub–processes), allowing the easy application of structured engineering principles.

3.4.1 Virtual channels

Each OS-Link of the original transputers implemented only two channels, one in each direction. To map a particular piece of software onto a given hardware configuration the programmer had to map processes to processors within the constraints of available connectivity. The problem is illustrated in figure 3.4 where 3 channels are required between two processors, but only a single link connection is available.

One response to this problem is the addition of more links. However this does not really solve the problem, since the number of extra links that can be added is limited by VLSI technology. Neither does this 'solution' address the more general communication problems in networks, such as communication between non-adjacent processors, or combining networks in a simple and regular way.

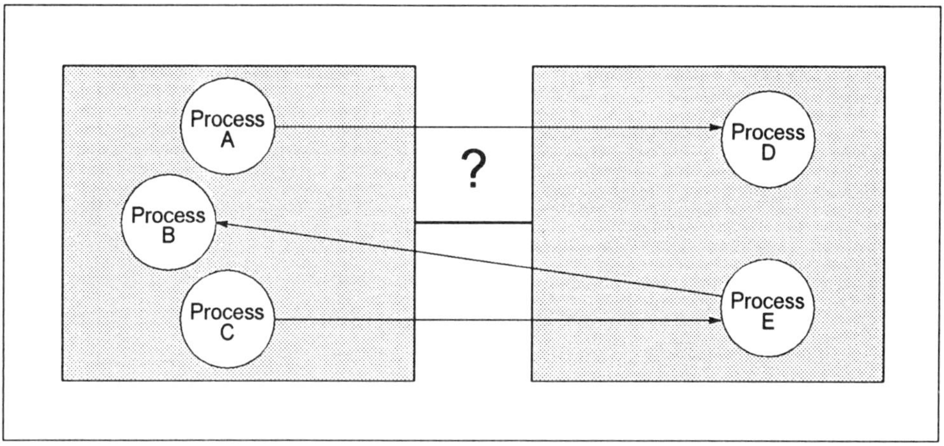

Figure 3.4 Multiple communication channels required between devices

A better solution is to add multiplexing hardware to allow any number of processes to use each link, so that physical links can be shared transparently. These channels which share a link are known as 'virtual channels'.

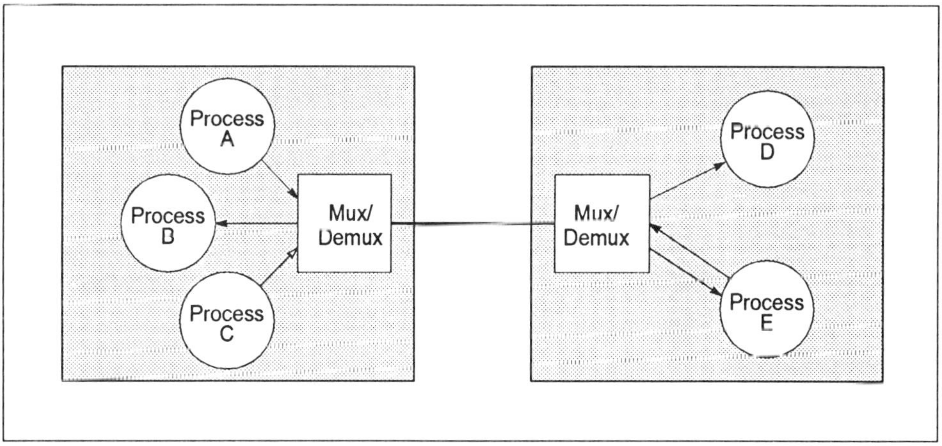

Figure 3.5 Shared DS-Links between devices

Virtual links

Each message sent across a link is divided into packets. Every packet requires a header to identify its channel. Packets from messages on different channels are interleaved on the link. There are two important advantages to this:

- Channels are, generally, not busy all the time, so the multiplexing can make better use of hardware resource by keeping the links busy with messages from different channels.
- Messages from different channels can effectively be sent concurrently – the device does not have to wait for a long message to complete before sending another.

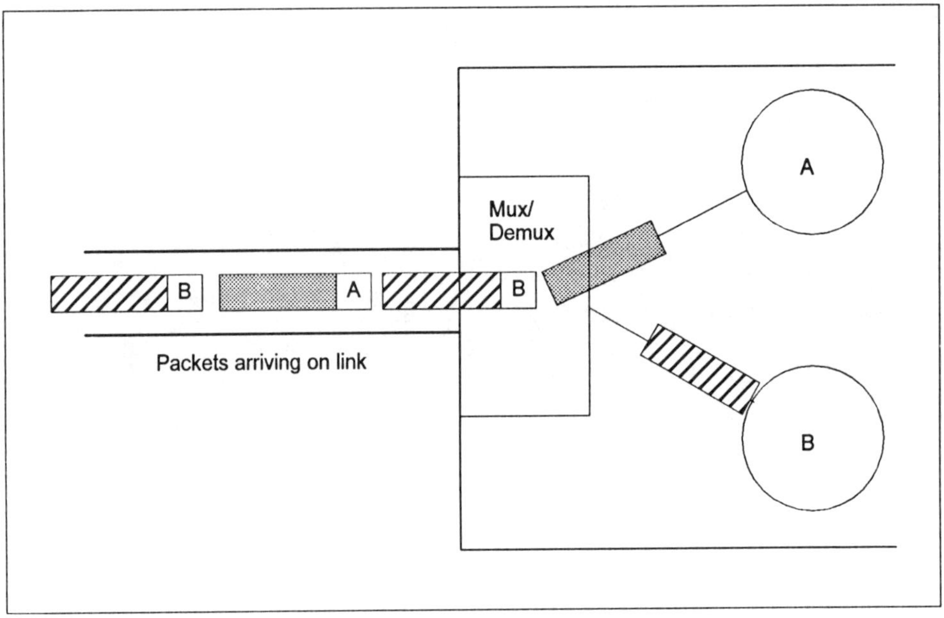

Figure 3.6 Multiple channels sharing a link

In this specific protocol, a packet can contain up to 32 data bytes. If a message is longer than 32 bytes then it is split up into a number of packets all, except the last, terminated by an 'end of packet' token. The last packet of the message, which may contain less than a full 32 bytes, is terminated by an 'end of message' token. Shorter messages can be sent in a single packet, containing 0 to 32 bytes of data, terminated by the 'end of message' token. Messages are always sent using the minimum possible number of packets.

Packet acknowledgements are sent as zero length packets terminated with an 'end of packet' token. This type of packet can never occur as part of a message because a zero length data packet must always be the last, and only, packet of a message, and will therefore be terminated by an 'end of message' token. Each packet of a message must be acknowledged by receipt of an acknowledge packet before the next can be sent. Process synchronization is ensured by delaying the acknowledgement of the first packet of a message until a process is ready to input from the channel, and delaying continuation of the outputting process until all the packets of the message have been sent and acknowledged.

Virtual channels are always created in pairs to form a 'virtual link'. This means it is not necessary to include a return address in packets, since acknowledgements are simply sent back along the other channel of the virtual link. The strict acknowledgement protocol means that it is not necessary to include sequence numbers in the packets, even when the routing network is non–deterministic!

The specific formats of packets used in this system are illustrated in figure 3.7.

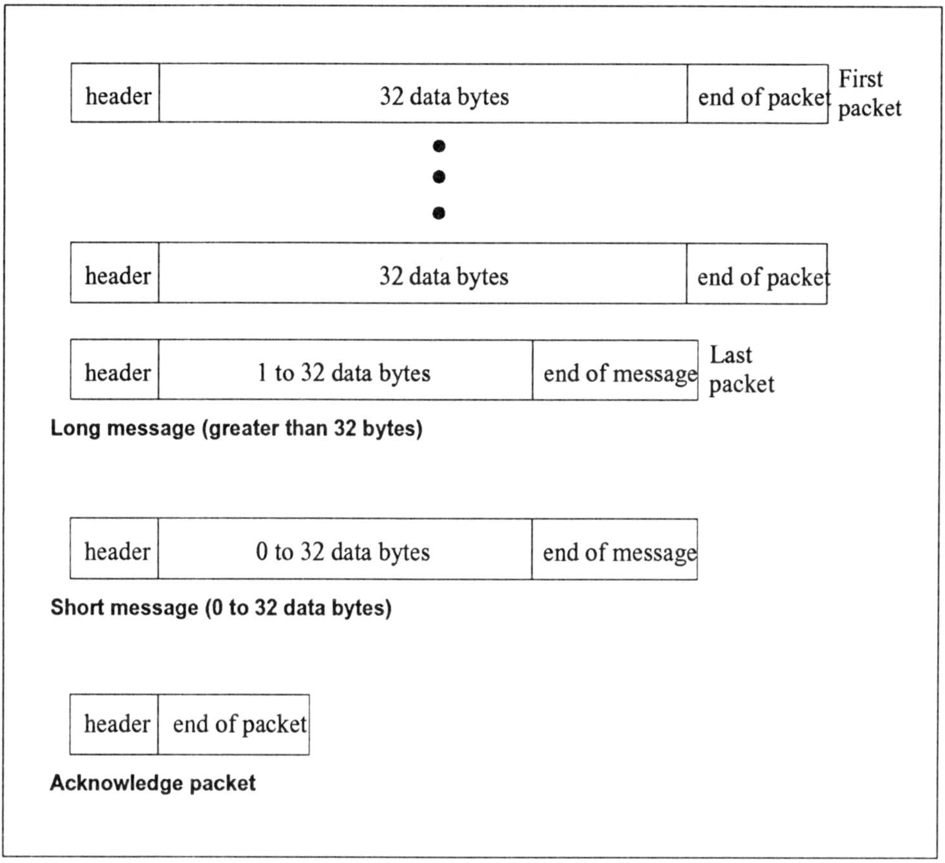

Figure 3.7 High Level protocol packet formats

3.5 Errors on links

The DS-Links are designed to be highly reliable within a single subsystem and can be operated in one of two environments, determined by a flag at each end of the link, called **LocalizeError**.

In applications where all connections are on a single board or within a single box, the communications system can reasonably be regarded as being totally reliable. In this environment errors are considered to be extremely rare, but are treated as being catastrophic should one occur. If an error occurs it will be detected and reported. Normal practice will then be to reset the subsystem in which the error has occurred and to restart the application. This minimizes the overheads on each communication, but if an error does occur there will be an interruption in the operation of the system.

For other applications, for instance when a disconnect or parity error may be expected during normal operation, a higher level of fault–tolerance is required. This is supported by localizing errors to the link on which they occur, by setting the **LocalizeError** bit of the link to 1. If an error occurs, packets in transit at the time of the error will be discarded or truncated, and the link will be reset automatically. This minimizes the interruption of the operation of a system, but imposes an overhead on all communications in order to deal with the possibility that data may be lost.

3.5.1 Errors detected

The DS-Link token protocol allows two common types of error to be detected. Firstly the parity system will detect all single bit errors at the DS-Link token level, and secondly, because each output link, once started, continues to transmit an uninterrupted stream of tokens, the physical disconnection of a link can be detected.

Disconnection errors

If the links are disconnected for any reason whilst they are running then flow control and token synchronization may be lost. In order to restart the link it is therefore necessary to reset both ends to a known flow control and token synchronization point.

Disconnection is detected if, after a token has been received, no tokens are seen on the input link in any 1.6 microsecond window. Once a disconnection error has been detected the link halts its output. This will subsequently be detected as a disconnect error at the other end, and will cause that link to halt its output also. It then resets itself, and waits 12.8 microseconds before allowing communication to restart. This time is sufficient to ensure that both ends of the link have observed disconnection and cycled through reset back into the waiting state. The connection may now be restarted.

Parity errors

Following a parity error, both bit–level token synchronization and flow control status are no longer valid, therefore both ends of the link must be reset. This is done autonomously by the DS-Link using an exchange–of–silence protocol.

When a DS-Link detects a parity error on its input it halts its output. This will subsequently be detected as a disconnect error at the other end, and will cause that link to halt its output also, causing a disconnect to be detected at the first end. The normal disconnect behavior described above will then ensure that both ends are reset (irrespective of line delay) before either is allowed to restart.

3.6 Network communications: the IMS C104

The use of DS-Links for directly connecting devices has already been described. The link protocol not only simplifies the use of links between devices but also provides hardware support for routing messages across a network.

The system described previously packetizes messages to be sent over a link and adds a header to each packet to identify the virtual channel. These headers can also be used for routing packets through a communication system connecting a number of devices together. This extends the idea of multiple channels on a single hardware link to multiple channels through a communications system; a communications channel can be established between any two devices even if they are not directly connected.

Because the link architecture allows all the virtual channels of a device to use a single link, complete, system-wide connectivity can be provided by connecting just one link from each device to the routing network. This can be exploited in a number of ways. For example, two or more networks can be used in parallel to increase bandwidth, to provide fault–tolerance, or as a ‘user’ network running in parallel with a physically separate ‘system’ network.

The IMS C104 is a device with 32 DS-Links which can route packets between every pair of links with low latency. An important benefit of using serial links is that it is easy to implement a full crossbar in VLSI, even with a large number of links. The use of a crossbar allows packets to be passing through all links at the same time, making the best possible use of the available bandwidth.

If the routing logic can be kept simple it can be provided for all the input links in the router. This avoids the need to share the hardware, which would cause extra delays when several packets arrive at the same time. It is also desirable to avoid the need for the large number of packet buffers commonly used in routing systems. The use of small buffers and simple routing hardware allows a single VLSI chip to provide efficient routing between a large number of links.

A single IMS C104 can be used to provide full connectivity between 32 devices. IMS C104s can also be connected together to build larger switch networks connecting any number of devices.

3.6.1 Wormhole routing

The IMS C104 includes a full 32 x 32 non-blocking crossbar switch, enabling messages to be routed from any of its links to any other link. In order to minimize latency, the switch uses 'wormhole routing', in which the connection through the crossbar is set up as soon as the header has been read. The header and the rest of the packet can start being transmitted from the output link immediately. The path through the switch disappears after the 'end of packet/message' token has passed through. This is illustrated in figure 3.8. This method is simple to implement and provides very low latency as the entire packet does not have to be read in before the connection is made.

Minimizing routing delays

The ability to start outputting a packet while it is still being input can significantly reduce delay, especially in lightly loaded networks. The delay can be further minimized by keeping the headers short and by using fast, simple hardware to determine the link to be used for output. The IMS C104 uses a simple routing algorithm based on interval labelling (described in section 3.6.3).

Because the route through each IMS C104 disappears as soon as the packet has passed through and the packets from all the channels that pass through a particular link are interleaved, no single virtual channel can monopolize a route through a network. Messages will not be blocked waiting for another message to pass through the system, they will only have to wait for one packet.

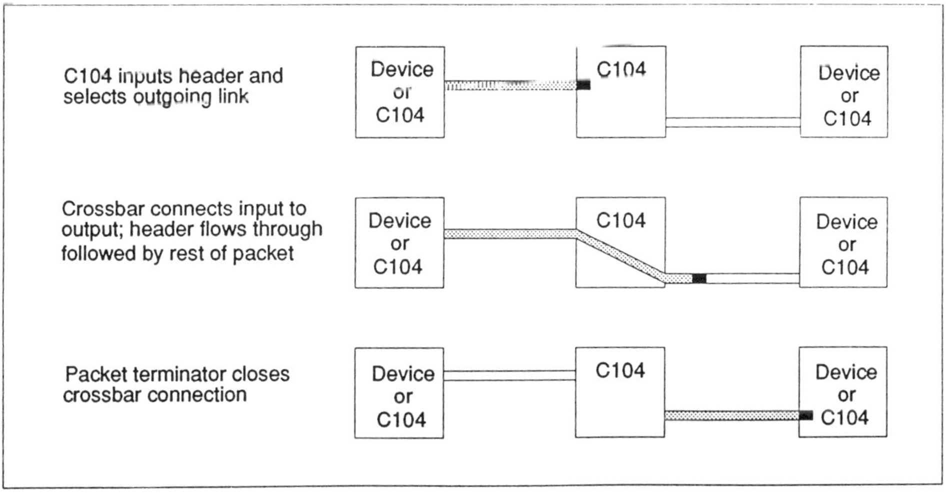

Figure 3.8 Packet passing through IMS C104

The IMS C104s that the packets pass through do not need to have information about the complete route to the destination, only which link each packet should be sent out of at each point. Each of the IMS C104s in the network is programmed with information that determines which output link should be used for each header value. In this way, each IMS C104 can route packets out of whichever link will send it towards its destination.

3.6.2 Header deletion

An approach that simplifies the construction of networks is to provide two levels of header on each packet. The first header specifies the destination device (actually, the output link from the routing network), and is removed as the packet leaves the routing system. This exposes the second header which tells the destination device which process (actually, which virtual channel) this packet is for. To support this, the IMS C104 can route packets of any length. Any information after the initial header bytes used by the IMS C104 is just treated as part of the packet, even if it is going to be interpreted as a header elsewhere in the system. Any output link of the IMS C104 can be set to do header deletion, i.e. to remove the routing header from the front of each packet after it been used to make the routing decision. The first part of the remaining data is then treated as a header by the next device that receives the packet.

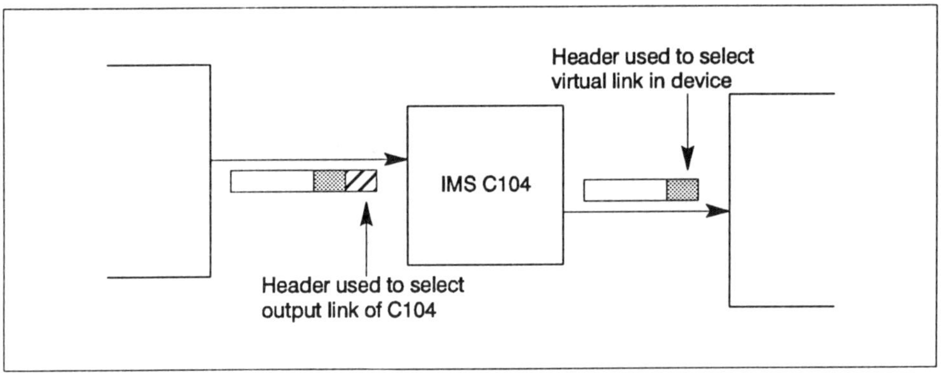

Figure 3.9 Header deletion

As can be seen from figure 3.10, by using separate headers to identify the destination device and a channel within that device, the labelling of links in a routing network is separated from the labelling of virtual channels within each device. For instance, if the same 2 byte header were used to do all the routing in a network, then the virtual channels in all the devices would have to be uniquely labelled with a value in the range 0 to 64K. However, by using two 1 byte headers, all the devices can use virtual channel numbers in the range 0 to 255. The first byte of the header will be used by the routing system to ensure that the packets reach the appropriate device before the virtual channel number is decoded.

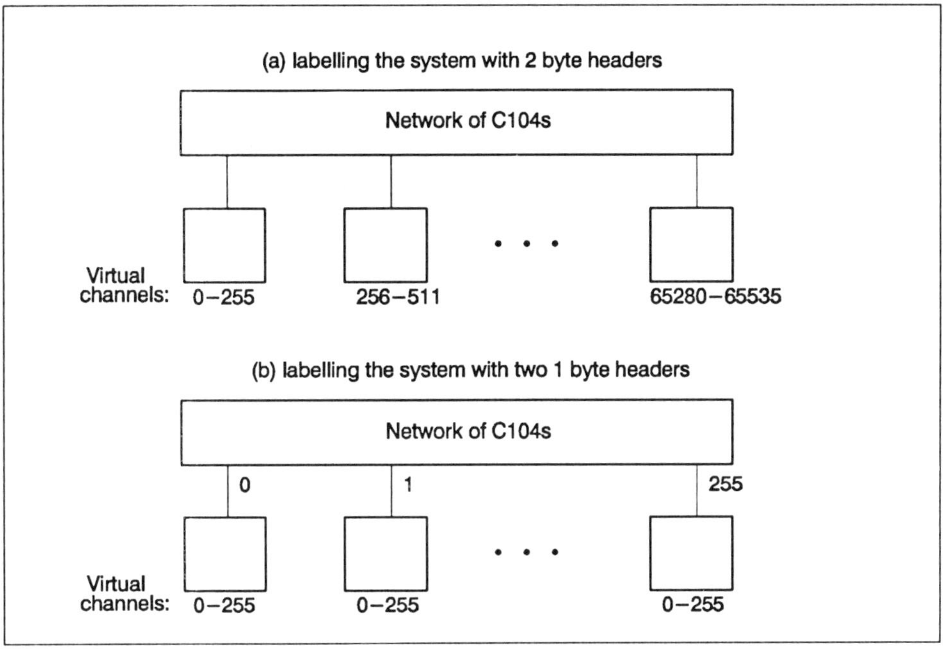

Figure 3.10 Using header deletion to label a network

The advantages of using header deletion in a network are:

- It separates the headers for virtual channels from those for the routing network.
- The labelling of the network can be done independently of the application using the network.
- There is no limit to the number of virtual channels that can be handled by a system.
- By keeping the header for routing short, routing latency is minimized.

Any number of headers can be added to the beginning of a packet so that header deletion can also be used to combine hierarchies of networks as shown in figure 3.11. An extra header is added to route the message through each network. The header at the front of each packet is deleted as it leaves each network to enter a sub-network. This is just like the local–national–international hierarchy of telephone numbers. Since the operation of the IMS C104 is completely independent of the length of the packets, the fact that header deletion changes the length of a packet as it passes through the network causes no problem at all.

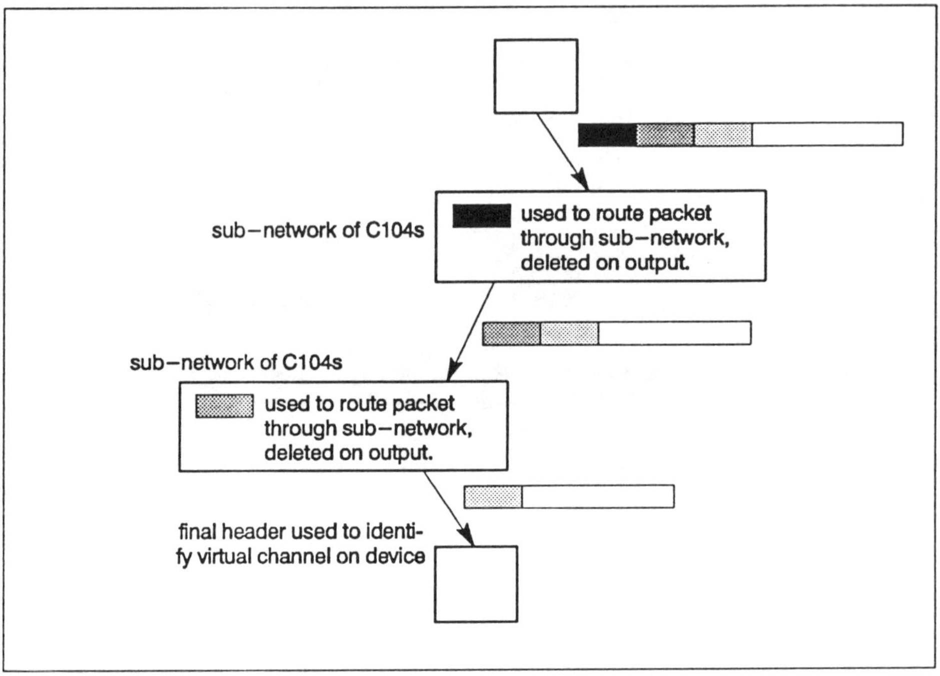

Figure 3.11 Using header deletion to route through sub-networks

3.6.3 Labelling networks

For each IMS C104 there will be a number of destinations which can be reached via each of its output links. Therefore, there needs to be a method of deciding which output link to use for each packet that arrives. The addresses that can be reached through any link will depend on the way the network is labelled. An obvious way of determining which destinations are accessible from each link, is to have a lookup table associated with all the outputs (see figure 3.12). In practice, this is difficult to implement. There must be an upper bound on the lookup table size and it may require a large number of comparisons between the header value and the contents of the table. This is inefficient in silicon area and also potentially slow.

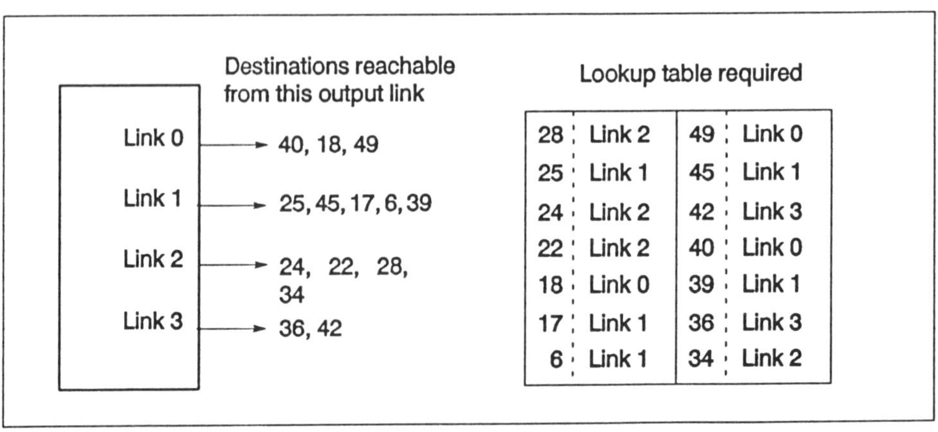

Figure 3.12 Labelling a network

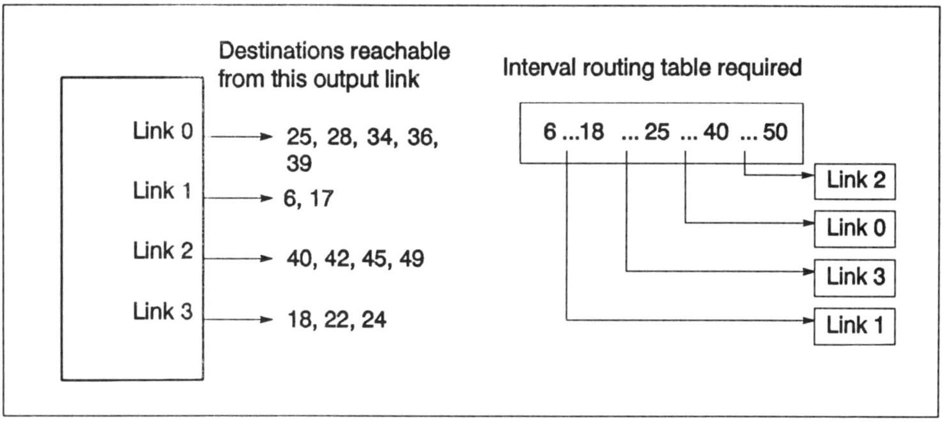

Figure 3.13 Interval labelling

However, a labelling scheme can be chosen for the network such that each output link has a *range* of node addresses that can be reached through it. As long as the ranges for each link are non-overlapping, a very simple test is possible. The header just has to be tested to see into which range, or interval, it falls and, hence, which output link to use. For example, in figure 3.13, a header with address n would be tested against each of the four intervals shown below:

Interval	Output link
$6 \leq n < 18$	1
$18 \leq n < 25$	3
$25 \leq n < 40$	0
$40 \leq n < 50$	2

The advantages of interval labelling are that:

- It is 'complete' – any network can be labelled so that all packets reach their destinations.
- It provides an absolute address for each device in a network, so keeping the calculation of headers simple.
- It is simple to implement in hardware – it requires little silicon area which means it can be provided for a large number of links as well as keeping costs and power dissipation down.
- Because it is simple, it is also very fast, keeping routing delays to a minimum.

Figure 3.14 gives an example of interval routing for a network of two IMS C104's and six IMS T9000 transputers showing one virtual link per transputer. The example shows six virtual channels, one to each transputer, labeled 0 to 5. The interval contains the labels of all virtual channels accessible via that link. The interval notation [3,6) is read as meaning that the header value must be greater than or equal to 3 and less than 6. If the progress of a packet with the header value 4 is followed from IMS $T9000_1$ then it is evident that it passes through both IMS C104s before leaving on the link to IMS $T9000_4$.

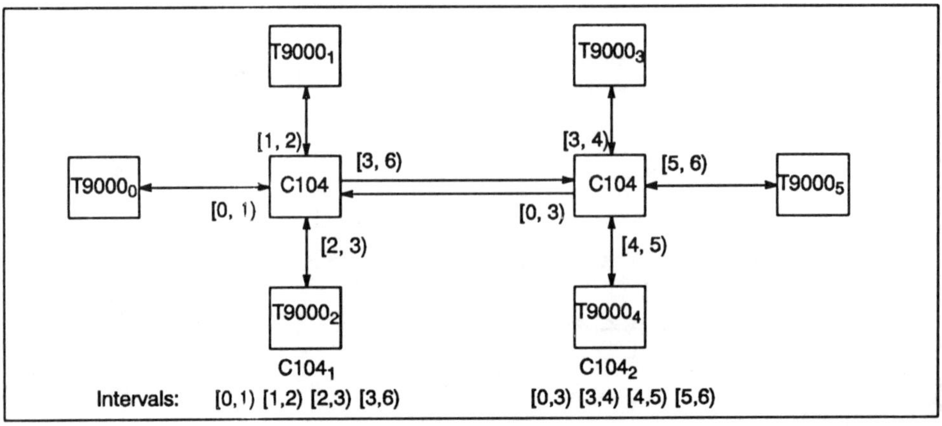

Figure 3.14 Interval routing

It is possible to label all the major network topologies such that packets follow an optimal route through the network, and such that the network is deadlock free. Optimal, deadlock free labelings are available for grids, hypercubes, trees and various multi–stage networks. A few topologies, such as rings, cannot be labeled in an optimal deadlock free manner. Although they can be labeled so that they are deadlock free, this is at the expense of not using one or more of the links, so that the labeling is not optimal. Optimal deadlock free labelings exist if one or more additional links are used.

3.6.4 Partitioning

All the parameters determining the routing are programmable on a per link basis. This enables an IMS C104 to be used as part of two or more different networks. For example, a single IMS C104 could be used for access to both a data network and a control network (see figure 3.15).

Partitioning provides economy in small systems, where using an IMS C104 solely for a control network is not desired, whilst maintaining absolute security. By ensuring that no link belonging to one partition occurs in any interval routing table in another partition, it is guaranteed that no packet can be routed from one partition to another, whatever the value of its header.

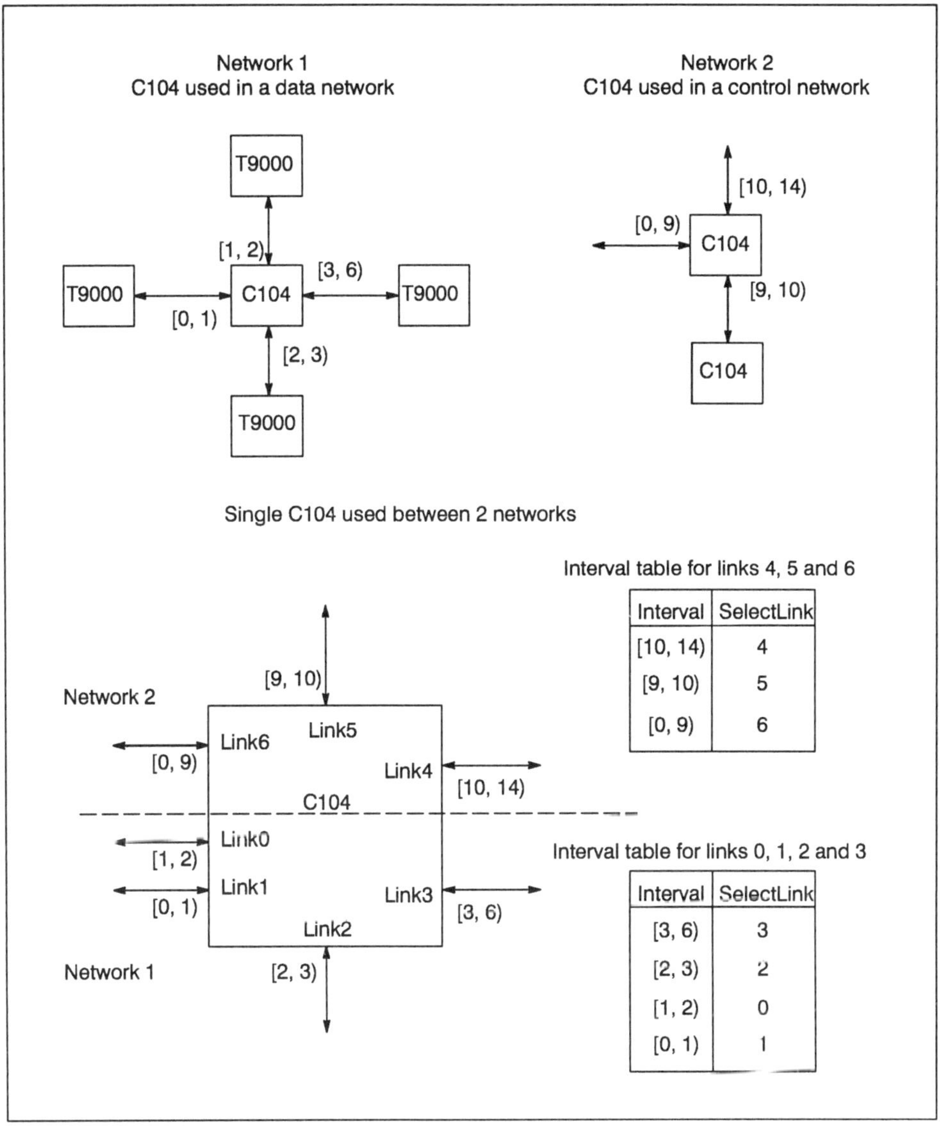

Figure 3.15 Using partitioning to enable one C104 to be used by two different networks

3.6.5 Grouped adaptive routing

The IMS C104 can implement *grouped adaptive routing*. Sets of consecutive numbered links can be configured to be grouped, so that a packet routed to any link in the set would be sent down any free link of the set[11]. This achieves improved network performance in terms of both latency and throughput.

Figure 3.16 gives an example of grouped adaptive routing. Consider a message routed from $C104_1$, via $C104_2$, to $T9000_1$. On entering $C104_2$ the header specifies that the message is to be output down **Link5** to $T9000_1$. If **Link5** is already in use, the message will automatically be

11. This is also sometimes called a *hunt group*.

routed down **Link6**, **Link7** or **Link8**, dependent on which link is available first. The links can be configured in groups by setting a bit for each link, which can be set to 'Start' to begin a group and 'Continue' to be included in a group.

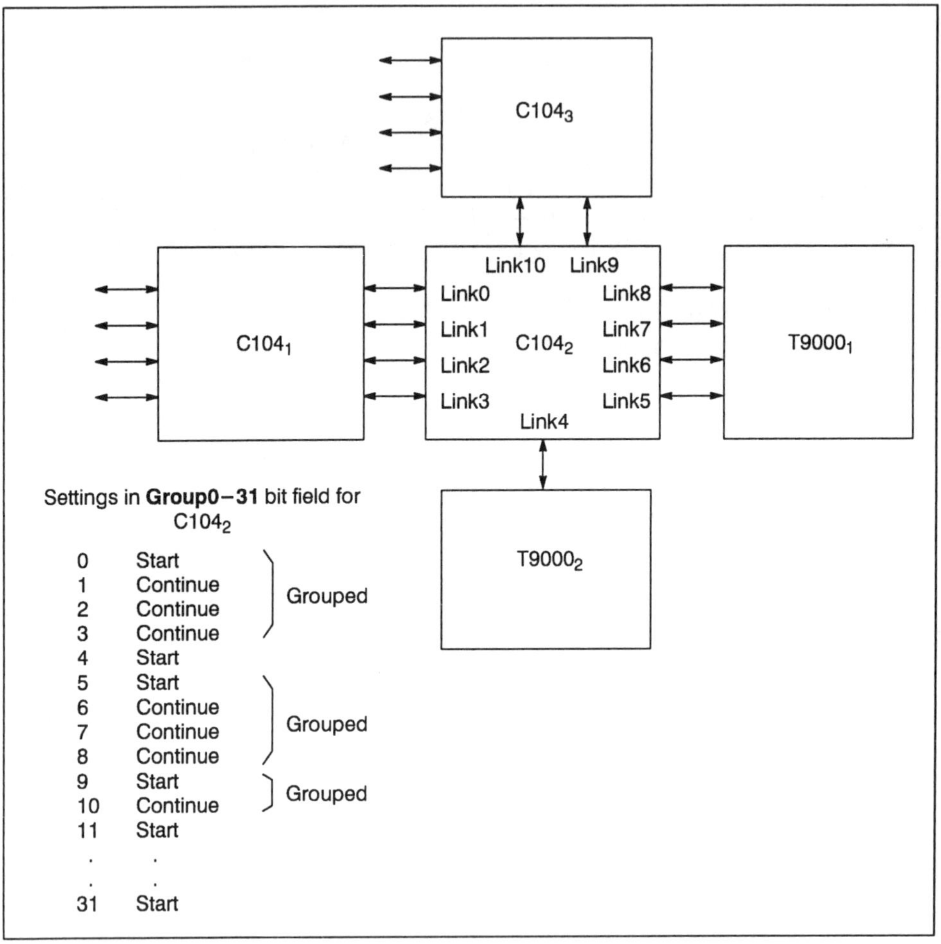

Figure 3.16 Grouped adaptive routing

3.7 Conclusion

DS-Link technology provides reliable, high–speed serial communications at low cost, in a simple form which is suitable for a wide range of applications. A simple protocol, implemented in hardware, keeps overheads down whilst allowing more complex functions to be layered on top of it. It also permits high–performance routing devices to be constructed, from which efficient systems of any size can be built to provide very high system bandwidth and fault–tolerance.

4 Connecting DS-Links

4.1 Introduction

Digital design engineers are accustomed to signals that behave as ones and zeros, although they have to be careful about dissipation and ground inductance, which become increasingly important as speeds increase. Communications engineers, on the other hand, are accustomed to disappearing signals. They design modems that send 19200 bits per second down telephone wires that were designed 90 years ago to carry 3.4KHz voice signals. Their signals go thousands of kilometers. They are used to multiplexing lots of slow signals down a single fast channel. They use repeaters, powered by the signal wires.

Digital designers do not need all these communications techniques yet. But sending 100Mbits/s or more down a cable much longer than a meter has implications that are more analog than digital, which must be taken care of just like the dissipation and ground inductance problems, to ensure that signals still behave as ones and zeros.

Actually, it is easy to overestimate the problems of these signal speeds. Engineers designing with ECL, even fifteen years ago, had to deal with some of the problems of transmitting such signals reliably, at least through printed circuit boards (PCBs), backplanes, and short cables. One of the best books on the subject is the Motorola 'MECL System Design Handbook' [1] by William R Blood, Jr., which explains about transmission lines in PCBs and cables. This shows waveforms of a 50MHz signal at the end of 50ft (15m) of twisted pair, and of a 350MHz signal at the end of 10ft (3m) of twisted pair, both with respectable signals.

This chapter first discusses the signal properties of DS-Links. PCB and cable connections are then described, followed by a section on error rates: errors are much less frequent on transputer links than is normal in communications. A longer section introduces some of the characteristics of optical connections including optical fibre, which should be suitable for link connections up to 500m, using an interface chip to convert between the link and the fibre. A pointer is given towards possible standards for link connections. Appendix A describes a connector that will assist standardization of transputer link connections. Appendix B shows waveforms of signals transmitted through cable and fibre. Appendix C gives detailed electrical parameters of DS-Links, and appendix D gives an equivalent circuit for the DS-Link output pads.

4.2 Signal properties of transputer links

Considerable design work has gone into making the DS-Link signals [4] well behaved. The bit-level protocol and the electrical characteristics both contribute to make the link signals unusually easy to use, for serial data at 100MBits/s.

The DS-Link information is carried by a pair of wires in each direction. The D signal carries data bits, and the S signal is a strobe, which changes level every bit time that the D signal does not change[12]. This is illustrated in figure 4.1. This bit-level protocol guarantees that there is a transition on either D or S every bit time. Effectively this provides a Gray code between the D and S signals.

12. Note that this differs from the usual meaning of a 'strobe', which is a signal which indicates *every* time the data signal is valid.

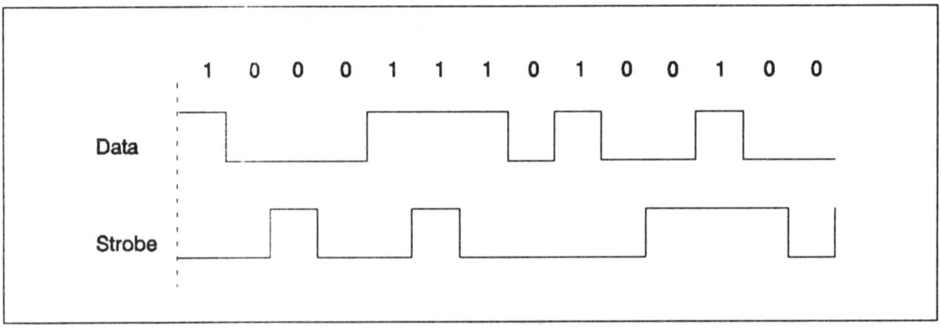

Figure 4.1 DS-Link signals

One result of the DS Gray coding is that the received data is decoded purely from the *sequence* of D and S transitions rather than depending on any absolute time. This means that the link receivers 'autobaud', receiving data at whatever speed it is sent (so long as the receiver logic is fast enough).

The Gray coding makes it much easier to design logic that is fast enough, because the timing resolution required is a whole bit time. Alternative codings would require a clock edge in the centre of a data bit, and hence require timing resolution of half a bit time. The more relaxed timing resolution needed by the DS-Links gives major benefits in terms of the performance that can be achieved in practical systems.

A further advantage of the coding, with only D or S changing at a time, is that the signal can be received without a phase-locked loop (PLL) – the clock is just the Exclusive-OR of the D and S signals. For the C104 routing switch, avoiding the need for 32 PLLs is very valuable, and it is likely that a 32 way routing switch would not be implementable had the PLLs been required.

Electrical aspects of the design include a controlled output impedance approximately matched to a 100Ω transmission line[13]. Obviously there is a tolerance on the impedance, which also may not be identical for high and low, but the DS-Link has been designed to minimize the effect of any such mismatch on the signal.

The link outputs have also been designed to give controlled rise and fall times. The full electrical characteristics will not be known until the devices are fully characterized, but a reasonable estimate of the transition times is 3ns fastest transition and 6ns slowest transition.

The DS coding gives as much tolerance as possible for skew between the D and S signals, and the outputs and inputs have been designed to have minimal skew at the TTL threshold of 1.5V.

These characteristics of the DS-Link signals make them ideal for connections on PCBs, and for DC coupled connections on short lengths of cable, up to 10m. Later sections will describe such connections, as well as much longer connections up to 500m using optical methods.

4.3 PCB connections

The following discussion assumes the use of multi-layer PCBs with power and ground planes; use of DS–Links on double-sided boards without ground planes is not recommended.

A 100Ω transmission line impedance is fairly easy to achieve on the surface of a PCB. PCBs have been made with long connections of 100Ω impedance which carry link signals faithfully. The 100Ω impedance requires a track width between 0.1mm and 0.3mm, depending on the board

13. See appendix C.

thickness and where the power planes are located within it. Figure 4.2 (derived from data given in Blood [1], from SONY [2], and from Coombs [3]) shows the approximate relationship between these parameters for standard FR4 PCB material with a dielectric constant of 4.7.

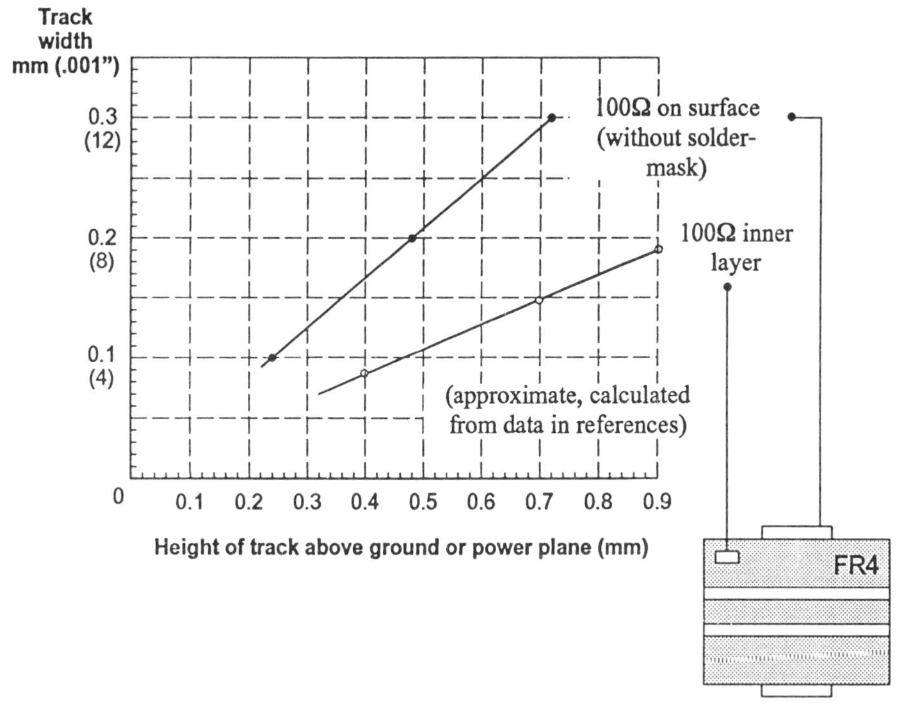

Figure 4.2 Graph showing approximate PCB transmission line impedance for FR4 laminate

Note that when a PCB track is buried in the fiberglass/epoxy laminate, its impedance is reduced by about 20% compared with a surface track. This requires the inner layer tracks to be narrower than surface tracks, to minimize differences in impedance. It is not possible, within the normal 1.6mm board thickness, to have 100Ω tracks sandwiched between power or ground planes.

If the transmission line impedance could be maintained with high precision, PCB DS-Link connections would be good for several meters, in theory. However in practice it is hard to maintain a tighter tolerance than +/– 20%. It is therefore advisable to limit the connections on PCBs to less than 1000mm with standard FR4 PCB material. If the impedance goes outside the range of 80Ω to 120Ω, it is advisable to limit the connection to 500mm.

Short discontinuities in the impedance are permissible, such as connectors, vias, and short sections of track of higher or lower impedance; such discontinuities should be kept to less than 50mm. Similarly, if it is necessary to use some PCB tracks of higher impedance than 100Ω, and some lower than 100Ω, it is best if they can be alternated in short sections, rather than having a 400mm length of 125Ω track and then a 400mm length of 80Ω track.

The controlled transition times of the DS-Links minimize crosstalk compared with the sub-nanosecond fall times of some of the fast families of 'TTL', but care still needs to be taken over crosstalk. Tests, simulations, and theory using typical PCB materials and DS–Link outputs suggest that backwards crosstalk increases as the length of the parallel tracks increase up to 25cm, and does not increase for longer parallel tracks. Track separation of 0.15mm over this length appears to give 1 volt of crosstalk, which is above the noise margin. Simulations of track separation of 1.25mm over a length of 20cm give crosstalk figures of less than 100mV.

The references [1], [2], and [3] do not give a great deal of information about PCB crosstalk, and the results above suggest that further work is required. In the meantime, it must be good practice to avoid long parallel runs and to space the tracks out as far as possible. Another technique is to use guard tracks (tracks connected to 0V) between link tracks, although the effects of this on the impedance of the link track may need to be taken into account.

The D and S pair of signals should be approximately the same length, but a difference in length of 50mm would only introduce a skew of 250ps, which should be totally acceptable.

4.4 Cable connections

This section looks at existing cable interfaces, comparing them with transputer links, and then discusses the loss and noise that occur in a cable, and what can be done to overcome their effects.

4.4.1 Existing cable interfaces and rough costs

Ethernet connections are now inexpensive, with a component cost well under $50 and an end-user cost around $150. Transputer links are even less expensive with a low cost T400 having two OS-Links each capable of 20Mbits/s full duplex, a total bandwidth four times that of ethernet.

Token Ring goes a little faster than Ethernet, but to go substantially faster the next standard is FDDI at 125 MBits/s (of which 100 Mbits/s are useful data). FDDI is expensive, not only in its protocol, but even in its components, and just the optical transceiver is not expected to fall below $100 even in volume for some time.

Links on the T9000 transputer run at 100 MBits/s, full duplex. The cost per link is considerably less than either the chipset or the transceiver for FDDI. The C104 routing switch, with 32 ports will give a cost per port well under $10 – at least an order of magnitude less than the FDDI component cost.

Ethernet, Token Ring, and FDDI are all local area networks, with many ports in a network and long distances between ports. Transputer links are point-to-point, and are generally expected to be comparatively short connections. In this respect they are more like the recent parallel interfaces such as SCSI2, IPI and HPPI. HPPI as an example has a maximum length of 25m, and runs at 800 Mbits/s in one direction down a cable with 50 twisted pairs. The same speed in both directions requires two cables, and the speed can be doubled by using two cables in each direction.

FibreChannel is a fibre connection with similar data rates to HPPI, using laser diodes. This will allow much longer connections than HPPI, at drastically lower cable costs, but possibly with a high cost per port.

4.4.2 Vanishing signals (High frequency attenuation)

Copper wire has a finite resistance: 28AWG wire is one of the smallest cross sections in widespread use and has a resistance of 0.23Ω/m, 1Ω in 4.3m. If the characteristic impedance of the cable is 100Ω, a resistance of 10 ohms is not going to affect the signal very much, so this cable should certainly be usable at 43m. The problem is that at high frequencies, the signal does not flow evenly throughout the conductor but concentrates at the outside of the conductor – the skin effect. So the higher the frequency of the signal, the more the resistance of the cable. Some of the energy does not flow in the conductor at all, but in the insulation and, if it can, in adjacent conductors causing crosstalk as well as loss. Some of the energy is sent into the atmosphere to interfere with radios and other users of the airwaves.

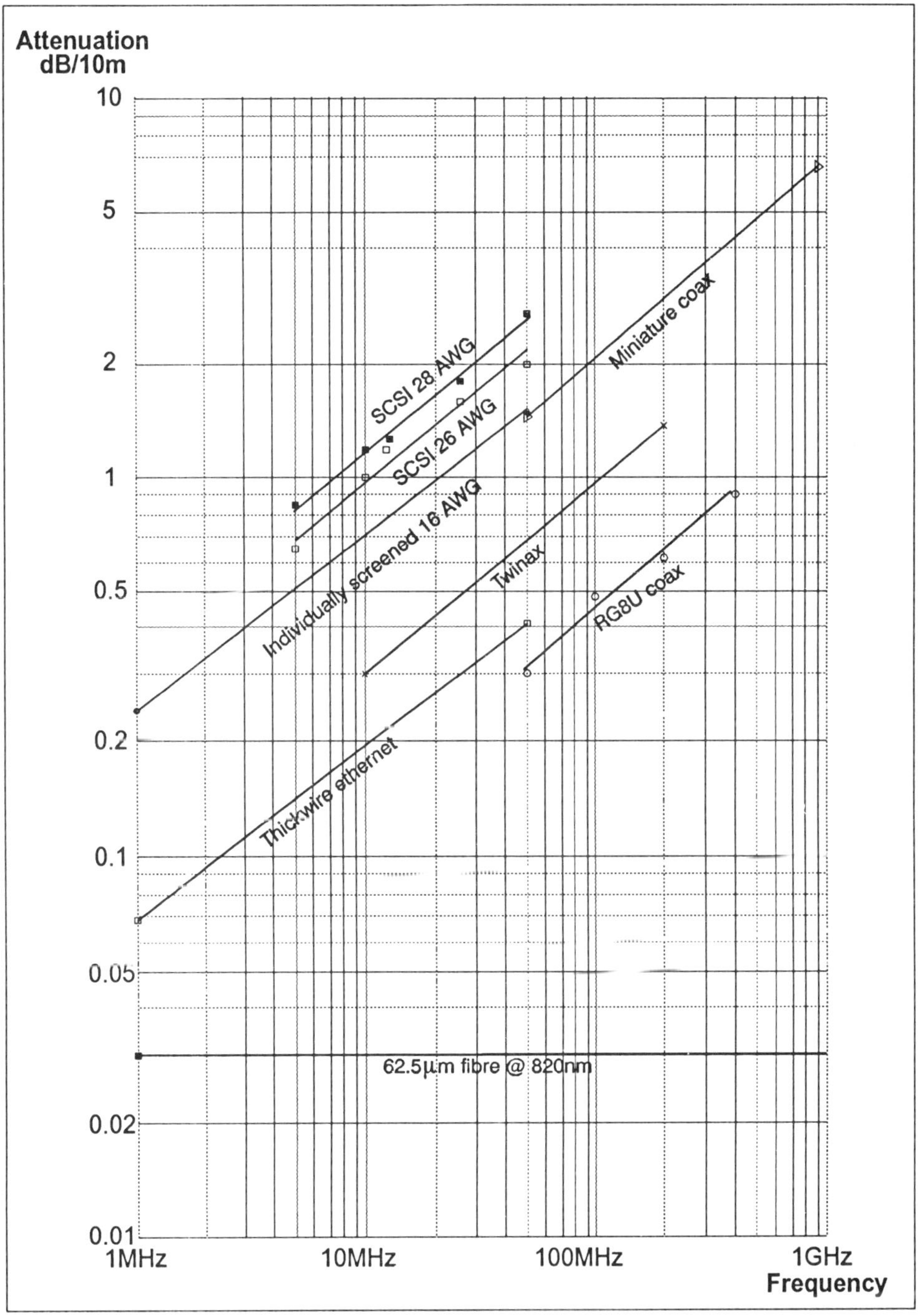

Figure 4.3 Cable attenuation against frequency for a variety of cables

The sum of these losses of energy which depend on frequency is measured in dB (deciBels) per unit length. Figure 4.3 plots these losses for a number of cables – some inexpensive, some extremely expensive. The detail is not important but note that for all of the electrical cables the loss increases with frequency.

The increase of loss with frequency means that the higher the frequency to be passed along the cable and the longer the cable, the less 'lossy' (and probably more expensive) the cable will have to be. Above some length of connection, the losses have to be compensated for somehow – as in Telecommunications – and more tricks have to be used, increasing the cost of the circuitry at the ends of the cable, and possibly adding repeaters in the cable. At some stage, it will become worth while to use optical fibre, an example of which is shown in figure 4.3.

The increased loss at high frequency can be overcome by using a cable short enough that the loss is minimal. At 100MHz, this could mean less than a meter for some of the cables illustrated. The effect of using a longer cable is distortion of the signal. Figure 4.4 shows the sort of thing that happens to an NRZ (Non Return to Zero) signal which has suffered a 10dB loss[14] at the frequency of the square wave. The dotted line represents the DC threshold of the receiver, which suggests that the signal will not be received correctly, even if there is no noise.

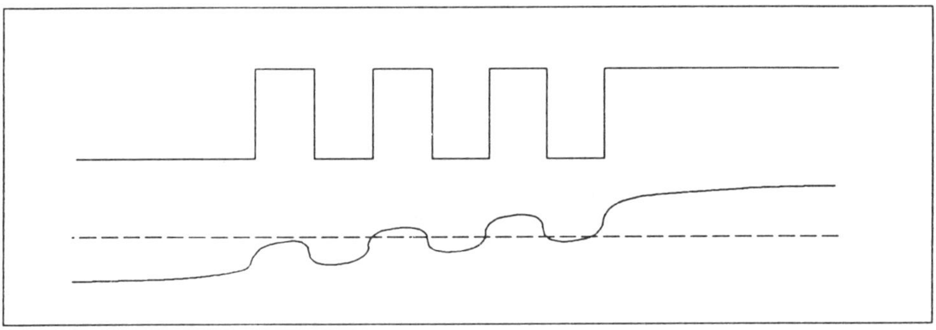

Figure 4.4 Cable as a low-pass filter

Figure 4.5 shows a similar effect to figure 4.4, but the received high frequency voltage is now about 0.6 times the transmitted voltage, representing a loss at this frequency of around 4.5dB. At 100Mbits/s, the 'sine wave' part of figure 4.5 is 50MHz, and the 28AWG IPI/SCSI2 cable[15] shown in figure 4.3 has a loss of 2.8dB for 10m at 50MHz, so in the absence of noise, and with a receiver which had sufficient gain and is tolerant of small errors in timing, this cable might just work not at 43m but at (4.5/2.8) × 10m or 16m. In practice the maximum length will be less than this.

14. The 10dB loss means that the power at the receiver is 1/10 of the power at the transmitter. As power is volts times amps, both of which are reduced in the same proportion, the received voltage for a 10dB loss is 0.33 times the transmitted voltage.

15. The 28AWG and 26AWG Madison cables, shown in figure 4.3, have also been designed to minimize the skew that can occur between any two pairs in the cable, resulting in a skew of 0.04ns/ft, which is an order of magnitude better than that of cables which have not been so designed. Skew is important for parallel interfaces such as SCSI or HIPPI, and is equally important for DS-Links.

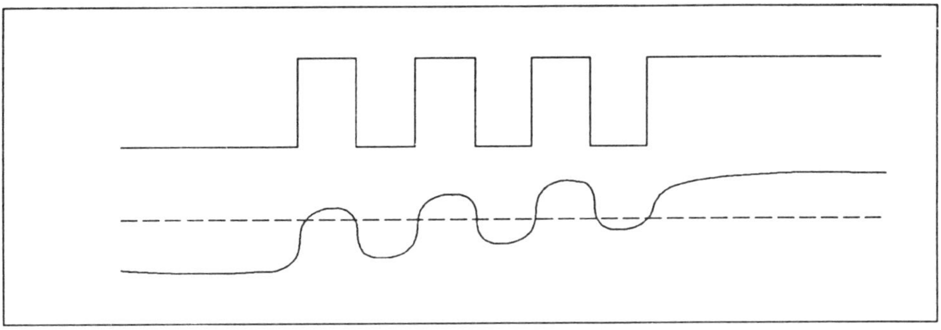

Figure 4.5 Almost enough signal

4.4.3 Boxes are not at the same voltage (Common mode, DC coupled differential signals)

For a cable several meters long between two boxes, there may be crosstalk and it can not be guaranteed that there will be no difference between the boxes' ground or logic 0V levels. Any difference will be seen as noise.

A good way to remove the effect of the difference in grounds between the two boxes is to send differential signals. These are shown in figure 4.6. Any difference in ground voltage will be seen as common mode by a receiving differential buffer.

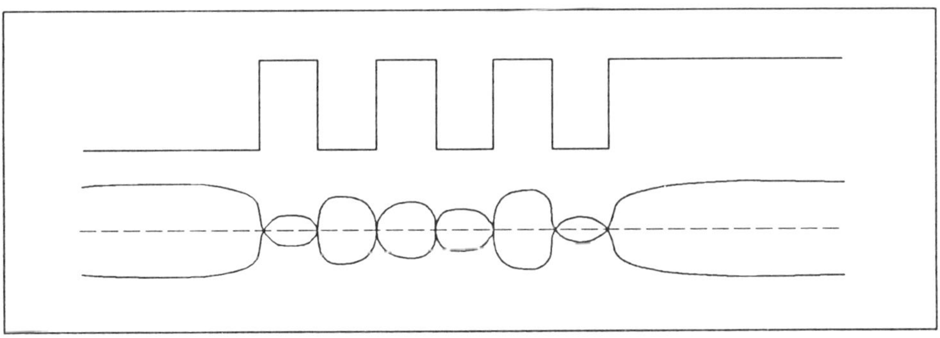

Figure 4.6 DC coupled differential signal

A popular standard differential signals is RS422, whose receivers have a common mode tolerance of +/– 7V. The RS422 components are limited to 10MBits/s or 20MBits/s, and so are not suitable for higher bit rate DS-Links. However they have been found to be extremely reliable when used to connect OS–Links between boxes, which shows that differential signalling is effective. DS-Links therefore simply require faster differential buffers.

ECL buffers are much faster than the RS422 components. Blood shows 'scope traces of a 350MHz signal after a receiver at the end of 10ft of twisted pair. Unfortunately the ECL common mode tolerance is much less than RS422, from +1V to -1.8V or -2.5V depending on the device used.

A family of devices from AT&T (41 series of High Performance Line Drivers, Receivers, Transceivers.) offers speed approaching that of ECL together with common mode tolerance approaching that of RS422. The transmitters have TTL inputs and pseudo-ECL outputs, and the receivers convert the pseudo-ECL back to TTL. One range of devices runs up to 100MHz (200MBits/s), another to 200MHz (400MBits/s). Common mode tolerance is from -1.2V to +7.2V, with the 1V signal approximately in the middle of of this range.

Tests have been done using these buffers which indicate that a 10m link running at 100 Mbits/s should work reliably.

The cable used for the tests was 30AWG individually shielded twisted pairs. The shielding and the use of 30AWG both increase attenuation compared with the 28AWG unshielded cable mentioned earlier; the shielding minimizes EMC emissions for FCC and other regulations, eliminates crosstalk, and the 30AWG reduces the size of the cable.

4.4.4 Ground differences more than a few volts (AC coupling, DC balance)

In the last section, we overcame some problems by using balanced, differential signals. Larger common mode voltages between two boxes can be overcome by using AC coupling, which requires a different sort of balance. Figure 4.7 shows a signal which has a mark-to-space ratio of 4-1: on the receive side of the AC coupling, the threshold is set by averaging the received voltage. As a result, the threshold is heavily offset, reducing the noise margin and changing timings.

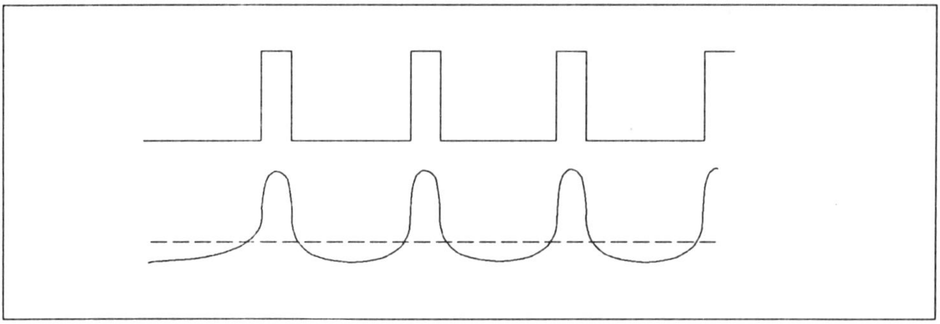

Figure 4.7 Effect of DC imbalance

In order to provide DC balance, so that the threshold is in the middle of the signal, the data is *coded* in some way, usually by adding redundant bits to achieve the desired signal characteristics. One of the most popular forms of DC balanced coding is Manchester Code, which provides DC balance over every bit period, at the expense of doubling the bit–rate. An alternative to coding is to *modulate* a carrier, in amplitude, in frequency, in phase, or in combinations of these, with different data values being represented by different amplitudes, frequencies or phases; the carrier is a sine wave which is inherently DC balanced.

Even when there is no DC component in the signal, a long period without a transition can cause the signal to disappear. Codes therefore have a maximum *run length* to limit this time between transitions; they also have a minimum run length, to ensure that two adjacent edges do not cancel each other out and appear as no edge. Figure 4.8 shows the effect of a long run length: the signal droops, reducing the margin between the signal and the threshold, until it eventually crosses over the threshold.

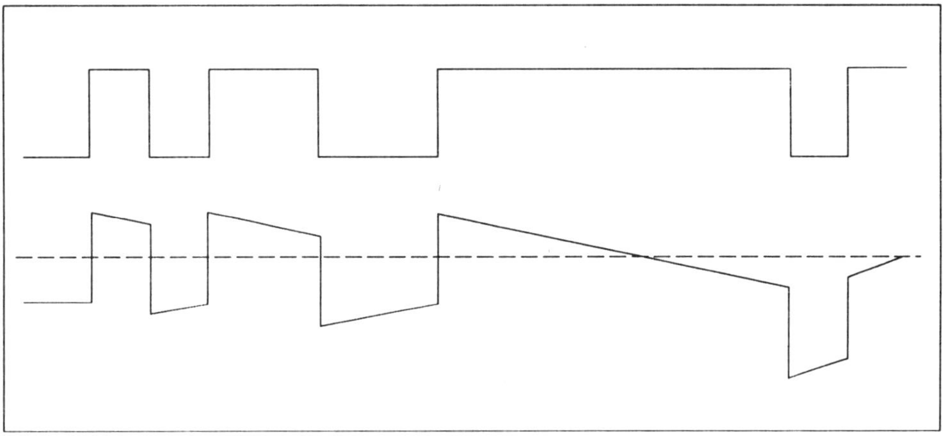

Figure 4.8 Effect of excessive run length

Some of the codes which are currently popular are not in fact completely DC balanced, but for most data patterns have minimal DC component. Such codes include the 2:7 *Run Length Limited* code used on disks, and the TAXI/FDDI code which is never worse than 40%/60% balanced. (The code used by FibreChannel has the same efficiency as the FDDI code, but is completely DC balanced.) A technique used on ISDN and on SONET is to *scramble* the data so that it is approximately balanced and very rarely has long run lengths; the scrambling has the advantage that no extra bits are added to the data.

An extreme form of AC coupling is to differentiate the signal, which provides inherent DC balance. The pre-compensation circuit used in twisted pair FDDI effectively produces the sum of the signal itself, plus a differentiated version of the signal. In magnetic recording, such differentiation occurs naturally, but it brings its own problems; any noise such as crosstalk is coupled through the differentiator, and any AC imbalance in common-mode coupling is translated into extra noise.

AC coupling can either be provided by transformers or capacitors. Transformers provide excellent common mode isolation and are readily available at low cost up to a few hundred MHz (Mini-Circuits T1-1 0.15MHz to 400MHz, $3.25 in low volume). Capacitors do not provide good common mode isolation, but can be used for frequencies up to many GHz. Low cost amplifiers are also available which *must* be AC coupled, with 7.5dB gain at 1.5GHz.

4.4.5 Limiting the frequency range and tuning

The constraints on run length and on the DC balance effectively reduce the bandwidth that needs to be received. If the highest frequency needed is 50MHz, and the lowest is 10MHz, the 28AWG cable referred to above loses 2.8dB in 10m at 50MHz and 1.2dB at 10MHz. So we only have to cope with a difference of 1.6dB per 10m between the frequencies. Instead of the 16m limit given above for the differential DC coupled case giving 4.5dB, we can AC couple, use more gain, and should be able to reach $(4.5/1.6) \times 10$m or 28m [16].

Even with a very wide bandwidth, it is possible to use tuning to compensate for the frequency characteristics of the cable. As with 'scope probes, it is easier to do if the tuning is built into the cable (otherwise it has to cope with a wide range of different cable lengths). As with 'scope probes, this can be expensive and liable to misuse.

16. A similar example is Ethernet, which uses Manchester coding, with a limited frequency range, and allows a total of 8.5dB loss at its frequency.

4.5 Error Rates

The form of serial communications that most engineers are familiar with are LANs and very long distance (tele-)communications. For these long distance connections, error rates tend to be around 10^{-9} or less, which at 100MBits/s is an error per link every five seconds (counting a link as bidirectional). Telecomms and LANs also need to cope with buffer overflow.

For these high error rates, it is absolutely necessary to have CRCs for error detection, and to have re-try mechanisms for corrupted or lost data – whether lost as a result of data errors or buffer overflow.

Another reason for needing CRCs is that most of the efficient communication codes, such as FDDI and FibreChannel, allow an erroneous single bit in the received data stream to be decoded as a valid (but incorrect) whole data symbol; both the FDDI and FibreChannel codes limit such decoded errors to less than a byte of data, but such error multiplication necessitates the use of checksums such as CRC.

The situation with transputer links is rather different: the specified error rates on PCBs are substantially better than 10^{-20}, which is a failure per link every 50 000 years. At such error rates, it is quite reasonable to consider a system as reliable, and to crash the system if an error occurs. Alternatively, it is possible to add software to detect the rare event and to take some form of recovery action. In practice, at these error rates, hardware errors are much more likely to be caused by lightening strikes or by mechanical damage than by electrical signal failure.

The parity check on the DS-Links is such that a single bit error, either in control or data, is detected. As long as the errors are infrequent (one every several thousand years), this is entirely adequate. If a user is concerned about the possibility of an error not being detected, software can be added to the processes at the end of the link to perform more rigorous data checks and to recover from data or control errors.

These software checks can be performed even if the suspected virtual channel goes through a routing switch. The suspected link can be configured in the routing switch to go to a single transputer which is programmed to check the messages, effectively ignoring a possibly corrupted routing header. If several transputers are programmed to check the messages, the routing switch can be configured to route the messages to any of these transputers – but not to another routing switch or to a transputer that is unable to check the message.

The specifications stated in the transputer data sheets are designed to ensure the very good error rates that are expected between logic devices on a PCB. As a result, the permitted skew specification for the T4xx and T8xx transputers is a few nanoseconds. Some users have observed that OS–Links work with larger skews, but with such large skews the error rates are more like the 10^{-9} of the telecommunications and LANs. At INMOS, there is a network of transputer links, buffered with RS422 buffers, with connection lengths of close to 100m – far outside the specification or recommendations; in practice, the incidence of software failure on this network is substantially higher than the incidence of hardware errors due to links.

DS-Links have been specified, therefore, so that they give such infrequent errors that the hardware can be considered reliable. This does not preclude any user from adding checking software; nor does it preclude the use of more elaborate checking hardware when connecting links over longer distances such as with optical fibre interconnections.

4.6 Optical interconnections

Included in this section on optical interconnection are optical isolators which retain electrical connection, but offer large tolerance of common mode noise, and optical fibre, which comes into its own for connections much above 10m.

4.6.1 DC coupling with common mode isolation (Optical Isolation)

Optical isolators appear to offer the best of both worlds, in that they do not require the DC balance or run length limits that AC coupling needs, but yet offer almost infinite tolerance to common mode. To make opto-isolators fast, however, most of the circuitry needs to be included that would be used in an optical fibre connection. As a fibre connection would cost less than the wire connection and go much further at a given speed, it may be preferable to use fibre. Whether this is the reason or not, it has not been possible to find opto-isolators that are specified to run at 100Mbits/s.

4.6.2 Long distance, high data rate, infinite isolation ... but... (Optical Fibre)

The fibre shown on figure 4.3 is inexpensive but is much better in terms of its attenuation than the best copper cable. Single mode fibre is still better. The problem is not in the attenuation in the cable, but in the losses (and consequent costs) in converting from electricity to light at one end and from light to electricity at the other end.

4.6.3 Losses, performance and costs of components for optical fibres

The light is produced by a LED or by a Laser Diode. An example LED outputs (infra-red at 1300nm wavelength) 0.25mW of optical power when driven by 100mA of electrical power. Laser diodes are more efficient, one for example produces 5mW of optical power for 50mA of input current. The fastest LEDs have an optical rise time of about 2.5ns, and a 1.5dB cutoff at 100 or 150MHz (6dB around 800MHz). The 1300nm laser diodes have sub-nanosecond rise and fall times: one example has a very sharp cutoff at around 1.5GHz.

Components with wavelengths of 820 or 850nm are in many respects more suitable for 100 MBits/s transputer links. Components from HP and from a number of other companies include LEDs which output around 0.1mW (-10dBm) of optical power into the fibre with optical rise and fall times of 4ns, for a current of 60mA.

The receivers are PIN[17] photodiodes, very often integrated into a hybrid with a pre-amp, and sometimes also with a power supply for the diode. The diodes are reverse biased, with a finite reverse (Dark) current. One example has a responsivity of about 0.5A/W. Assuming no attenuation in the fibre, 100mA into the LED becomes 0.25mW in the fibre which becomes 0.125mA in the PIN diode; this loss is far more than the electrical cable loss but fibre has the important advantage that, over short distances at least, there is much less variation of loss with frequency.

The received current needs to be amplified up to logic levels, and this amount of amplification, at these frequencies, is easier with AC coupling. So the requirements of bandwidth limiting, DC balance and run length limiting are present for optical fibre as much as for electrical wire. The FDDI transceivers and the HP 820 nm 125MHz receiver module amplify up the current into a voltage – ECL levels from the FDDI transceivers, 10mV to 1V from the HP receiver.

The costs are radically dependent on the technology used, as illustrated in table 4.1 (all figures are approximate and for large volumes).

17. PIN = P doped, Insulator, N doped

Table 4.1 Optical components cost/performance

Wavelength (nm)	Data rate	Light source	Cost	Availability
820	200KBits/s	LED	less than $10 per transceiver	now
820	125MBits/s	LED	$30 per transceiver	now
1300	125 to 350 MBits/s	LED	over $300 per FDDI transceiver	now
			$100 per FDDI transceiver	long term goal
1300	125MBits/s to 2.5GBits/s	Laser diode	$1000 to $10000 per transceiver	now

Notice that there is nearly an order of magnitude cost difference between the 820nm and 1300nm wavelengths, and another order of magnitude between LEDs and lasers. The one exception to this is the 780nm laser diodes used for Compact Disks, which are discussed below.

4.6.4 Expensive or affordable, long or short distances, 1300 or 820nm?

Most of the work on fibre has have been to make it go long distances, often at very high speed; or to make it cheap, where speed and distance do not matter. FDDI seems to come in between these, in asking for 2km at 125Mbits/s, but they have chosen the more expensive 1300nm. In fact FDDI connections using lasers are now being developed to go further than the 2km, as Medium or Metropolitan Area Networks (MANs).

The 820nm components are limited in distance to about 500m at 100 or 125 MBits/s, which is more than adequate for transputer links.

The laser diodes that are used in compact disks have a wavelength of 780nm, which ties in well with the HP 820nm receivers for 100MBits/s, and it is possible that the CD lasers could be used with faster receivers to provide 400Mbits/s. FibreChannel has specified a CD laser as one of its options. These laser diodes are inexpensive because they are made in such large volumes for CDs, but the laser is not ideal for use by non-experts, and the laser diodes are not as reliable as LEDs.

At present, the cost, availability, and performance of the 820nm components appear to offer the preferred choice for DS-Links.

4.6.5 Interfacing between links and fibre

The last few subsections have described a number of characteristics of the fibre connection which are not handled directly by the DS-Link:

- The fibre connection is a single fibre in each direction, so both D and S need to be encoded onto a single signal;
- This signal needs to include sufficient transitions that a clock can be extracted by a PLL at the receiver;
- The LED (or laser) is driven by a current rather than by a voltage, and the receiver needs to see a signal of possibly only 10mV, certainly no more than ECL;
- The fibre allows connection up to 500m, whereas the buffering in the standard link logic is enough for some distance between 10m and 50m.

- Longer distance connections, with the amount of amplification required for the optical signal, is such that the connection must be considered as less reliable than normal short connections on a PCB. In fact the indications are that it may be possible to achieve worst case error rates of the order of 10^{-20}, far better than is achieved by normal communications. It may nevertheless be reasonable to offer additional error checking and possibly alternative means of handling errors compared with short distance links.

The best way to do these various interfacing functions would be with a link-to-fibre interface chip, designed for the purpose.

INMOS is collaborating on projects in the European ESPRIT program with other partners developing optical fibre connections. Indications suggest that fibre connection over 200m to 500m will be achievable with low-cost optical components. The signalling system used for the optical connection should allow isolated copper connection over 100m, possibly with unshielded twisted pair cable.

4.7 Standards

A number of users have asked that standards for interconnections between equipments be proposed, so that different manufacturers' equipments can be connected by their transputer links. In some respects this provides a 'small area network' of transputer or link based systems.

The proposal for electrical cable connection is to use DC coupling with the 41 series buffers mentioned earlier. Earlier in this chapter, it was suggested that these cable connections should work well up to 16m, and although tests have given good results at 30m, for a reliable link it is necessary to limit this to 10m using the 30 AWG shielded twisted pair cable suggested.

If isolation is required the proposal is that it should be done with low cost optical fibre.

In drafting early versions of the proposed standard, it was found to be necessary to specify four different types of connector for different applications. There was no single connector which provided separate cables for each link, while meeting the other requirements, so INMOS produced an outline specification of a single connector which would satisfy all the various requirements. This connector has been developed by AMP, Harting and Fujitsu, in cooperation with INMOS/SGS-THOMSON. Sample plugs and intermateable sockets have been manufactured by Fujitsu and Harting, and the connector closely follows an IEC standard which was originally put forward by AMP. It is shielded, polarized, latched and robust, and has a leading pin for 0V for reliable hot-swap. An outline description of this proposed connector is included as an appendix.

The four connectors specified in the draft standard were 9-way D type, LEMO, SCSI2, and METRAL. Pinouts will be defined for these, for the MiniDIN, and for the new connector.

Proposed standards for optical fibre connection are based on a fibre interface chip, with the low cost 820nm optical components, 62.5µm fibre (which is being installed into buildings for FDDI) and SC connectors (which appear to give a good combination of repeatability, density, and ease of use for the end-user).

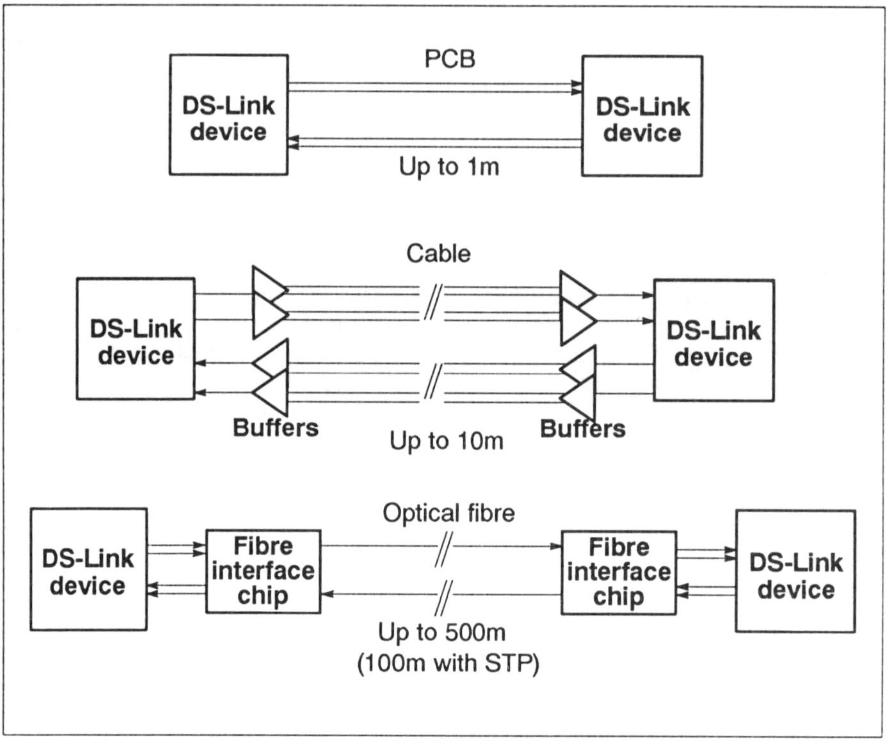

Figure 4.9 Distances that can be covered by DS-Links

4.8 Conclusions

DS-Links have been optimized for short connections on printed circuit boards, for which they are ideal. The Gray coding means that the receiver does not need a PLL, that there is a wide tolerance of skew, and that the receivers can 'autobaud' without requiring a status register to set their speed. The comparatively slow edges – at least for 100 MBits/s – minimize crosstalk.

Link specifications are designed to ensure that errors are sufficiently infrequent that connections can be treated as logic connections rather than as telecommunications or LAN connections. If users violate these specifications for links, systems will often work, but with error rates approaching the error rates seen by LANs. For these error rates, it is necessary to add software to handle the more frequent errors. Such software is not required when the specifications are met.

For PCB connections up to 20cm, the characteristic impedance of the PCB track is not critical. Up to 1m the impedance should be kept within a reasonable tolerance, between 80Ω and 120Ω. Some care should be taken to avoid crosstalk. Beyond 1m, PCB connections may be possible, but the characteristic impedance should be more tightly controlled.

INMOS will be proposing link standards for long distance connections. Such standards will enable different manufacturers' equipments to interconnect and, with cooperation on software, to inter-operate.

The proposal for short cable connections up to 10m is to use the fast 41–series buffers from AT&T, which have good common mode performance, in a DC coupled arrangement. For longer connections, up to 200 or 500m, or for electrical isolation, it seems best to use low cost optical fibre components, with a purpose designed interface chip.

Standards remove from the user some of the need to understand fully the principles on which they are based. At 100 MBits/s, over the distances suggested here, the problems are not especially severe, but the faster the signals and systems go, the more necessary it is to engineer them to avoid problems such as attenuation in the connection. It is hoped that this chapter is of assistance in understanding these issues.

4.9 References

1 *MECL System Design Handbook*, William R Blood, Jr, Motorola.
This is an excellent book on the subject of high frequency digital logic signals on PCBs and cables. It also shows that the ECL system builders needed careful thermal design some years ago.

2 *SONY data book of SPECL*, 1990 edition.
This has a short application note with some comprehensive graphs of transmission line impedance, capacitance, and delay.

3 *Printed Circuit Handbook*, third edition, edited by Clyde F Coombs, Jr, McGraw-Hill, New York, 1988 ISBN 0-07-012609-7.
This book covers all aspects of printed circuits.

4 *The T9000 Transputer Products Overview Manual*, INMOS/SGS-THOMSON, 1991, order code DBTRANSPST/1.

There are many textbooks on communications but one of the most useful, which explains the concepts for a non-specialist and without excessive mathematics, is the Open University course 'T322: Digital Telecommunications'; this comprises a number of books, which are available separately or as a set from Open University Educational Enterprises in Milton Keynes, England. The three most useful in the course are Blocks 4, 5, and 6: Digital Signals; Noise; Coding and Modulation.

More mathematical, and covering more ground, is 'Digital Communication' by Edward A Lee and David G Messerschmitt, ISBN 0-89838-295-5, reprinted 1990 and published by Kluwer Academic Publishers, Boston.

Remember, when reading these texts on communications, that (while the principles involved need to be understood) the distances required and the error rates obtained make transputer links much easier than telecomms.

A great deal of development is taking place in fibre connections, and probably the easiest way to keep in touch with the developments is by taking magazines, such as Lightwave or Laser Focus World, both from PennWell. More technical is IEEE Lightwave Communication Systems.

A good introduction to fast, low cost, optical fibre connections is given in HP's Application Bulletin 78, document 5954-8478 (3/88).

A number of standards are mentioned in this chapter, including SCSI and HPPI which are parallel interfaces, RS232, Ethernet, and Token Ring which are copper cable based LANs, and FDDI, FibreChannel and SONET which are optical fibre standards for LAN, computer interface, and long-distance telecomms respectively. After these standards are formally issued, they may be obtained from the standards authorities such as ANSI and IEEE. Obtaining drafts before the standards are published is not always easy, and may require contact with the working group responsible for the particular standard.

4.10 Manufacturers and products referred to

AT&T: 41 series of high performance line drivers, receivers, and transceivers;

Hewlett Packard: 820nm low cost 150MBits/s fiber optic LED and receiver modules;

Honeywell: 820nm low cost 150MBits/s fiber optic LED and receiver modules;

Madison Cable: 'SCSI' type cable with specified and low skew.

5 Using Links for System Control

5.1 Introduction

The T9000 family of devices includes processors and routers which have subsystems and interfaces which are highly flexible to match the requirements of a wide range of applications. In addition to the static configuration requirements of subsystems such as the memory interface of the T9000, the more dynamic aspects of a network of devices must be configured before application software is loaded. These more dynamic items include:

- cache organization;
- data link bit–rates;
- virtual link control blocks;

If T9000 processors are configured as stand-alone devices, the configurable subsystems will be initialized by instructions contained in a local ROM. When the devices are integrated as part of a network with a static configuration every processor in the network could also initialize these subsystems independently by executing code contained in a local ROM. Typically, however, networks of T9000 family devices contain routers as well as processors and executing code from a ROM is not an option for a routing device. As a consequence, routing devices must be configured under external control. During system development or for systems which are used for multiple applications a flexible configuration mechanism for processors is also required.

Debugging of software and hardware on networks consisting of many devices is not a simple problem. The major difficulty is in monitoring the behavior of the system as an integrated whole rather than observing the individual behavior of the separate components. A flexible mechanism which allows monitoring tools to observe and manage every device in a network in a simple manner is essential in designing a system-wide debugging environment.

5.1.1 Virtual channels

Connecting processors together with point-to-point serial links overcomes many of the problems of shared memory multi-processor systems. Point-to-point links, however, introduce a different set of problems. Of these problems, two of the most critical for system design are, firstly, the difficulty of mapping a software structure on to an arbitrary hardware topology and, secondly, routing messages between processes running on processors which are not adjacent. A great deal of effort has gone in to seeking solutions to these problems and the most flexible and readily implementable technique for overcoming the difficulties is the concept of virtual links. Processes in a network communicate via channels and so the collection of processes and channels define the software topology of a system. The IMS T9000 has multiplexing hardware (the *Virtual Channel Processor*) which allows any number of channels to share the available physical links in such a manner that processes communicating via the channels are unaware of the sharing. Virtual channels are naturally paired to form virtual links, as described in chapter 2. The use of virtual channels allows the software structure of a system to be developed independently from the hardware on which it is to be executed.

Control virtual channels

An ideal way of configuring and monitoring a network of T9000 family devices would be to create a control network in which a master control process running on a host is connected to a client control process on every configurable device in the network. Using virtual links to implement this control network gives exactly the level of control and flexibility required. The remote end of the control virtual link must be managed by an autonomous process which is active and able to obey the instructions of the control process even if the device itself is in a completely unconfigured or stopped state. To achieve this, this process is implemented by an independent hardware module called a *control unit.*

Figure 5.1 illustrates how control virtual channels appear to the control processes involved.

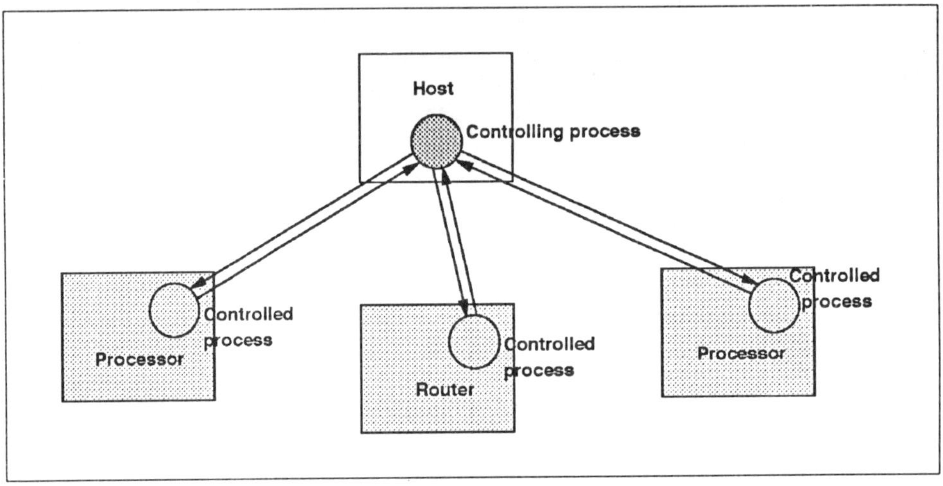

Figure 5.1 Control virtual channels

Providing all device types with an identical control unit allows:

- host system control software to be consistent for every member of the product family;
- the control network on a mixture of devices to be explored and the device types determined;
- processor–free routing networks to be initialized and monitored for error;

A virtual channel from a system control process to every device in a network means that each device can be controlled and monitored as if it were the only device in the network. The ability to control and monitor routing devices is an important capability especially in networks containing no processing devices. Facilities provided by the control system must include the ability to:

- start the device;
- stop the device;
- reset the device;
- identify the device;
- configure the device;
- examine and modify memory (if any);
- load boot code (if the device uses loadable code);
- monitor the device for error;
- re-initialize the control system after an error.

Control links

Because of the critical function of the control system in system initialization and error recovery it is vital that is highly reliable. To guarantee the integrity and reliability of the control system it is essential that it exists in an entirely different domain from the normal operation of the communication system. This separation is achieved by providing each device in the T9000 family with two dedicated control links (`CLink0` and `CLink1`, also called the '*up*' and '*down*' links) and a dedicated control unit. Implementing the control links with a data link is not desirable because it adds complexity to the implementation (by mixing functions which can otherwise be implemented separately) and reduces security, since for example an error in the data network might be impossible to report.

The control links of every device in a network are connected to form a control network. The communication links of the devices will be connected to form a data network. The control network is kept completely separate from the data network and is intended for use by the control system exclusively. It is an important feature that the control links are not accessible to software running on a T9000 processor; the control system is a mechanism designed exclusively for initializing and monitoring the various *hardware* subsystems of the T9000 family of devices. The type of error which would be reported via the control system includes system crashes such as link failure. The control system could not be used for run-time system messages to report failure of a user application. In the latter case the failure messages would be routed via established virtual channels across the data network but in the former case these channels may no longer be reliable. The control network may be run at a lower speed or use different interconnect technology from the data network for increased reliability if necessary.

5.2 Control networks

In a network of T9000 family devices, the control system of each device will have a virtual link to a process running on the processor being used to manage the initialization and monitoring of the system (typically a host). The managing processor, referred to as the control processor, is connected to the network via the *control port,* which consists entirely of one or more standard DS-Links. If the control processor is a T9000, one of its serial links could be used as the control port and the *Virtual Channel Processor* would then implement the virtual channels to the controlled devices. If the control processor is not a T9000, the control port would need to be implemented by a device such as a DS-Link adapter and the virtual channel handling would need to be implemented by software.

Within the control network every control unit obeys a simple protocol on its virtual link. Each message from the control process to a device is acknowledged by a handshake message back to the control process. Each unsolicited message from a device to the control process is acknowledged by a handshake message from the control process to the device as shown in figure 5.2.

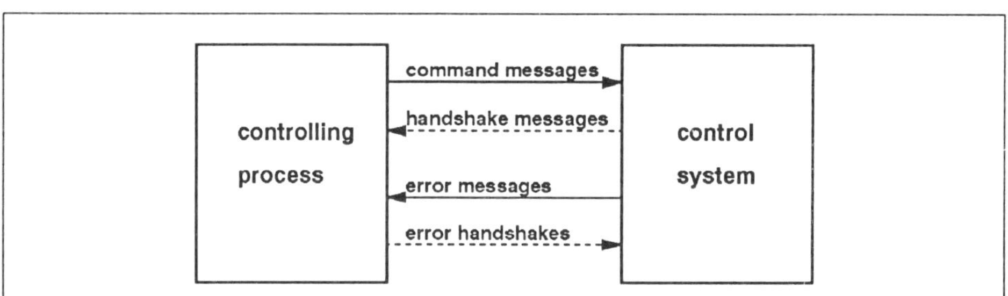

Figure 5.3 Communication between control process and control system

This strict exchange of a handshake message for each command or error message means that the controlling process can be implemented entirely sequentially without danger of deadlock. Even if the control system sends an error message at the same time as the controlling process sends a command, the controlling process subsequently performs an input in any case in order to receive the handshake for its command. When it receives an error message instead it knows that a further pair of messages must be exchanged.

The messages received by a control unit have the form of a command byte followed by parameters specific to that command. Of the thirteen commands in the protocol some are common to all device types and some are specific to particular device types. The physical implementation of the part of the control unit which handles the common commands is generic to all device types. The commands common to all device types are those to start, reset, and identify the device, and to recover from an error in the control network. Other commands are specific to particular devices. The meaning of the commands is detailed in section 5.8.

5.2.1 Implementation

After hard (power-on) reset the virtual links between the control process and the control unit of all the devices in the network must be established. The virtual link to a device is established by the first message received by the network device on `CLink0`; this must be a *Start* command. The *Start* command will be used to set the device 'label' as well as the return header used by the device on every packet sent back to the control process. The label is the header which identifies the virtual link to this device; all packets received from `CLink0` with this label are directed to the device control unit and all those with a different label are passed to `CLink1`. Packets received on `CLink1` are passed directly to `CLink0`. By connecting the control links of all devices into the control network and establishing a virtual link to every device, the control process can initialize and monitor every processor and router in the network independently of the behavior and topology of the data network.

Each device has a single control link pair so in a network consisting entirely of processors these must be daisy-chained as shown in figure 5.4.

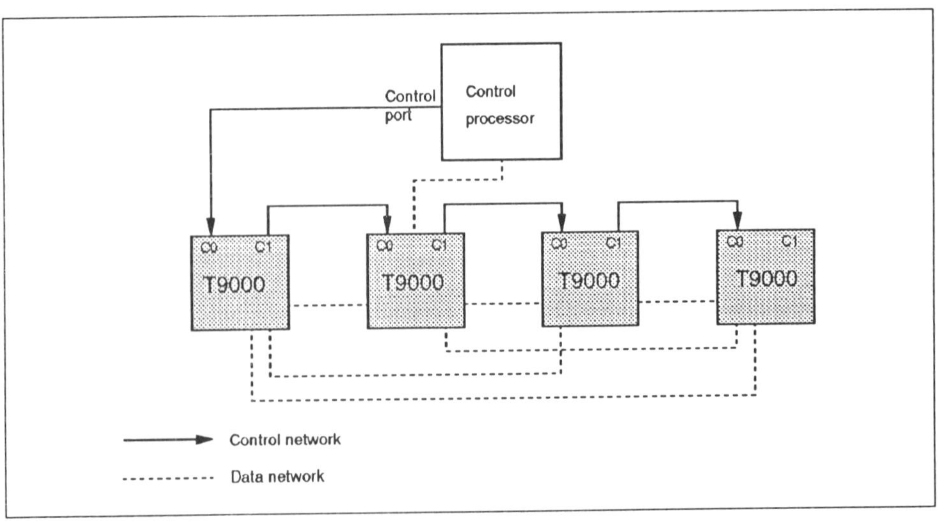

Figure 5.4 Daisy chained control links

For large networks containing IMS C104 devices daisy-chaining is undesirable because of command latency and possible physical routing constraints. In these networks it is better to route the control network via C104s as shown in figure 5.5.

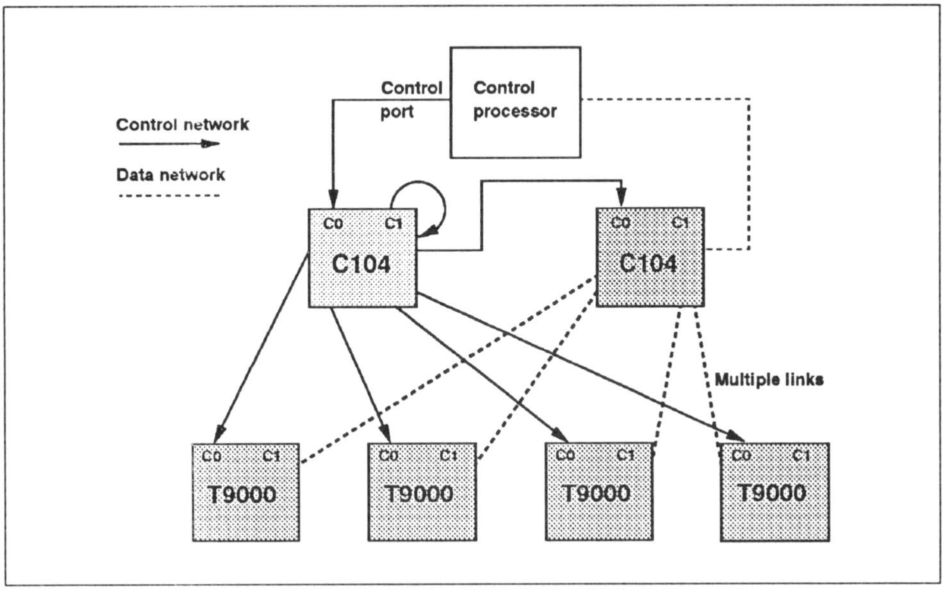

Figure 5.5 Routing control links through an IMS C104

It is possible to use C104s for control network routing because control links use the same electrical and packet–level protocols as the standard data links. When data links on a C104 are used to route the control network, its *down* control link, `CLink1`, can be connected into one of its own data links and thus the control network can fan out in a similar manner to the data network. It is strongly recommended that C104 devices which are part of the control network are used exclusively for the control network and are not part of the data network. If it is unavoidable that a C104 is part of the data network as well as part of the control network it must be partitioned into separate logical devices so that no link can be in both networks (as described in section 3.6.4 of chapter 3). In this case special actions must be taken during reset sequences to avoid losing the control network when resetting the data network. When the control network includes C104 devices the routing tables of the C104 must be initialized using *CPoke* commands before the control network can be fully established.

`CLink0` is started automatically by the arrival of the first token. `CLink1` must be started explicitly via a *CPoke* command received by the control process. If a message is received for downward transmission and `CLink1` has not been started a protocol error will be reported.

5.3 System initialization

System initialization is the sequence of actions from receipt of a hard reset (i.e. assertion of the reset pin) until the devices in the system are ready to perform the application for which the system is intended. In a network containing processors, the application may be an operating system ready to run user software or an embedded application ready to start receiving its control data. In a network consisting entirely of routers the system is fully initialized when all of the routing information of the network is established. A possible sequence of actions for a network containing processors and a host, referred to as *levels of reset* and shown in figure 5.6, is as follows:

- Label the control network (including configuring any C104s in the control network) - the network is now at level 1.
- Configure the devices in the network using the control network - level 2.

- Set up virtual links over which to load the network and then run boot code in each processor -level 3.
- Load the network with the application and then set up the virtual links required by the application software -level 4;
- Start the application on the network and a server on the control process - level 5.

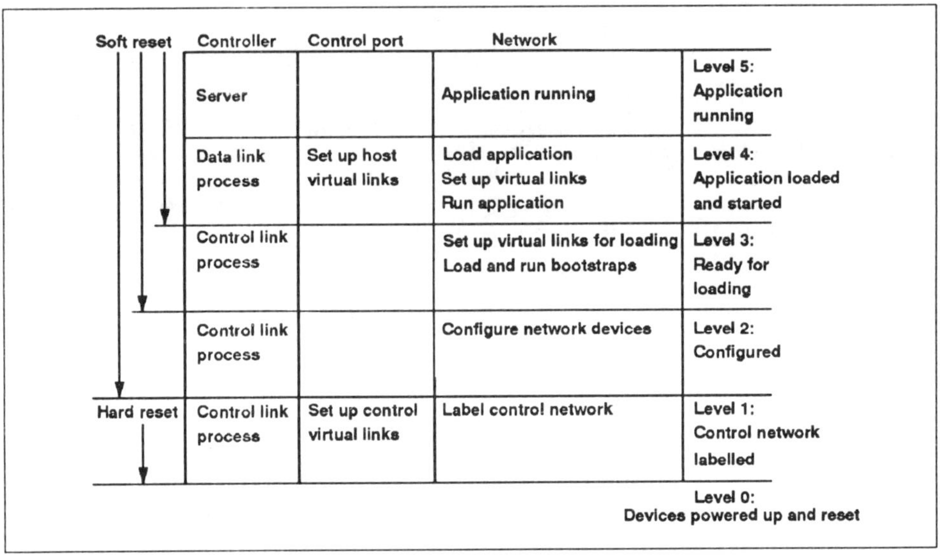

Figure 5.6 Levels of reset

The sequence can be performed one device at a time or network wide one level at a time. For a processor some of the configuration actions can be performed either across the control network or by local software. Because a richer protocol with higher data transfer rates and (possibly) shorter paths can be implemented across the data network than exists on the control network it is generally desirable to establish the data network as early as possible in the initialization cycle.

Using the sequence outlined, application software is loaded onto processors in the network via virtual channels established within the data network. A loader must first be loaded and connected to the virtual channels to load the application at the desired locations. This loader must be loaded and started using the control network and the control channel protocol contains the commands *Boot*, *BootData* and *Run* to facilitate this. The *Run* command provides a workspace pointer and an instruction pointer to start the T9000 CPU. The *Run* command and the *Stop* command are the two commands by which the control system can modify the behavior of the T9000 CPU.

The control network can only be re-labelled after a hard reset so no packet corruption can result in control messages re-configuring the control network. The control process can, however, issue a *Reset* command to any device in the network. The *Reset* command directs the device to reset to level 1, 2 or 3 so the control process can restore individual processors to a known state ready for re-loading an application or, perhaps, to load a debugging kernel.

Some or all of the processors in a network may be set to boot from ROM. Boot-from-ROM devices might be used simply to the configure the local environment or, alternatively, in embedded applications they can be used to configure and then load the whole system.

5.3.1 Local ROM

In many networks it is desirable to localize configuration information. For example it is often useful to program the memory interface locally with the the characteristics of the memory system connected to that processor. Suppliers of special purpose interface boards can build a ROM onto the board which sets up all of the specific characteristics without having to worry about the environment in which the board is going to be used. While a network processor is executing code from its local ROM it is important that the control process does not attempt to load and configure the device. A simple convention to prevent this from happening is for the code in the ROM to set error when it has completed its local configuration, and thereby cause the processor to halt and transmit an *Error* message. The receipt of the *Error* message then signals to the control process that the device is now ready to receive the rest of the initialization sequence.

The local ROM could contain code to take the device to a higher reset level. It might be desirable to bootstrap the device to level 3 ready for the application to be loaded. The same convention as above could be adopted to indicate to the control process that the ROM has completed its initialization sequence.

Boot-from-ROM will only occur automatically after a hard reset. The control process can, however, instruct a T9000 to boot from ROM by sending a *Reboot* message. This allows the control process to be in complete control of the system initialization sequence.

5.3.2 System ROM

A T9000 network may be configured to boot from ROM. The processor which is the root of the network will have access to the system ROM, and will be connected so that one of its data links is the control port at the 'top' of the control network. Its own control links will not be connected as part of that same network. This processor will be the control processor as well as the root processor for the system initialization. Configuration information, bootstraps and application code will be drawn from the system ROM rather than from a local file store which would typically be the case if the network was booting from link. After booting the network, the root processor can execute its own application from RAM or continue executing from the ROM. All processors in the network, other than the root processor, are initialized and configured across the control network as shown in figure 5.7. These processors could boot from local ROMs for local configuration if necessary.

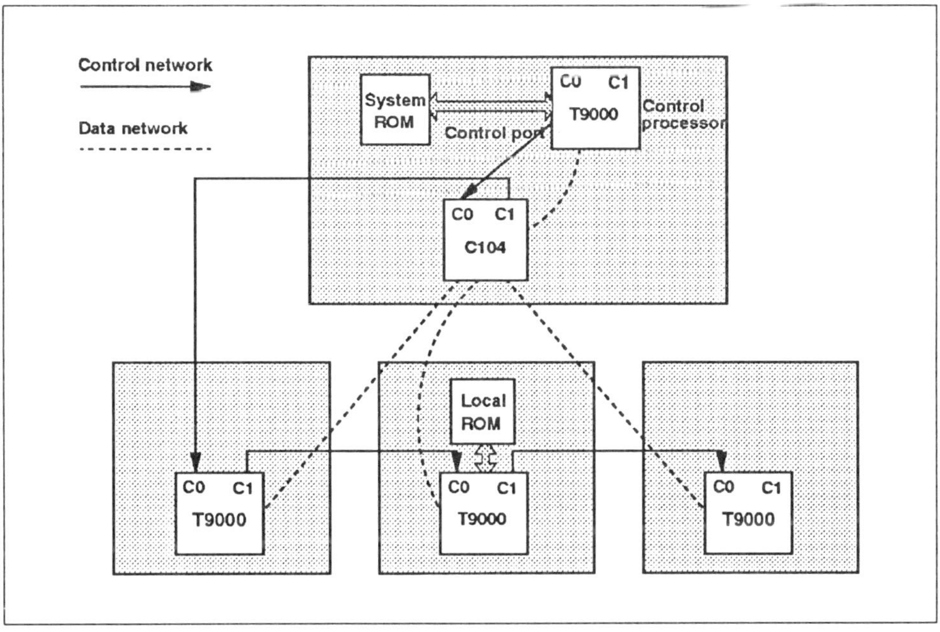

Figure 5.7 Booting from system ROM

A similar mechanism could be employed for a network consisting entirely of routing devices; a single (cheap) processor could initialize the routing tables for the whole network. The processor could then monitor the control system for errors taking appropriate recovery actions and logging information for later analysis.

5.4 Debugging

The normal mechanism for dealing with errors on a working T9000 processor is to execute a trap handler which takes recovery and repair actions to restore the processor to a known valid state. The trap handler may report its actions via the data network to a supervisory process in the system. During development of software and hardware, however, it may be desirable to halt the processor which has caused the error and examine the system state in some detail.

Errors generated by a T9000 subsystem (other than those detected in the CPU and caught by a trap handler) will result in an *Error* message being generated on the virtual channel back to the controlling process and the CPU being halted. The control process can then bring the whole system to a quiescent state by sending a *Stop* command to every T9000 in the network. The *Stop* command stops the processor cleanly, preserving register values and allowing a debugging kernel to retrieve processor state and thus trace the cause of the error. If a processor initiated the situation because of an error, that processor will have halted at the point of error. On all other processors the CPU will continue until the next deschedule point or timeslice. The links are unaffected, and the timers continue to run until a *Reset3* command is received, but no processes will be scheduled.

After the control process has received handshakes for all of its *Stop* messages it must allow time for the system to become quiescent and then issue a *Reset3* command to every T9000. When every device has received a *Reset3* command, all of the CPUs will be halted and the system is guaranteed to be static. At this stage the control process can make certain that the configuration is correct by using configuration 'peek' and 'poke' (*CPeek* and *CPoke*) commands.

If a debugging kernel is to be loaded into the network it may be necessary to save the area where it is to be loaded to guarantee that no processor state is lost to the analysis tools. This space can be retrieved across the control network using the *Peek* command and stored on the host processor. The debugging kernel can be loaded and started using a *BootData* and *Run* sequence which will not interfere with the preserved state of the data network.

The debugging kernel now has access to all of the previous processor state and can be directed by the debugging tools running on the control processor to retrieve information on all of the processor's subsystems. The network is thus a distributed data base containing the memory state, register contents and call history of the whole system rather than of just a single processor. The debugging tools can piece together the cause of the system failure and observe the interaction between the different processes and processors. The combination of access to the state of every processor, access to the sources from which the system was built and knowledge of the compiling, linking and loading strategies enables debugging tools to produce an integrated picture of the behavior of the whole system at a symbolic level rather than at an instruction stream level. Once the debugging kernel is loaded onto the network, the debugging tools would, typically, establish virtual channels across the data network to communicate with the individual kernels.

The mechanism described above is called *post-mortem* debugging. *Interactive* debugging can be accomplished by running a debugging kernel on every processor in the system in parallel with the application. In this way breakpoints, watchpoints, single stepping and many of the other facilities delivered by ICE systems are provided without using expensive and intrusive additional hardware. An additional benefit of using links to assist in debugging is the ability to monitor the behavior of a complete multi-processor system observing the interactions across processor boundaries at source level. The debugger running on the control processor communicates with the debugging kernels through virtual channels additional to those established for the data network so that the applications are entirely unaware of the presence of the debugging system.

Much of what has been described in this section is familiar to developers of software for multiprocessor systems. The T9000 family of devices introduce many features to decouple software and hardware development and as a consequence access to the state of routing devices is a vital requirement in system debugging. Access to the state of routing devices is particularly important for networks which contain no processors. The post-mortem mechanisms described earlier are equally relevant for routers. A control process can examine the configuration of a routing device and proceed to access the state of every serial link and thus locate the point of failure and determine what recovery action must be taken. When a data link disconnect error is detected on a router it will cause an error message to be generated on the virtual link to the monitoring process running on the system control processor. As a consequence networks of routers do not require special hardware monitoring devices, a significant amount of fault detection and isolation can be built into the system by the addition of a single monitoring device.

5.5 Errors

The control system provides an error reporting mechanism for all errors, other than those detected by a CPU and caught by trap handlers. The reporting of errors by the control system to the control process is the only time that the controlled device is the initiator of a communication on the control network. The controlling process must acknowledge receipt of the *Error* message by sending an *ErrorHandShake* message back to the device generating the *Error* message. The *Error* message includes a field to indicate the source of the error. The control system will not send an error message if a handshake has not yet been received for a previously sent error message.

The control system handles three distinct classes of error, as listed below.

1. Errors on the control links, which include:
   - parity/disconnect on `CLink1`;
   - unexpected acknowledge;
   - invalid messages;
   - handshake protocol error;
2. System errors - errors from one of the subsystems when stand alone mode is not set.
3. Stand alone mode errors

The effects of the errors are given in table 5.1. The `ErrorSinceReset` flag is a flag in the IMS T9000 which is provided to assist self–analysis of stand–alone systems.

Table 5.1 Error effects

Error class	Result of error		
	Stops CPU	ErrorSinceReset flag set	Error message sent on CLink0
Control link error	No	No	Yes
System error	Yes	Yes	Yes
Stand alone mode error	Yes	Yes	No

The control unit will record a single error which is cleared by the error handshake from the control process. A hard reset, reset 1 or reset 2 will cause the record of untransmitted errors to be cleared.

5.5.1 Control link errors

The basic reliability of DS-Links used within their specifications, as discussed in chapter 4, is very high, and this reliability can be further enhanced for the purposes of the control network by reduced the operating speed somewhat and by paying particular attention to the connection of links. However since an error – however unlikely – in the control network is potentially very serious for the whole system, extra mechanisms are provided to report and recover from such errors.

A parity or disconnect error on `CLink1` will be reported by the control system to the control process via `CLink0`. A parity or disconnect error on `CLink0` will cause the link to halt. This halt will be detected by the device connected to the other end of the link which will in turn report the error.

After an error has occurred some virtual links in the control network may be in an invalid state. The controlling process ends of the virtual links must be reset and then the process can restore the control network to a valid state by sending *RecoverError* commands (which can be sent in violation of the normal protocol). A *RecoverError* command will reset the remote end of a control virtual link and cause any un-handshaken error message (which may have been lost) to be resent. A sequence of *RecoverError* messages sent by the control process to each of the devices in turn can thus systematically restore the control network and at the same time recover information which may help to determine the cause of the failure.

5.5.2 Stand alone mode

When a T9000 processor is operating in stand-alone mode, errors are handled in a distinct way. If an unmasked/untrapped error occurs the control system will reset all of the subsystems on the T9000 and then cause a boot from ROM. The `ErrorSinceReset` flag will be set so that the ROM code can determine that an error has occurred.

5.6 Embedded applications

The root processor in an embedded application which has booted from ROM takes over the role of the control processor on a system which has booted from a host. The control process can monitor and log errors, restarting and re-configuring processors after failure and recovering from errors in the control system. As described in section 5.5.2 above, errors in the control processor result in the processor rebooting. The control process can determine that an error occurred since the last reset and can recover and log information from the previous processor state for later analysis.

5.7 Control system

The control system of each device consists of a pair of control links, a packet handler, a control unit and system services as shown in figure 5.8. The functionality within each unit of the control system is described in more detail below.

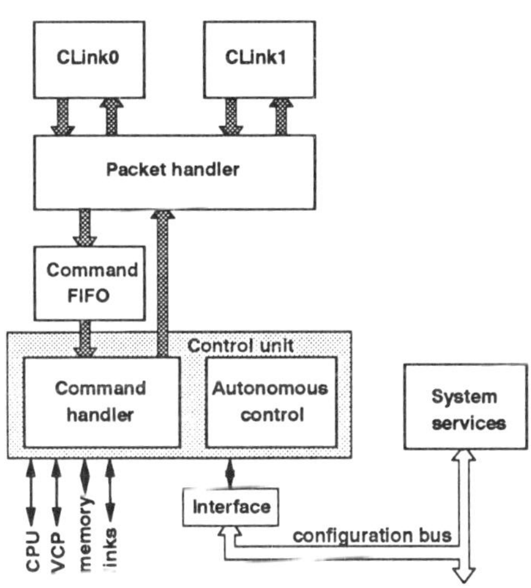

Figure 5.8 Control system components

5.7.1 Control links

A network of devices is controlled by a set of virtual links, one for every device in the network. A simple physical implementation of these virtual links can be achieved by connecting together the control links of a number of devices into a pipeline. The virtual links are multiplexed down this control link pipeline so that, as far as the network is concerned, each device has a single virtual link to the control process which is carried by `CLink0`. `CLink1` carries virtual links for devices further down the pipeline.

The virtual link is established by the first message received on `CLink0` after a hard reset. The physical management of the virtual links by routing packets received on `CLink0` to the correct destination is performed by the packet handler.

5.7.2 Packet handler

The packet handler manages the packet stream performing the following functions.

- Records the first header received on CLink0 after hard reset as the device label.
- Records the return header from a received *Start* command.
- Checks incoming CLink0 packet headers. Any with a different label from the one recorded after reset are forwarded to CLink1.
- Adds the return header to outgoing CLink0 packets.
- Forwards incoming CLink1 packets to CLink0.
- Detects and handles acknowledge packets received on CLink0.
- Validates that commands are correctly formed and forwards correctly formed commands to the control unit.
- Detects the commands *Reset*, *RecoverError* and *ErrorHandshake*.
- Rejects a command, other than the previous three, if another is already in progress

. The format of the packets is shown in figure 5.9.

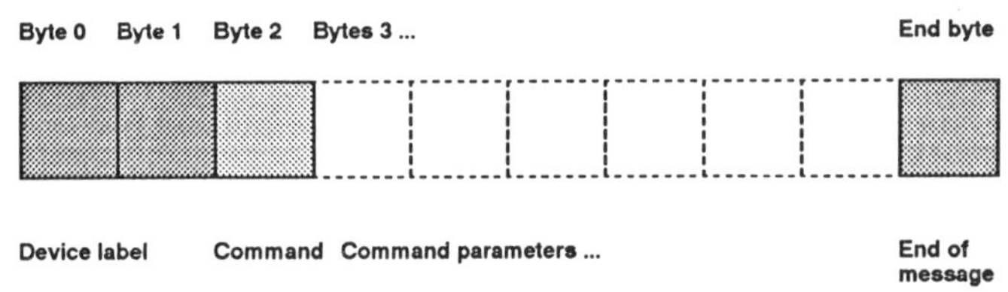

Figure 5.9 Command packet structure

5.7.3 Control unit

The control unit includes a command handler for acting on messages received from the control network and an autonomous control block which controls the behavior of the device when it is operating independently of a control network.

Command handler

The command handler

- captures errors from error inputs and forwards them to the control process via CLink0;
- responds to errors with appropriate stop/halt to sub-systems;
- arbitrates between command responses and errors, and forwards via CLink0 to the control process;
- filters illegal and inappropriate commands as errors;
- Controls sub-system reset after receipt of a *Reset* command;
- handles access to the configuration bus after receipt of *CPeek*, and *CPoke* commands;
- handles access to the memory system after receipt of *Peek*, *Poke*, *Boot* and *BootData* commands;
- stops the processor cleanly after receipt of a *Stop* command;
- starts the processor with with a given workspace and instruction pointer after receipt of a *Run* command;

- starts the processor with with a workspace and instruction pointer read from a ROM after receipt of a *Reboot* command.

5.7.4 System services

The system services is a block of registers in the configuration space containing control and general device information.

5.8 Commands

The commands to which the control unit responds are as follows.

5.8.1 Commands applicable to a variety of devices

Start

This must be the first command received by a device after a hard reset. It is used to program the return header of the device. After a hard reset it will also set the label of the device.

Reset

Reset is used to reset the device to a chosen state specified by a parameter. The parameter can typically have the values *1*, *2* or *3*.

1. Equivalent to hard reset but the control system is unaffected.
2. Resets all subsystems except the control system, and leaves the configuration unchanged.
3. Just halts the processor.

Identify

The *Identify* command causes the device to respond with a handshake containing an identifier unique to that device type.

Stop

This command causes the processor to come to a 'clean' stop ready for post-mortem debugging.

RecoverError

RecoverError is used to restore the protocol after a link error in the control link system.

CPeek

CPeek commands are used to examine registers in the configuration space. The handshake message contains the contents of the selected register.

CPoke

CPoke commands are used to initialize registers in the configuration space.

5.8.2 Commands applicable to processors

Peek

Peek commands are used to read the normal address space of a T9000. The handshake message contains the contents of the selected address.

Poke

Poke commands are used to write data to memory locations in the normal address space of the T9000.

Boot

This command initiates a booting sequence. Parameters to the command specify the length of code to be loaded and where it is to be loaded in memory. The *Boot* and *BootData* allow code to be loaded much more efficiently than it would be by using a sequence of *Poke* commands.

BootData

A sequence of *BootData* commands follow a *Boot* command. Each *BootData* command will contain 16 bytes of code which will be loaded into consecutive locations starting from the address specified in the *Boot* command until the length specified by the *Boot* command has been reached.

Run

The *Run* command specifies a workspace pointer and an instruction pointer and causes the processor to start executing with these values.

ReBoot

The *ReBoot* command re-initiates a boot-from-ROM sequence.

5.9 Conclusions

Using the same electrical and packet protocols for system control as for data transfer allows large concurrent systems to be programmed, monitored and debugged in a very straightforward way using virtual links. A small set of commands, supported directly in hardware, provides precise control over individual devices and the whole system. A simple handshaking protocol at the message level ensures that a simple, sequential control process can be used without any difficulty. Using a separate network for system functions improves the reliability and security of the system.

The provision of a two links and a basic through–routing function on each device allows a low–cost daisy–chain topology to be used for small systems. Larger systems can employ C104 routers in the control network to improve fan–out.

Facilities have been added to recover use of the control network even after the temporary disconnection of one of its links. The *RecoverError* command provides a 'remote channel reset' function to enable the control virtual links to be restored to a known state. Error information which might have been lost is re–transmitted.

6 Models of DS–Link Performance

This chapter contains analytic studies of the performance of DS-Links, the IMS T9000 virtual channel processor and the IMS C104 packet routing switch.

The first section considers the overheads imposed by the various layers of the DS–Link protocol on the raw bit–rate. Results are presented for the limiting bandwidth as a function of message size, which show that the overheads are very moderate for all but the smallest messages (for which the cost of initiating and receiving a message will dominate in any case).

The next section analyses the diminution of bandwidth caused by latency at both the token flow–control and packet–acknowledge layers of the protocol. The losses due to stalls at the packet level of the protocol when only a single virtual channel is active are plotted in the latter part of the section.

The final section considers the performance of the C104 routing switch under heavy load, both in the average and the worst case.

6.1 Performance of the DS–Link Protocol

This section looks at the maximum throughput of user data on a DS-Link implementing the virtual channel protocol (described in chapter 3) for a given message size. Two values are calculated, for unidirectional and bidirectional link use. These give bounds on the data transfer rate for a given message size. The DS–Link protocol requires use of flow–control tokens, packet headers and termination tokens. The analysis calculates how many bits have to be transmitted along a DS-Link in order to transfer a message, taking all of these overheads into account.

It is useful to define the ceiling function $\lceil x \rceil$:= (least integer greater than or equal to x).

6.1.1 Unidirectional data transfer

Assume that we have a message of size m bytes. This will be transmitted as n_p packets. If the message is sent as a single large packet, $n_p = 1$. If the message is split into packets of a maximum size 32 bytes,

$$n_p = \left\lceil \frac{m}{32} \right\rceil$$

Let s be the header size, in bytes. The number of bits transmitted for the message is

$$b_d = 10m + (10s + 4)n_p$$

since there are 10 bits for every byte of data, and a header-terminator overhead per packet. This overhead is 10 bits for each byte of header, and 4 bits for the terminator.

In the synchronised message–passing protocol used by the IMS T9000, each packet of a message must be acknowledged by an acknowledge packet, which we assume uses the inbound link. Since there will be one acknowledge for every outbound packet of data, the whole message will require n_p inbound acknowledge packets. The inbound acknowledge packets require outbound flow control tokens. There are s data tokens in the header of each acknowledge packet, and one data token in the terminator of each acknowledge packet. The total number of inbound data tokens for the acknowledge packets is

$$n_{dt} = (s + 1)n_p$$

For every eight inbound data tokens, there is an outbound flow control token. The number of flow control tokens is rounded up to the nearest integer for the purposes of the model

$$n_{ft} = \left\lceil \frac{n_{dt}}{8} \right\rceil$$

A flow control token is 4 bits. The total number of outbound bits, ***B***, required to transmit a message is the sum of the data bits and the flow control bits.

$$B = b_d + 4n_{ft}$$

The number of bits in the message transferred is 8***m***, and this requires ***B*** bits to be transmitted on the 100 MBit/s link. Thus the data rate on the link, *D*, is given by:

$$D = \frac{8m}{B} \times 100\ Mbits/s$$

6.1.2 Bidirectional data transfer

The message to be transferred has ***m*** bytes of data, and the number of packets required to transfer this data, n_p, is, as in the unidirectional case, given by

$$n_p = \left\lceil \frac{m}{32} \right\rceil$$

The data rate will differ from the unidirectional case because the outbound will have to carry a greater number of flow–control tokens corresponding to the increased amount of data on the inbound link, and also acknowledge packets for the message packets received on the inbound link.

Without loss of generality, the message analyzed is assumed to be on the outbound link. The inbound link is assumed to carry the same amount of data as the outbound link.

The outbound link will carry the data packets for the outbound message, the acknowledge packets for the inbound message, and the flow control tokens for all packets on the inbound link. The number of outbound data packets is n_p. The number of outbound acknowledge packets equals the number of inbound data packets, which in turn equals the number of outbound data packets (since the inbound link is assumed to carry the same amount of data as the outbound link). The number of acknowledge packets is therefore also n_p. Each acknowledge packet is transmitted as (10 *s* + 4) bits. The number of bits transmitted for the outbound message and the outbound acknowledgement packets is

$$b_d = (10m + (10s + 4)n_p) + (10s + 4)n_p$$

Now consider the flow control requirements. The outbound link will carry the flow control tokens for the packets received on the inbound link. The data tokens on the inbound link will be the sum of the number of data tokens for the inbound data transfer, and the number of data tokens for the inbound acknowledge packets. Recall that the inbound link carries the same amount of data as the outbound link. The number of data tokens on the inbound link is

$$n_{dt} = (m + (s + 1)n_p) + (s + 1)n_p$$

The number of flow control tokens required on the outbound link is (rounded up for the purposes of the model)

$$n_{ft} = \left\lceil \frac{n_{dt}}{8} \right\rceil$$

The total number of outbound bits for the message transfer is given by the sum

$$B = b_d + 4n_{ft}$$

and the outbound link data bandwidth is, as before,

$$D = \frac{8m}{B} \times 100 \ Mbits/s$$

Note that the bandwidth on the inbound link is the same, by assumption.

6.1.3 Asymptotic Results

Consider first the case where the message is split into packets of maximum size 32 bytes. For large messages, the overhead of the final, possibly not full size, packets will become negligible. In this case, the asymptotic values for throughput may be calculated.

Unidirectional link use

From the previous derivations, assuming that only 32–byte packets are used, we have

$$n_p = \frac{m}{32}$$

$$b_d = (10m + (10s + 4)n_p) = 10m + (10s + 4)\frac{m}{32}$$

$$n_{dt} = (s + 1)n_p = (s + 1)\frac{m}{32}$$

$$n_{ft} = \frac{n_{dt}}{8} = \frac{(s + 1)m}{8 \times 32}$$

$$B = 10m + (10s + 4)\frac{m}{32} + 4\frac{(s + 1)m}{8 \times 32}$$

collecting terms,

$$B = m\left(\frac{649 + 21s}{64}\right)$$

giving D in terms of s,

$$D = \frac{8m}{B} \times 100 = \frac{51200}{649 + 21s} \ Mbits/s$$

Bidirectional Link use

The bandwidth for the bidirectional case is calculated similarly, giving the asymptote

$$D = \frac{25600}{345 + 21s} \ Mbits/s$$

6.1.4 Results

The model is used to calculate data throughput for varying message size. This is the throughput in the outbound direction only, for both unidirectional and bidirectional link usage. This is calculated for both 1-byte and 2-byte header sizes. The graphs show data throughput, in Mbytes per second, for varying message size, header size and link usage. The asymptotic values are calculated below. The graphs also show the bandwidth that would result from sending the entire message as a single packet. This illustrates the relatively small cost of dividing messages into packets, which has considerable advantages in terms of fine–grain multiplexing and small buffer requirements.

Consider figure 6.1. It shows the data throughput for unidirectional and bidirectional link usage, with 1-byte headers, for messages up to 128 bytes. The larger discontinuity in the throughput curve occurs when an extra packet is required to transmit a message, for the maximum packet size of 32 bytes. The small discontinuities are due to the requirement to send an additional flow–control token. This is more pronounced in the bidirectional case. The overhead of the extra packet has less effect on throughput for the larger messages. Note that the knee in the graph occurs for very small messages. Only messages of 10 bytes or less cause appreciable degradation in the throughput rate.

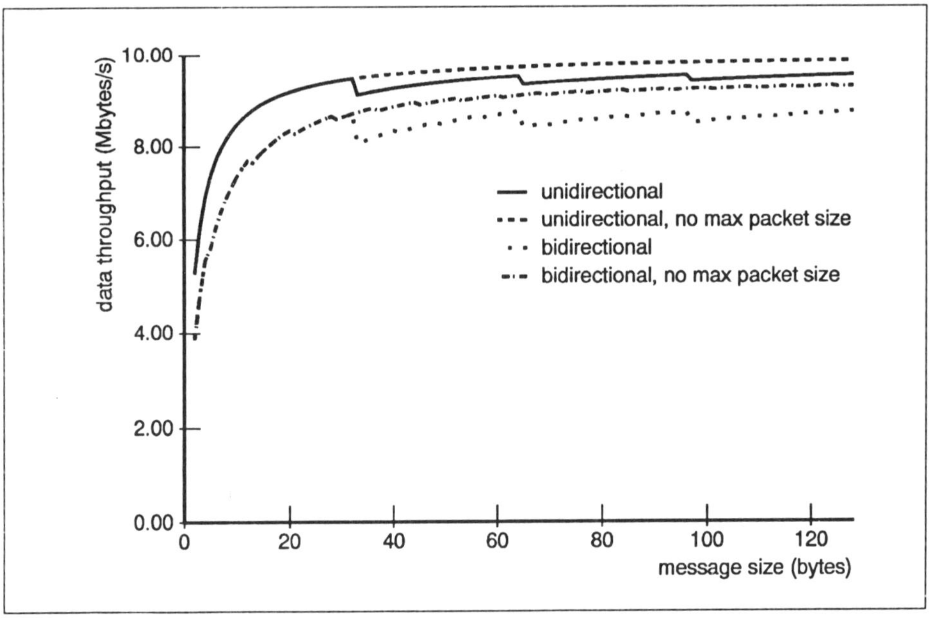

Figure 6.1 Outbound link throughput for small messages (1 byte headers)

The second graph, figure 6.2, shows the throughput for larger messages. Again a 1-byte header is assumed. Throughput is calculated for messages of size $32 \times i$ and for size $(32 \times i) + 1$ for integer values i.

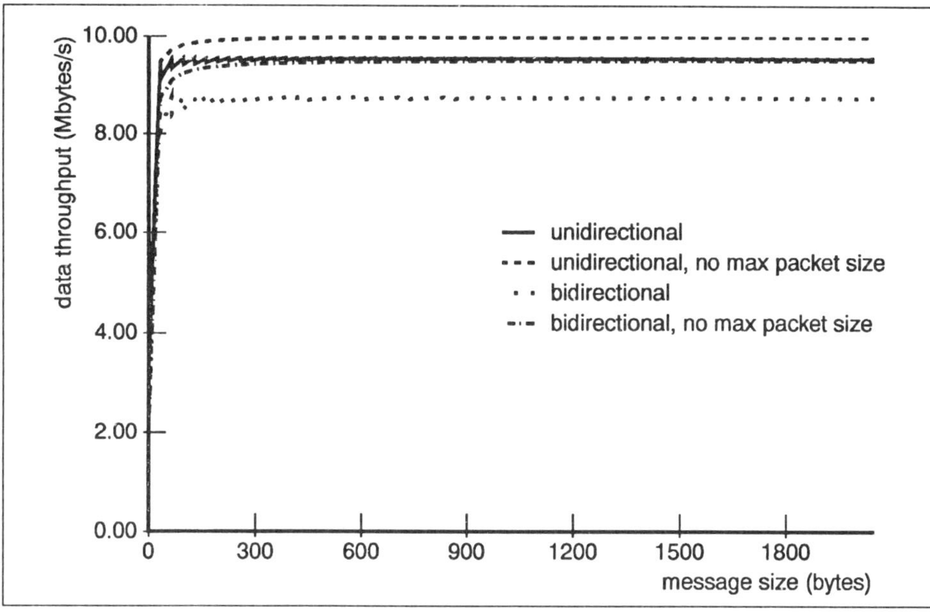

Figure 6.2 Outbound link throughput for large messages (1 byte headers)

The use of a two-byte header increases the overhead of each extra packet needed for the message. In figure 6.3, the data throughput for small messages with 2-byte headers, the overhead shows as a larger "dip" in the curve when an extra packet is used for the 32 byte maximum packet size. Figure 6.4 shows the use of 2-byte headers with larger message sizes.

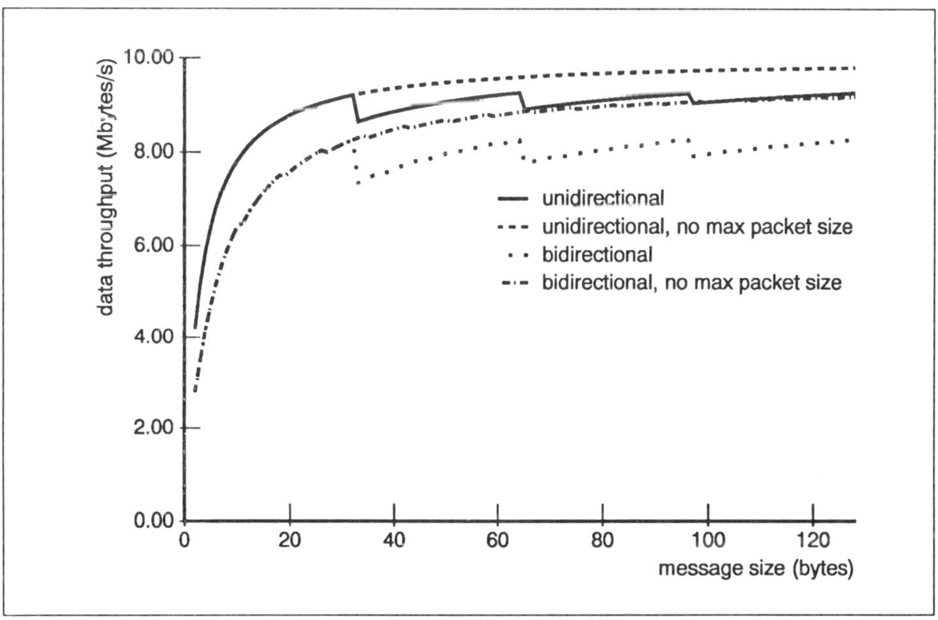

Figure 6.3 Outbound link throughput for small messages (2 byte headers)

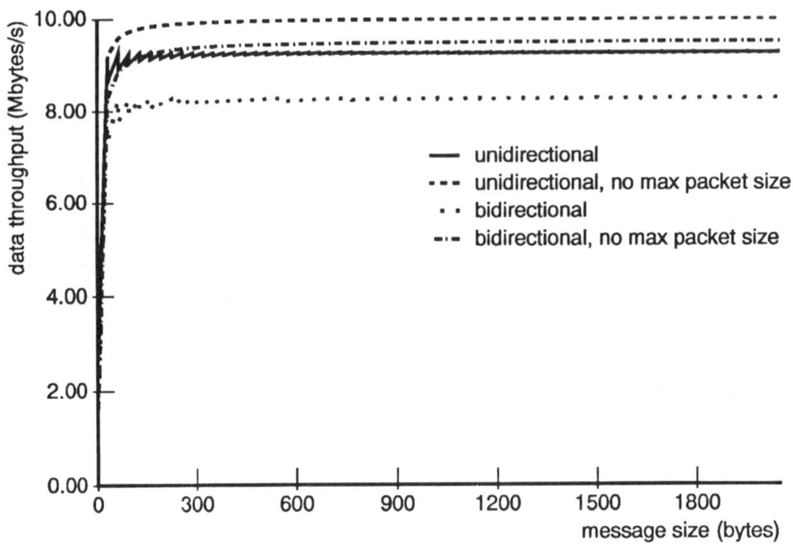

Figure 6.4 Outbound link throughput for large messages (2 byte headers)

6.1.5 Asymptotic Results

The values s=1 and s=2 are substituted into the limiting expressions for D given earlier. The results for the 32 byte maximum packet size are shown in table 6.1. The figures given are in Mbytes per second. Note that these figures are the asymptotes of the graphs.

Table 6.1 Effect of header size and usage on link throughput

s	Unidirectional	Bidirectional
1	9.55	8.74
2	9.26	8.27

Effect of maximum packet size

If the message is not split into packets then, for unidirectional data transfer the expressions for throughput derived above give

$$D = \frac{8m}{10m + 10s + 8} \times 100 \rightarrow 80 \ Mbits/s$$

For bidirectional data transfer, there is a slightly larger overhead due to the flow control information. Again from the previous derivations,

$$D = \frac{8m}{10.5m + 21s + 9} \times 100 \rightarrow 76.19 \ Mbits/s$$

6.2 Bandwidth Effects of Latency

In practice the bandwidth achieved at the user level is sometimes less than the theoretical peak calculated in the previous section, because latencies in the system cause the link to become idle for part of the time. In this section we first of all consider the effect of device–to–device latencies on the token-level protocol, and then consider the effect of end–to–end latency on the upper levels of the virtual channel protocol.

6.2.1 Bandwidth of Long Link Connections

Signals propagate through wires with a finite speed, and so long lengths of wire are themselves a source of latency, which can be significant at the speed of DS-Links,. What follows is a formal model of the flow–control mechanism of the DS–Links, which is used to calculate the maximum tolerable device–to–device latency before a link is forced to become idle.

Specification of DS–Link Flow–control

We consider a pair of links connected together. Each link is connected to both a source and a sink of data. Transmission/buffering delay between the links is modelled by a pair of buffers between them. The picture is shown in figure 6.5.

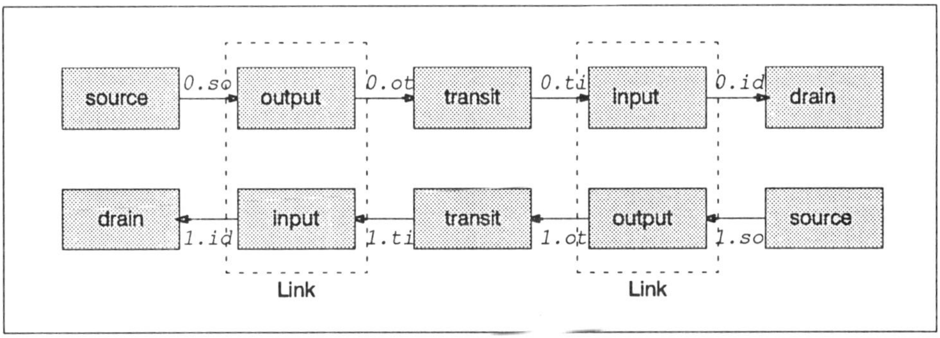

Figure 6.5 Token streams in a bi–directional DS–Link connection

Formally, we regard each labelled channel as a *trace*, i.e. a sequence of tokens transmitted upto the current time.

There are 256 different data tokens, an end-of-packet token (*EOP*), an end-of-message token (*EOM*), the flow-control token (*FCT*) and a null token. The set of tokens is thus $T = D \cup F \cup S$ where $D = \{data, EOP, EOM\}$, $F = \{FCT\}$ and S is the null token. We indicate the restriction of a trace to a sub-alphabet by $\lceil$, and the length of a trace by #. $<>$ is the empty trace. $a \preceq b$ means that the trace a is an initial subsequence of the trace b (so b can be thought of as a 'continuation' of a).

Almost all relations are given in one direction only; an exactly equivalent set hold with '**0**' and '**1**' interchanged.

Firstly, note that the streams from the source and to the drain contain only data, EOPs and EOMs; there are no flow–control or null tokens other than between the two link interfaces, so the restriction of the other traces to the set $F \cup S$ is empty:

$$0.so \lceil (F \cup S) = 0.id \lceil (F \cup S) = 1.so \lceil (F \cup S) = 1.id \lceil (F \cup S) = <>$$

The sequence of tokens is preserved, so the trace of data tokens received by the drain is a strict initial subsequence of the trace of data tokens sent by the source (the difference being those still in transit):

$$\mathbf{0}.id \preccurlyeq \mathbf{0}.ti \lceil D \preccurlyeq \mathbf{0}.ot \lceil D \preccurlyeq \mathbf{0}.so$$

$$\mathbf{0}.ti = \mathbf{0}.ot$$

The number of tokens held in each box is the difference between the number of tokens input and the number output. All the boxes (except the sources and drains) have finite capacities, thus:

$$\begin{aligned} 0 &\leq \#\mathbf{0}.so - \#(\mathbf{0}.ot \lceil D) \leq output.cap.\mathbf{0} \\ 0 &\leq \#\mathbf{0}.ot - \#\mathbf{0}.ti \leq t.delay \\ 0 &\leq \#(\mathbf{0}.ti \lceil D) - \#\mathbf{0}.id \leq input.cap.\mathbf{0} \end{aligned}$$

The total credit received is the number of *FCT*s received times the flow-control batch–size ***bsize***. The output credit remaining for that link is the difference between this and the number of data tokens sent. The total credit sent is the number of *FCT*s sent times the flow-control batch–size; the input credit remaining is the difference between this and the number of data tokens received[18]. Since we have a 'credit' based system all of them must be positive, and from the sequence relations above we can deduce:

$$\begin{aligned} input.credit.\mathbf{0} &= \#(\mathbf{1}.ot \lceil F) \times bsize - \#(\mathbf{0}.ti \lceil D) \geq output.credit.\mathbf{0} \\ output.credit.\mathbf{0} &= \#(\mathbf{1}.ti \lceil F) \times bsize - \#(\mathbf{0}.ot \lceil D) \geq 0 \end{aligned}$$

The input credit must never exceed the buffer space available, which is the difference between the size of the buffer and the number of tokens held. Thus we require:

$$input.cap.\mathbf{0} - \#(\mathbf{0}.\mathrm{ti} \lceil D) + \#\mathbf{0}.id \geq input.credit.\mathbf{0}$$

Combining the above gives the simple relation:

$$input.cap.\mathbf{0} + \#\mathbf{0}.id \geq \#(\mathbf{1}.ot \lceil F) \times bsize$$

This shows that the total credit issued must not exceed the buffer capacity of the input plus the amount sent to the drain.

Initially all the traces have zero length. The condition for actual transfer of data is that at least one of the traces into the drains (e.g. $\mathbf{0}.id$) must become non-empty. By the above this implies that $\#(\mathbf{0}.ot \lceil D)$ becomes non-zero. Now for this to happen $\#(\mathbf{1}.ti \lceil F) \times bsize$ must become non-zero, this is bounded from above by $input.cap.0$, since at the start $\#\mathbf{0}.id = 0$. Since the length of traces is integral, this shows that no data can ever be transferred unless $input.cap.0 \geq bsize$. Thus this form of flow–control requires an input buffer at least as large as the flow–control batch–size.

6.2.2 Effect of Inter–Link Delay

Now consider the consequences of the transit delay. If the delay is constant, it behaves as a fixed-size buffer which can only output when it is *full*. This means that in the steady-state there is always a fixed difference in the lengths of its input and output streams, i.e.

$$\#\mathbf{0}.ot = \#\mathbf{0}.ti + t.delay.\mathbf{0}$$

Thus, for any set A:

$$\#(\mathbf{0}.ot \lceil A) \leq \#(\mathbf{0}.ti \lceil A) + t.delay.\mathbf{0}$$

18. The difference between the input and output credits is due to tokens in transit.

Equality only occurs if *all* the tokens held in transit belong to A. If we assume (for the moment) that data flows only on the **0** channels and transmission is continuous (i.e. no tokens from S are interspersed) this means:

$$\#(\mathbf{0}.ot \lceil D) \quad = \quad \#(\mathbf{0}.ti \lceil D) \ + \ t.delay.0$$

On the **1** channels, to maintain the steady state we must send an *FCT* for every ***bsize*** tokens transmitted on the **0** channels (since these are, by assumption, all tokens from *D*). Thus, on average,

$$\#(\mathbf{1}.ot \lceil F) bsize \quad = \quad \#(\mathbf{1}.ti \lceil F) \times bsize \ + \ t.delay.1$$

Thus,

$$\begin{aligned} input.credit.0 \quad &= \quad \#(\mathbf{1}.ot \lceil F) \times bsize \ - \ \#(\mathbf{0}.ti \lceil D) \\ &= \quad \#(\mathbf{1}.ti \lceil F) \times bsize \ + \ t.delay.1 \ - \ \#(\mathbf{0}.ot \lceil D) \ + \ t.delay.0 \end{aligned}$$

Thus:

$$input.cap.0 \ \geq \ input.credit.0 \ + \ \#(\mathbf{0}.ti \lceil D) \times bsize \ + \ \#\mathbf{0}.id$$

$$= (t.delay.0 \ + \ t.delay.1) \ + \ (\#(\mathbf{1}.ti \lceil F) \times bsize \ - \ \#(\mathbf{0}.ot \lceil D) \ + \ (\#(\mathbf{0}.ti \lceil D) \ + \ \#\mathbf{0}.id)$$

By the above, the third term of the last equation is ≥ 0.

The second term is ***output.credit***.0, which can attain $\left\lfloor \frac{in.cap.0}{bsize} \right\rfloor \times bsize$ when $\#(\mathbf{0}.ot \lceil D)=0$ and $\#(\mathbf{1}.ti \lceil F)$ is equal to the maximum number of flow-control tokens that can be sent.

From the starting condition we can write ***input.cap***.0 = ***bsize*** + ***extra*** (where ***extra*** is non-negative) so that the previous expression is simply ***extra***.

Thus we deduce:

$$extra \ \geq \ t.delay.0 \ + \ t.delay.1$$

So we see that the input buffer must have a minimum capacity of ***bsize*** for transmission to start, but to maintain continuous transmission of data through a delay, there must also be some some 'slack' to deal with tokens in transit, which depends on the latency of the connection.

If we assume that data flows on both sets of channels, by a similar argument we obtain the result:

$$extra \ \geq \ (t.delay.0 \ + \ t.delay.1) \ \times \ \left(\frac{bsize}{1 \ + \ bsize} \right)$$

Inverting this equation gives a restriction on the maximum delay through which full bandwidth can be sustained:

$$t.delay.0 \ + \ t.delay.1 \ \leq \ extra \times \left(\frac{1 \ + \ bsize}{bsize} \right)$$

Thus for the DS-Link, for which ***bsize*** = 8, a total buffer capacity of 20 tokens means that *extra*=12, so the maximum delay which can be endured without loss of bandwidth is:

$$max.delay = 12 \times \left(\frac{9}{8} \right) = 13.5$$

where the unit of time is the average time to transmit one token. This depends on the ratio of data tokens to *EOP/M* tokens, the worst case being 1:1. This makes the average token length 7 bits, so at 100 MBits/s the average token transmission time is 70ns. Thus the maximum delay is 945ns. In practice there is some latency associated with the front-end circuitry of the DS-Link, buffers etc.. This could be added explicitly to the model by introducing more buffer processes, but the effect will simply be to reduce the latency budget for the wires. Latencies in the link account for approximately 400ns, so a conservative estimate would allow 500ns for the round–trip wire delay, which corresponds to a distance of about 80m. Allowing for delays in buffers leads to the conclusion that 50m would be a suitably conservative figure.

6.2.3 Bandwidth of a Single Virtual Channel

The T9000 VCP is pipelined in order to sustain the high rate of packet processing required by the virtual channel protocol, just as the DS-Link is pipelined internally to achieve a high bandwidth. When many virtual channels are active simultaneously on a link, the VCP ensures that the link is never idle so that its full bandwidth is exploited. The disadvantage of pipelining is that it introduces latency, which can become a limiting factor on bandwidth when only one virtual channel is active on a link.

The reason that latency can limit bandwidth is because of the requirement that each data packet must be acknowledged before the next may be sent. Although the VCP sends the acknowledge packet as soon as possible, so that its transmission can overlap that of the bulk of the data packet, if the data packet is short and/or the latency of the system is large, it is possible for the acknowledge to arrive too late to prevent a stall in data transmission. When the VCP has packets to send for other channels this does not matter, but if only a single channel is active, the bandwidth may be reduced by the system latency.

Analysis

We consider the particular case of two processes communicating over a single virtual channel.

```
CHAN OF [message.size]BYTE channel :
PLACED PAR
  [message.size]BYTE message :
  SEQ
    channel ! message
    .
    .   (repeat n times)
    .
    channel ! message
  [message.size]BYTE message :
  SEQ
    channel ? message
    .
    .   (repeat n times)
    .
    channel ? message
```

We ask: what is the bandwidth that this pair of processes observes, as a function of the message size? The bandwidth is defined as the total amount of message data transferred divided by the total time taken (as measured by the outputting process). Whenever the time is limited by the latency of the system, the bandwidth is proportional to the length of the message, since the time is constant. When the time to transmit the data exceeds the round-trip latency it is this which limits the bandwidth. In this case the time to transmit the header is significant, and so there is a difference in bandwidth depending on the size of header used.

We assume that all data is in the cache, the inputting process is initially ready, and that only one process is using each machine. Communication is thus mainly unidirectional, and so we ignore the effects of token level flow-control, since this has been analyzed in the previous section. We assume that the two T9000s are directly connected by short wires.

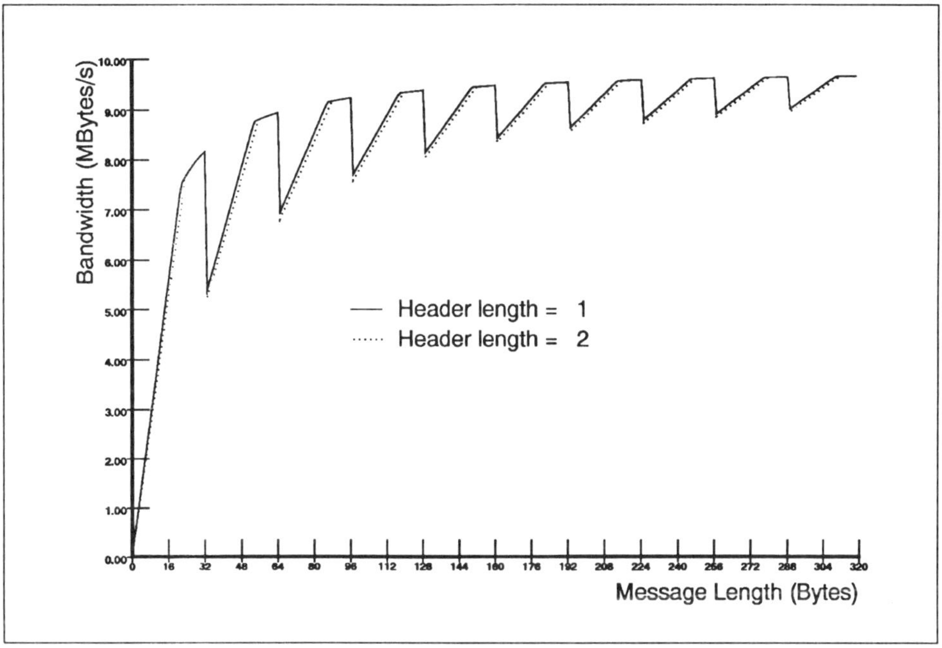

Figure 6.6 Single channel bandwidth vs. message size

The results are illustrated in figure 6.6. It can be seen that for messages of less than about 20 bytes, latency dominates. Packet transmission time becomes limiting until the message size exceeds 32 bytes, when a second packet is required. The time to acknowledge the second packet then becomes limiting until the message size reaches about 50 bytes. This pattern is repeated at each multiple of 32 bytes, but as the message size increases the effect of latency on the final packet becomes proportionately less significant, and so the dips in the graph become smaller. The envelope of the curve is that derived in section 6.1. If the length of the individual connections is greater, and/or the message is routed via one or more C104 routers, the latency is larger, and so the dips in the curve become both wider and deeper. Latency can be hidden by having more channels active at once, since in this case an acknowledge does not have to be received until a packet has been sent for *each* active channel.

6.3 A model of Contention in a Single C104

In this section we develop a statistical model of contention for the C104. The model allows a number of C104 input links to be trying to route packets to a number of C104 output links. The C104 will allow one packet which requests an output link to succeed, for each output link[19]. Each packet has a header, which is one or two bytes, and a terminator. A byte of information is transmitted as 10 bits on the link, and the packet terminator is transmitted as 4 bits.

19. Grouped adaptive routing is not considered in this model.

The model allocates time in slots. Conceptually, at the start of the time slot all of the input links attempt to route a packet to their selected destination link. A subset of these transmissions will succeed, and the other packets are discarded – note that this is *not* what occurs in the implementation. The model developed here assumes that the destination links are chosen at random, and this assumption is appropriate for the the actual behavior of stalling and buffering of unsuccessful packets for the next time slot, because the destinations of all the packets in the next slot will again be independent and random. The model describes the probability that a packet is successfully transmitted from its chosen outbound link.

6.3.1 Time slots

The size of a time slot is the time for which a packet occupies the input/output pair of links, given that it is successfully routed. This is the sum of the header routing time and the time taken for the following bits to cross the switch.

Let h denote the header delay, and b denote the bit delay. Then the slot time, S, for k-bit packets is $S = h + k'b$, where k' is the number of bits transferred after the header. For one-byte headers, this is $k + 4$ since the bits transferred are the data bits and the 4 terminator bits. Two-byte headers may be modelled by setting $k' = k + 10 + 4$, where the extra 10 bits correspond to the extra byte of header to be transferred.

6.3.2 The Contention Model

At the start of a time slot, each input link submits a packet. If there is contention for the output links, then one packet for each output link is successful.

Let the number of input links in use be in, and the number of output links in use be out, with the ratio $r = out/in$. Then the probability that an output link is not used by any of the inputs is given by

$$p(free) = \left(1 - \frac{1}{out}\right)^{in}$$

The probability that an output link is used is therefore

$$p(use) = 1 - p(free) = 1 - \left(1 - \frac{1}{out}\right)^{in}$$

The data throughput, T, of an input link is given in bits/s by

$$T = \frac{1}{slot\ time} \times p(use) \times rk$$

Substituting in the above expressions gives

$$T = \frac{1 - (1 - \frac{1}{out})^{in}}{S} \times rk$$

6.3.3 Average delay

The model so far describes the expected throughput of each input link. This may be used to calculate the expected number of time slots it will take for a submitted packet to cross the switch. This time is the delay due to the contention within the switch. In order to look at system delays, the time taken to reach the front of the input queue also needs to be taken into account.

The expected delay of a packet, in terms of time slots, is given by

$$L = \sum_{i=1}^{\infty} i \times p(i)$$

where i is the time slot number. Now $p(i)$ is the probability of an input success on the ith trial, so that $p(i) = p(failure)^{i-1} \times p(success)$. Substituting into the expression for L and taking the common factor outside of the summation we get:

$$L = \frac{p(success)}{r} \times \sum_{i=1}^{\infty} i \times p(failure)^{i-1}$$

summing the series, this gives

$$L = \frac{1}{r} \times \frac{1}{p(use)}$$

The absolute expected delay, D, is the value L multiplied by the length of the time slot, $D = L \times (slot\ time)$. Substituting,

$$D = \frac{1}{r} \times \frac{S}{1 - (1 - \frac{1}{out})^{in}}$$

6.3.4 Summary of model

The throughput per terminal link, in units data bits per second is

$$T = \frac{1 - (1 - \frac{1}{out})^{in}}{S} \times rk$$

The total bandwidth of the system is $B = in \times T$.

The expected delay of a packet, in seconds, is

$$D = \frac{1}{r} \times \frac{S}{1 - (1 - \frac{1}{out})^{in}}$$

where the slot–time $S = h + k'b$, for k bit packets where k' is the number of bits transferred after the header, and

- h is the time taken to route a header, in seconds
- b is the time taken to transmit a bit, in seconds
- k is the number of bits in the packet
- in is the number of input links used, $in \leq 32$
- out is the number of output links used, $out \leq 32$
- r is the ratio $r = out/in$

6.3.5 Asymptotes of the model

The expression $\left(1 - \frac{x}{n}\right)^n$ tends to the value e^{-x} as $n \rightarrow \infty$. As both in and out grow, the asymptotic throughput and delay for a particular set of switch parameters may be calculated. The limit of the expressions is

$$\left(1 - \frac{1}{out}\right)^{in} = \left(1 - \frac{1}{r \times in}\right)^{in} \rightarrow e^{-1/r}$$

$$T_{lim} = \frac{1 - e^{-1/r}}{S} \times rk$$

$$D_{lim} = \frac{1}{r} \times \frac{S}{1 - e^{-1/r}}$$

In the special case where $r = 1$, i.e. the numbers of input and output links in use are the same,

$$T_{lim} = \frac{0.632 \times k}{S}$$

$$D_{lim} = 1.582S$$

6.3.6 Results

The IMS C104 chip will have a header routing time, ***h*** of approximately 500ns, and a bit delay, ***b*** of 10ns. The throughput of each input link is calculated as a function of the number of links in use, and of the packet size (in data bits).

The model is first used to describe the throughput of the chip when the number of input links in use is the same as the number of output links in use. In the equations, this is setting ***in=out***, or $r = 1$. Figures 6.7 and 6.8 show the resulting throughput and delay respectively for one-byte packet headers. All of the message is sent in a single packet, with one header and one terminator. The value of S is $S = h + (1.25k + 4) \times b$. Note that the curves for both the throughput and delay quickly flatten.

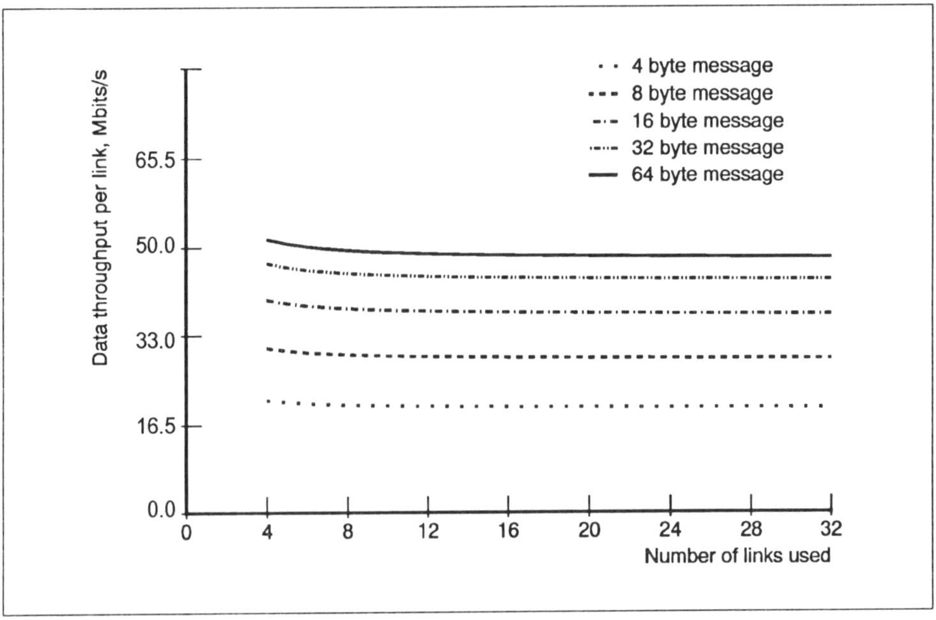

Figure 6.7 Throughput per link vs. packet size

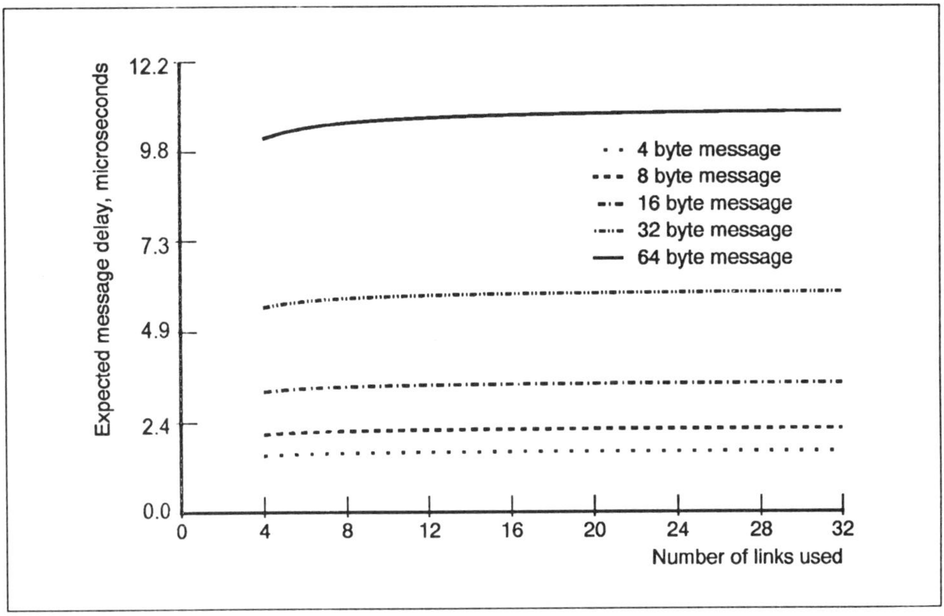

Figure 6.8 Mean packet delay vs. packet size

The model is now used to illustrate the case when $in \neq out$. The number of input links is varied, with the number of output links held constant at 32. The message size is varied. The throughput for each input link is shown in figure 6.9, and the corresponding expected packet delay is shown in figure 6.10.

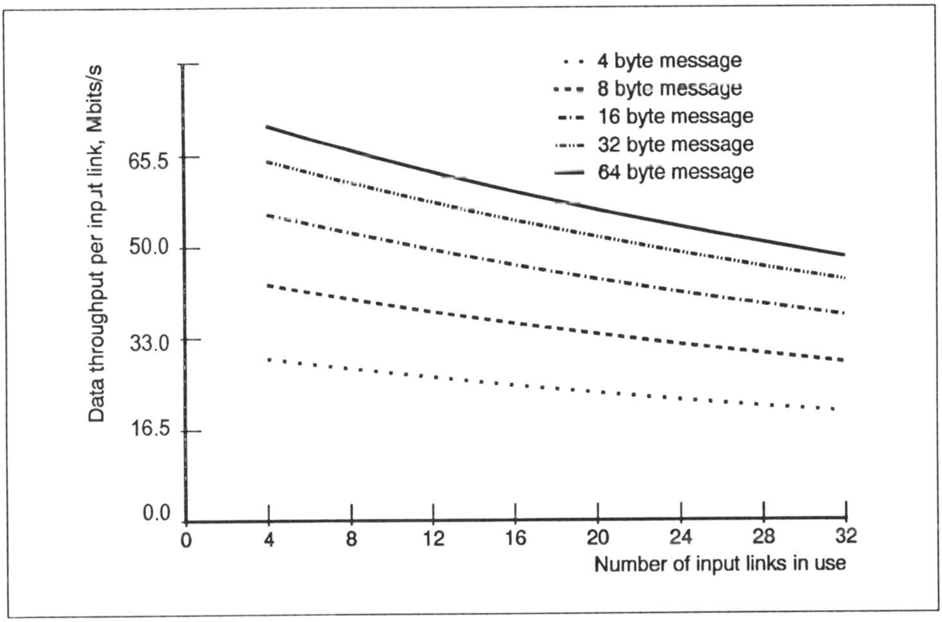

Figure 6.9 Throughput per link vs. no inputs used (32 outputs)

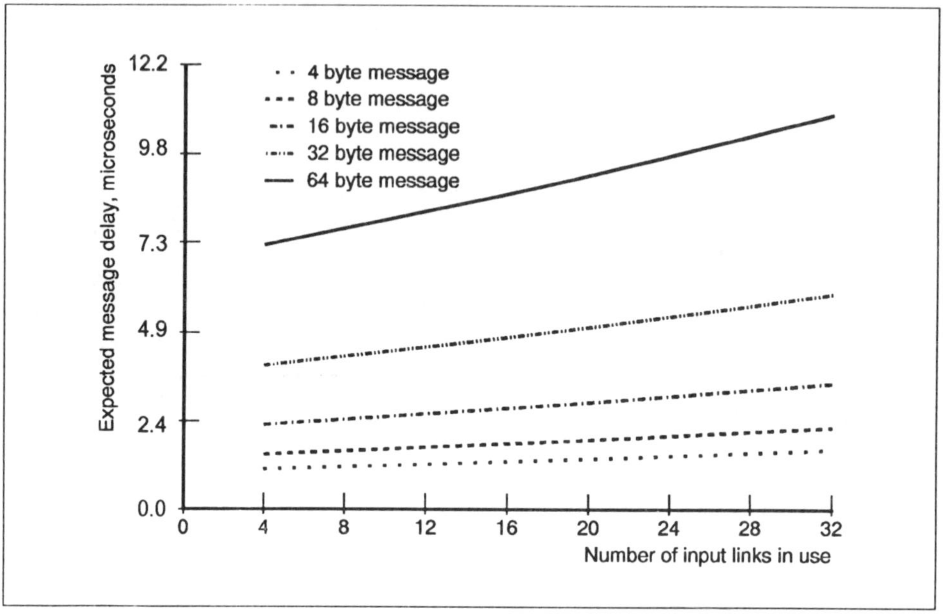

Figure 6.10 Mean delay vs. no inputs used (32 outputs)

The asymptotic results for the case ***in*** $\neq$ ***out*** describes the expected behaviour. The number of output links is held constant, first at *out* = 32, then at *out*=8. The number of input links is varied, for 32 byte messages. The throughput and delay are compared to the asymptotic curves in figures 6.11 and 6.12 with 32 output links in use. Figures 6.13 and 6.14 show 8 output links in use.

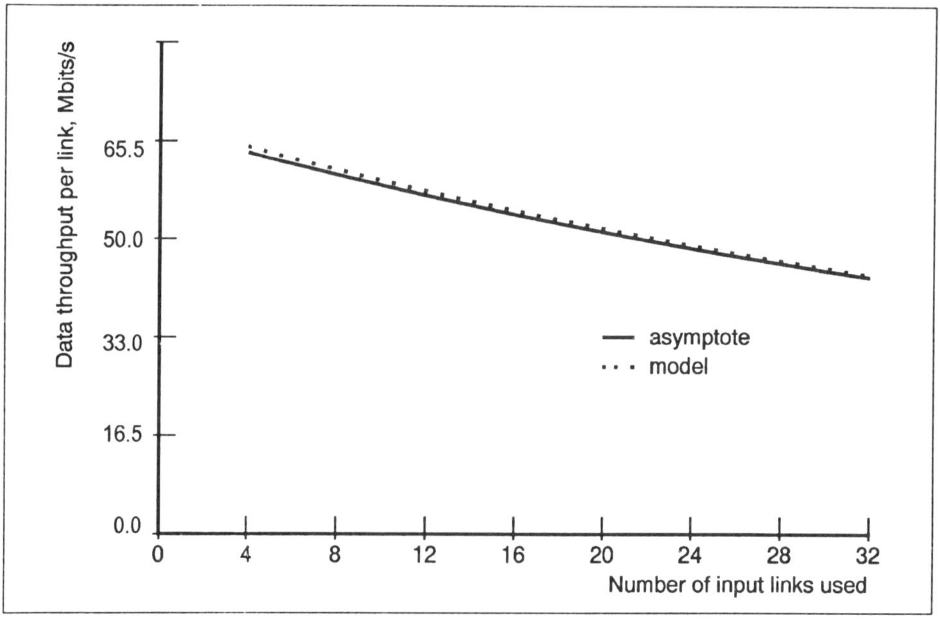

Figure 6.11 Throughput per link vs. no inputs used (32 outputs)

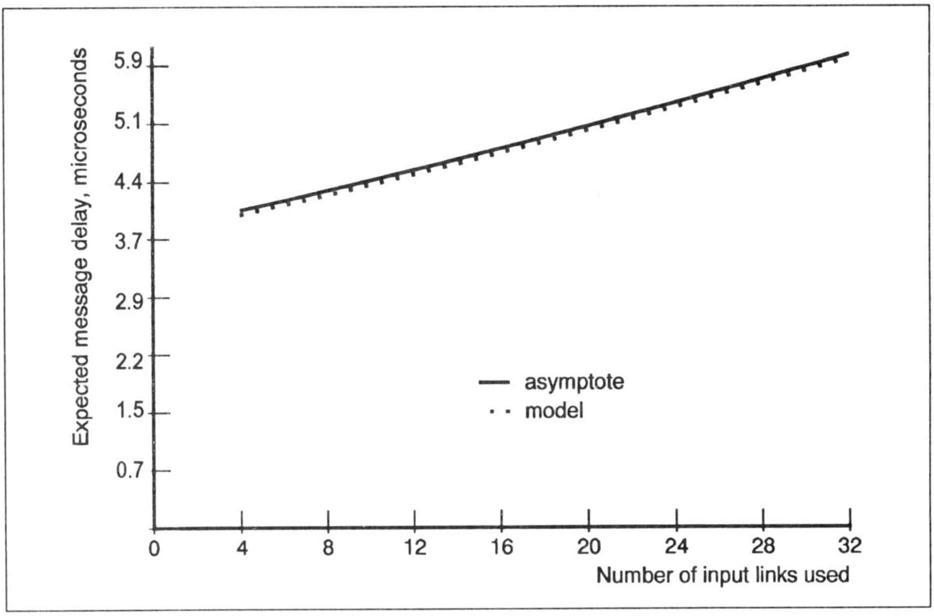

Figure 6.12 Mean delay vs. no inputs used (32 outputs)

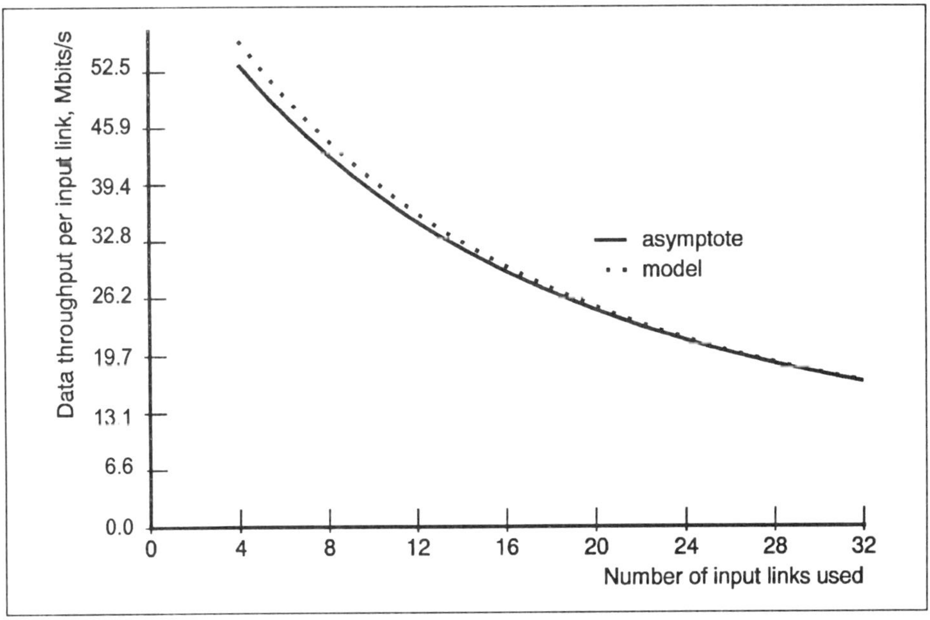

Figure 6.13 Throughput per link vs. no inputs used (8 outputs)

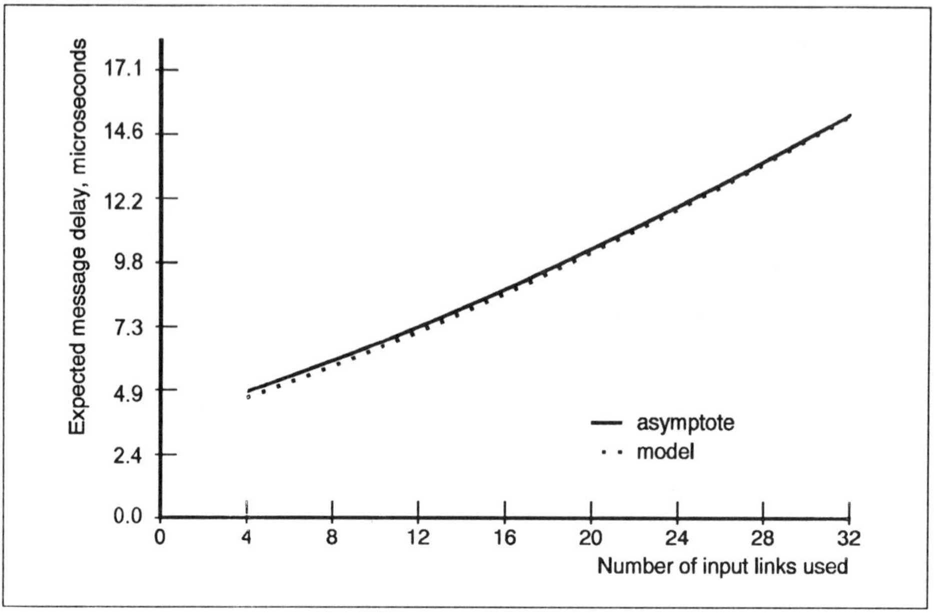

Figure 6.14 Mean delay vs. no inputs used (8 outputs)

These graphs show that the limits of the expressions are actually a very good approximation to the exact model as long as there are more than a few links in use for both input and output. The factor common to the expression for link throughput, and delay, is $r\left(1 - e^{-1/r}\right)$. This is plotted in figure 6.15.

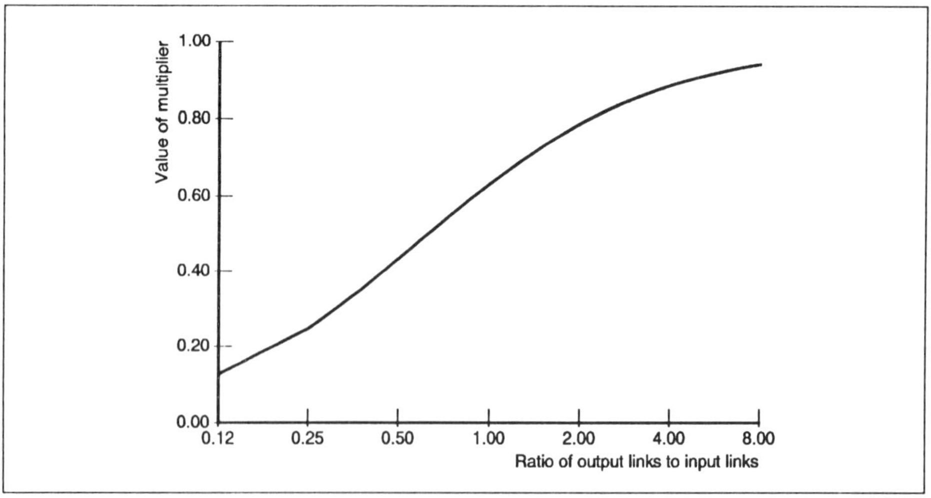

Figure 6.15 Variation of $r\left(1 - e^{-1/r}\right)$ with r

The approximation is dependent upon the ratio of output links to input links, and not the absolute number of input links and output links in use. This suggests that the throughput for each of 8 input links, choosing among 16 output links, will be about the same as the throughput of each of 16 input links, choosing between 32 output links.

In the expression for throughput, the value k/S describes the amount of data in time S: the data throughput rate. The factor $r(1 - e^{-1/r})$ describes the proportion of output links which are used.

The expression for delay depends on S, with the factor $\frac{1}{r(1 - e^{-1/r})}$ determining the number of slot times which the packet takes to get across the switch.

6.3.7 Maximum Routing Delay

Finally we consider the effect of the very worst case contention on the transit time of a packet through a C104. This means the time between the header arriving on an input link of the C104 to the time that the header is transmitted from the chosen output link.

In the worst case, 32 inputs contend for the same output[20], so the unlucky packet must wait for 31 others to be routed before it can proceed. The very worst case is when all 32 packets arrive simultaneously; in all other cases some of the routing of the first packet will have been done by the time the unlucky packet arrives.

In this case, every packet header must be received and the corresponding routing decision taken. The worst case is with two-byte headers, which take 2×100ns + *(link input latency)* to receive. Making the routing decision and performing the arbitration takes about 60ns; the first packet can then start to be transferred across the crossbar. Each successive packet will start to be transferred immediately after the previous one finishes; the whole process will be limited by the speed of the output link[21].

Thus a total packet transfer time of $31 \times L_{packet} \times 100$ns is required before the unlucky packet gets across the crossbar; it then has to reach the outside world through a FIFO and the link output circuitry.

Thus the total is: $(L_{header} + 31 \times L_{packet}) \times 100\text{ns} + 4 \times 20\text{ns} + (\textit{link latency})$. In a T9000 system packets (in the worst case) are 32 bytes plus a terminator plus a routing header of length L_{header} plus (usually) a virtual channel header (typically another two bytes), so L_{packet} is typically at most 37. The link latency is small compared to the other terms, so this gives a total of about 115μs.

Note that this analysis assumes that the congested output link transfers data at full speed the whole time. If this is not the case (for example if it is connected to another C104, where there is contention for an output link...) then the time must be increased. Note however that the effect of this multiplication is minimized by using large fan-out routers such as the C104.

6.4 Summary

A variety of models have been developed to describe data throughput on the DS-Link and through the C104 router. The first takes into account the overhead of acknowledge packets and flow control, use of one or two byte headers, and unidirectional or bidirectional link use. This model has been used to give the asymptotic throughput of the DS-Link, as the message size gets very large. For large messages and a maximum packet size of 32 bytes, the lowest throughput value of the link is 8.27 Mbytes per second. This occurs when two-byte headers are used along with bidirectional link use. Further models consider the effect of latency on bandwidth given the particular protocols used, both at the token and the message levels of the protocol. The final models show the effect of output contention in a single C104, both in an average and a worst case.

20. Note that this includes the unusual - but not impossible - case that one packet is being routed directly back out of the link on which it arrived.

21. All the links are assumed to run at the same speed.

7 Performance of C104 Networks

The use of VLSI technology to design specialised routing chips makes the construction of high-bandwidth, low-latency networks possible. One such chip is the IMS C104 packet routing chip, described in chapter 3. This can be used to build a variety of communication networks.

In this chapter, interconnection networks are characterized by their throughput and delay. Three families of topology are investigated, and the throughput and delay are examined as the size of the network varies. Using deterministic routing (in which the same route is always used between source and destination), random traffic patterns and systematic traffic patterns are investigated on each of the networks. The results show that on each of the families examined, there is a systematic traffic pattern which severely affects the throughput of the network, and that this degradation is more severe for the larger networks. The use of universal routing, where an amount of random behavior is introduced, overcomes this problem and provides the scalability inherent to the network structure. This is also shown to be an efficient use of the available network links.

An important factor in network performance is the predictability of the time it will take a packet to reach its destination. Deterministic is shown to give widely varying packet completion times with variation of the traffic pattern in the network. Universal routing is shown to remove this effect, with the time taken for a packet to reach its destination being stabilized.

In the following investigation, we have separated issues of protocol overhead, such as flow control, from issues of network performance.

7.1 The C104 switch

The C104 is a packet routing chip. The use of VLSI to create such a chip means that routing is fast, and the flexibility of the C104 ensures that the chip can be used in many situations. The C104 contains a 32-way crossbar switch, in which all of the 32 inputs can be routed simultaneously to the 32 outputs. Routing delays are minimized by the use of wormhole routing, in which a packet can start to be output from a switch whilst it is still being input.

A packet arriving at a switch is routed according to its header. If the required outbound link is available, the packet utilizes the link. However, if the link required is currently in use, the packet will be blocked. The tail of the packet may now start to catch up with the head. If there is enough buffering, the whole packet may be taken into a buffer, waiting to have access to its required output. Therefore if the network is very busy, the performance will approximate to the performance of a store-and-forward network. The simulations model the C104, which provides roughly one packet of inbound buffering, and one packet of outbound buffering on each link, for packets of a small average size, such as those used by the virtual channel protocol.

The C104 supports universal routing, which requires a packet to be sent to a randomly chosen intermediate node before it travels to its real destination. Any of the links on the C104 can be set to create a random header for each inbound packet on that link. At the randomly chosen intermediate node, this random header is deleted, leaving the original header to route the message to its real destination.

All routing, header creation and deletion is performed on a per link basis. There is no shared resource within the C104. This has the effect of making the links of the network the shared resources, rather than the nodes of the network.

7.2 Networks and Routing Algorithms

In a communication network connecting p terminals, we can realistically expect the distance a packet will travel to increase with $log(p)$. Consequently, if we wish to maintain throughput per terminal, the number of packets in flight from each terminal will scale with $log(p)$. Therefore network capacity required for each terminal will scale with $log(p)$. The total capacity of a network with p terminals must therefore scale as $p \times log(p)$. One structure which achieves this is the hypercube or binary n–cube. Another structure is the (indirect) butterfly network, which has constant degree. Conversely, the two–dimensional grid and indirect multistage networks do not maintain throughput per node as the network scales.

Three topologies are considered. The first structure is the binary n-cube. The second structure is the two-dimensional grid, which is appealing practically. The last structure is the indirect multistage network.

In a binary n-cube, node i is connected to node j in dimension k if the binary representation of i and j differ only in the kth bit. The n-dimensional cube has $N=2^n$ nodes, diameter n and uses n links per network node for network connections.

A grid is a 2-dimensional array of routing chips. Each routing chip has one processor connected to it. If the network is drawn onto integer axes, there is a router at each of the intersections, and links in both the x and the y directions. Only links internal to the grid are used, since, although it is possible to construct toroidal networks using the C104, the number of links used to 'wrap around' must be doubled to avoid the possibility of deadlock. This contrasts with the appealing simplicity of the grid, and so such networks are not studied here.

The indirect multistage networks considered in this chapter provide a low cost switch for small networks, and make economical use of the C104 switches for large networks. An example of an indirect multistage network, with 512 terminals, is shown in figure 7.1.

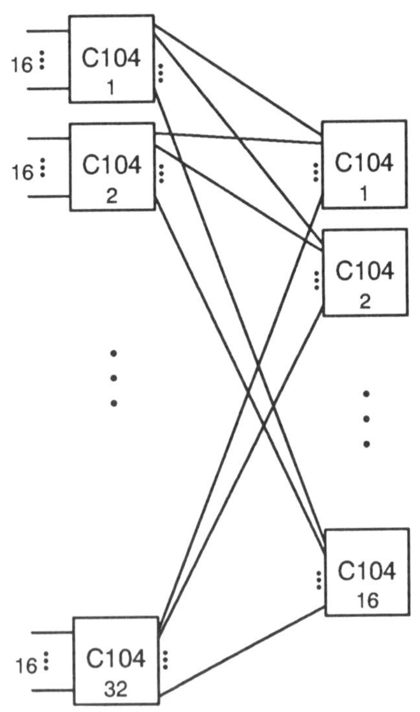

Figure 7.1 A 512–way multistage network

There are 16 external links on each C104 in the left hand column, and there are 32 switches in the column. There are 16 switches in the right hand column. Indirect multistage networks can also be built using 8 links to the left of the left hand column, and 24 links to the right, providing greater throughput per terminal. Similarly, 24 links to the left and 8 to the right provide less throughput per terminal. For very large networks, where the switches in the right column need to switch more than 32 links, small indirect networks can be used.

7.3 The Networks Investigated

In the following performance evaluation, three sizes of network are considered, where the size of a network is measured as the number of terminals from it. The networks studied are mostly not practical, in that they do not make efficient use of the routing chips[22], but they are such that the results can be easily interpreted in terms of scalability, and extended directly to other networks of similar form.

Three sizes of network are considered: 64, 256 and 1024. These are natural sizes for the topologies considered.

7.3.1 The binary n–cube

The network sizes are all powers of 2. The smallest network is constructed from 64 C104 switches. These form a six-dimensional cube. On each switch there are six links in use for the network, and one more for the traffic source and sink (the terminal link).

The 256 size cube is constructed as 256 switches, connected as a degree 8 cube. The 1024 size cube is 1024 switches, constructed as a degree 10 cube. For all three sizes, smaller "fatter" cubes would more fully utilize the C104s. These are cubes of lower dimension, with several links in parallel where only a single link would otherwise be used.

Deterministic routing on the hypercube is done from the highest dimension downwards, providing the deadlock free routing described in chapter 1.

7.3.2 The two–dimensional grid

The grids examined are all square. Each switch uses one link in each direction $(+x, -x, +y, -y)$ and there is one terminal at each switch. The links at the edges of the grid are not used.

The 64 size grid is therefore made from 64 switches, arranged as an 8 by 8 square. The 256 size is 16 switches square, and the 1024 size is 32 switches square. The same number of terminals would be given by using smaller grids with, say, four terminals per node, and parallel links between the nodes.

Deterministic routing on the grid is first in the y direction, then in the x direction, providing the deadlock free routing described in chapter 1.

7.3.3 Indirect multistage networks

The indirect multistage networks considered here are all *low-cost* networks. A larger number of switches can be used to make the network more highly connected: this tends towards the indirect butterfly. The networks examined therefore indicate the performance characteristics of the "cheaper" networks in the class. The 64-way network illustrated in figure 7.2 has eight links

22. In most cases a far larger number of terminals could be connected with the number of switches used.

for each one from left to right shown in the diagram, and the 256-way network illustrated in figure 7.3 has two. A 1024–way network can be constructed from 32–way routers by using a 64–way network for each of the center stage switches, as illustrated in figure 7.4.

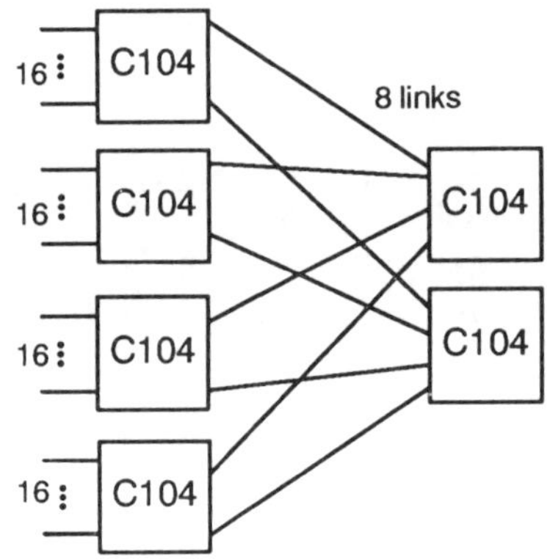

Figure 7.2 64–way multistage network

Deterministic routing on the indirect multistage network routes an inbound packet at the left hand side via an appropriate right hand side node to the destination terminal at the left hand side.

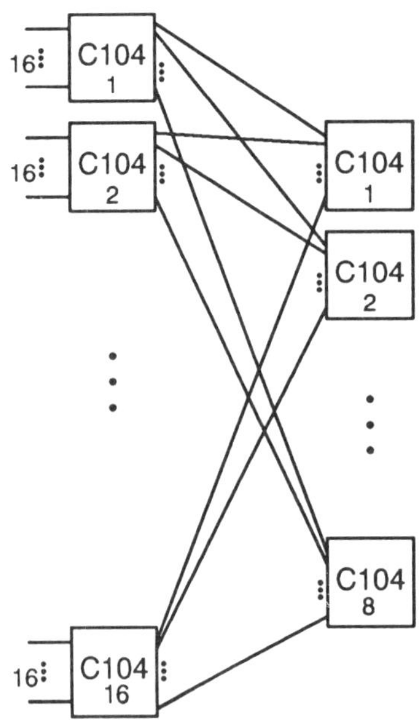

Figure 7.3 256–way multistage network

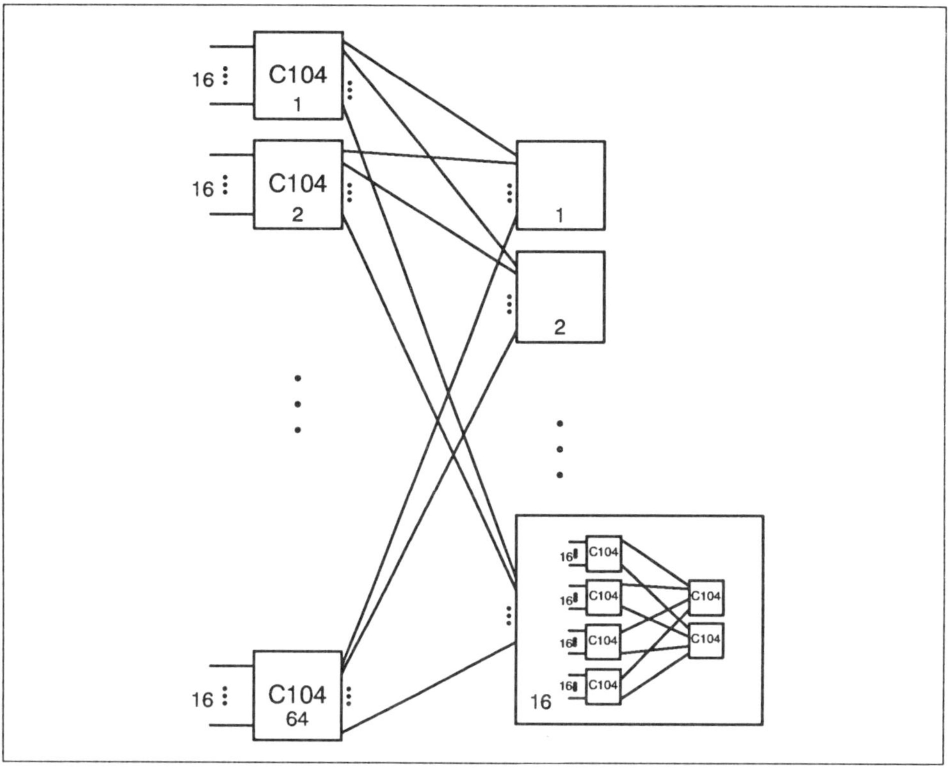

Figure 7.4 1024–way multistage network

7.4 The traffic patterns

In designing universal communication networks, we are interested in network throughput where network properties are not exploited by the traffic pattern. The important features are the local throughput and delay for continuous operation, and the way in which throughput and delay scale with network size. Once the continuous throughput of the network has been determined, the load may be adjusted to take advantage of the throughput.

The symmetry of the cube and multistage networks mean that for continuous traffic approximately the same number of packets are injected at each node. On the grid network, one would expect the edge nodes to inject a smaller number of packets than the centre nodes. To understand these effects, we also measured a traffic pattern in which a fixed number of messages was injected from every terminal, but the difference produced by this traffic pattern was not significant.

7.4.1 Continuous Random traffic

The continuous traffic is created at each source. Whenever an input queue is empty, a new packet is created and put on the queue. The destination of this packet is chosen at random from all possible destination addresses. This is a good pattern as it dissipates traffic over the network, in a similar manner to that of universal routing. However, such random behavior will obviously create a number of packets from different sources which are going to the same destination. This causes contention at the destination, and the effects of this are discussed later on.

7.4.2 Systematic traffic patterns

For a systematic pattern, each source sends to a specific destination. When an input queue is empty, a packet is created to this pre-defined address. Each of the patterns chosen is a permutation, so that no two source nodes send to the same destination. Therefore the contention seen in these patterns is wholly a feature of the network and routing algorithm.

For each network, a systematic traffic pattern is chosen. The patterns seem harmless enough, and represent an operation which could be reasonably expected to be performed. However, in each case the pattern chosen will create severe hot–spots in the network. These are, in a sense, worst-case traffic patterns.

7.5 Universal Routing

For a communication network, we would like to be able to bound delay and achieve scalability of throughput. The bound on delay will, with deterministic routing, depend on the traffic patterns currently in transit in the network. Some of these patterns will be fast, others slow. Universal routing overcomes this problem by bounding the amount of time a set of communications is likely to take. The probability of exceeding this time can be made arbitrarily small. Improvement of the upper bound is of considerable benefit, and since we are only interested in the upper bound any detrimental effect on fast patterns is inconsequential.

The practice of universal routing is straightforward. An amount of random behavior is introduced. This "upsets" systematic traffic patterns which cause the exceptional delays, and disperses the load across the network so that more links can be used concurrently. The realization of the random behavior depends on the underlying topology.

On the cube, a packet is sent to a random intermediate node in the network, then it continues to its destination. The journey to the random intermediate node and the final destination node makes use of the appropriate deterministic routing algorithm. This means that the average packet travels twice as far, so in order to maintain throughput, twice as many links are needed. The links are partitioned into two parallel networks, one of which carries the traffic on its journey to the random intermediate node, and the other carries the traffic from the random intermediate node to the required destination.

On the grid, it is only necessary to randomize in one dimension. This is the second direction in which the packet would normally travel. So for routing which goes first in the y direction, then the x direction, universal routing takes a packet first to a random node in the x direction. An extra set of links is used in the x direction specifically for this random step.

Universal routing on the multistage network sends a packet via a randomly chosen node on the right hand side, see figure 7.1. This does not increase the number of links required in the network. In practice, even better results can be obtained by using grouped adaptive routing to make the selection of link to the right hand switches.

7.6 Results

The simulation examines continuous traffic in a network in equilibrium. The throughput is measured as a percentage of the maximum possible throughput of each input link. Delay is measured in terms of header times: this is the amount of time it takes a header to be output from a switch, received at the next switch, and processed ready for output at that switch, which for the C104 is approximately 500ns. Time units are therefore consistent throughout.

7.6.1 The n–cube

The systematic traffic pattern

The n–cube is perhaps the most difficult of the three structures to visualize, especially for the larger examples. Therefore the systematic traffic patterns on the cube will be described for a small part of the network, then extended.

A seven dimensional cube can be partitioned into a number of three-dimensional cubes. Two of these 3-cubes can be joined by a "middle dimension" link. The 7-cube can be partitioned so that each node lies in exactly one such sub-structure.

For a permutation, which is one-to-one by definition, the maximum congestion will occur at the middle dimension. Therefore the 3-cube on one end of the middle link is mapped to the 3-cube at the other end of the middle link, and vice versa. This is the essence of the underlying permutation for systematic traffic on the cubes.

The cubes which are examined are all of even dimension. So the traffic pattern for one dimension less is used, and each packet moves along the first dimension. (This will not increase the contention, but will increase slightly the time taken). On the 6-cube, a 2-cube (square) maps to a 2-cube, therefore giving four-way contention. On the 8-cube, a 3-cube maps to a 3-cube, giving eight-way contention. The 10-cube gives 16-way contention. So with the increase in the dimension of the cube, we can expect the throughput per terminal of the network to halve. The delays for the systematic traffic are expected to double with the increase in dimension of the cube.

Results

Table 7.1 Random traffic on the n–cube

Network size	Mean delay	Max delay	Throughput(%)
64	48	322	78.8
256	59	546	70.2
1024	64	655	71.1

Table 7.2 Systematic traffic on the n–cube

Network size	Mean delay	Max delay	Throughput(%)
64	188	376	25.1
256	383	1618	12.5
1024	722	3679	6.3

Table 7.3 Universal Routing on the n–cube

Network size	Mean delay	Max delay	Throughput(%)
64	59	260	84.7
256	80	514	67.5
1024	91	605	71.7

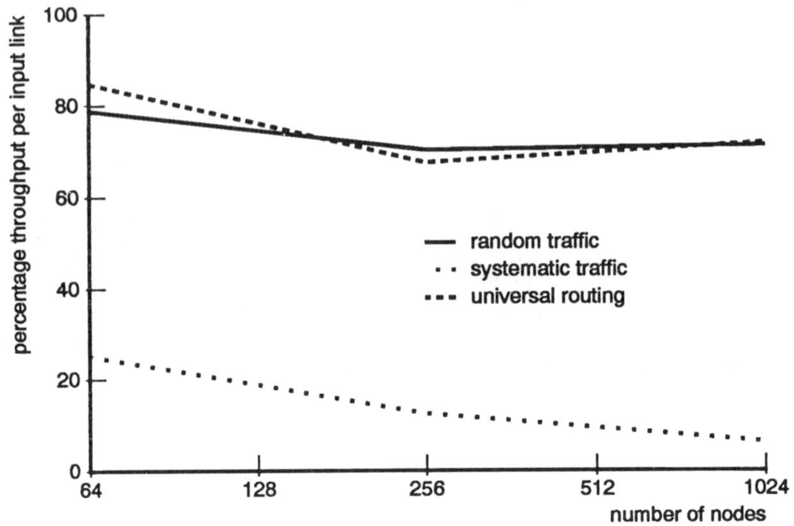

Figure 7.5 Throughput varying with network size on the n–cube

Discussion

The continuous random traffic shows the throughput and delay to scale, as predicted. Universal routing has the effect of adjusting the nature of the systematic permutation towards that of the random traffic. The variation of throughput with network size is due to variation within the random number generator.

The results show the behavior of the systematic permutation to be as expected, with a large increase in delay and a large decrease in throughput for an increase in network size. Note the relative decrease in throughput as network size increases. For the 6-cube, throughput is about one third of that for random traffic, the 8-cube reduces to one sixth of the random traffic throughput, and the 10-cube to a mere twelfth of the random traffic throughput.

As an aside, there is an interesting aspect of the delay figures. Comparing the random traffic with the universal routing shows that the universal routing does not double the delays. This is counter-intuitive, as the universal routing sends messages, on average, twice as far. However, this anomaly is explained by the nature of random traffic. As noted earlier, random traffic will send several packets to the same destination. This is a major cause for delay for the random traffic. However, the universal routing on the systematic traffic does not cause the same destination contention (and does not cause contention at the randomly chosen node because random headers are removed at each link in the switch).

7.6.2 The two–dimensional grid

The systematic traffic pattern

On a grid, a block move provides the permutation on which to base the systematic traffic. The grid is divided into four sets of nodes, with the nodes being bisected in both the x and y directions. The top left corner is translated onto the bottom right, and vice versa. This means that messages are delayed in both the y and x direction when travelling to their destination. Note that the four separate block moves are independent of each other.

The amount of contention doubles in both the x and y direction with an increase in network size. This suggests that throughput will decrease by a factor of 4, and that the average delay will at least double with each increase in network size.

Results

Table 7.4 Random traffic on the 2–D grid

Network size	Mean delay	Max delay	Throughput(%)
64	116	1135	34.2
256	223	4442	17.5
1024	336	19937	7.9

Table 7.5 Systematic traffic on the 2–D grid

Network size	Mean delay	Max delay	Throughput(%)
64	302	1311	12.6
256	861	7126	3.1
1024	1916	36833	0.8

Table 7.6 Universal Routing on the 2–D grid

Network size	Mean delay	Max delay	Throughput(%)
64	187	1095	21.9
256	368	2178	11.2
1024	826	4725	5.1

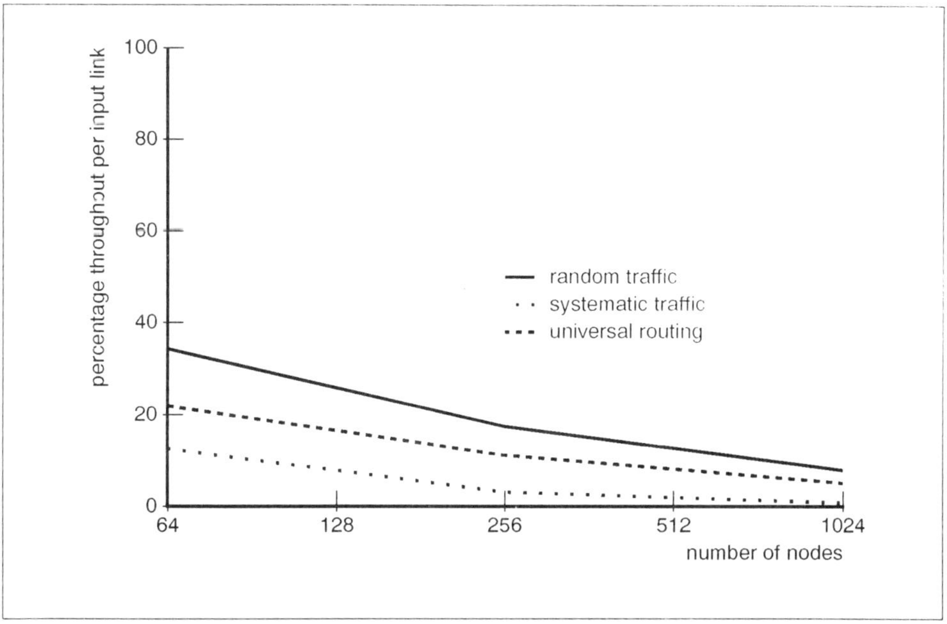

Figure 7.6 Throughput varying with network size on the 2–D grid

Discussion

The continuous random traffic shows that throughput per node degrades with increasing network size. This is to be expected, as the grid does not increase network capacity at a suitable rate. The delay increases quickly with network size.

Systematic traffic shows that the throughput and delay on a grid can both be affected considerably by the traffic pattern. Again, the throughput per terminal decreases with the network size. Universal routing pulls the behavior back towards the random traffic, providing similar scalability in both throughput and delay. Throughput is now limited only by the overall capacity of the network. For the grid, the universal routing takes longer than the random traffic, as expected.

7.6.3 Indirect multistage networks

The systematic traffic pattern

The systematic traffic pattern is built upon a very straightforward permutation. In each case, the source node adds a particular value (modulo the number of nodes), to its own identity number. This number is chosen so that all traffic is routed through a single mid-layer switch. Note that there is no contention within the switch, as messages contend for the links. However, this ensures a large amount of contention for both the inbound and the outbound links of that switch.

Consider these patterns compared to random traffic. For the 64-way network, shown in figure 7.2, traffic all goes via the top switch on the right hand side. As there are two central switches, this can be expected to reduce bandwidth by about a half compared to the random traffic, as only one half of the links out of the left hand side are used.

Results

Table 7.7 Random traffic on the MIN

Network size	Mean delay	Max delay	Throughput(%)
64	36	442	56.8
256	46	512	48.8
1024	78	1078	30.0

Table 7.8 Systematic traffic on the MIN

Network size	Mean delay	Max delay	Throughput(%)
64	44	44	36.0
256	204	364	8.6
1024	408	622	4.4

Table 7.9 Universal Routing on the MIN

Network size	Mean delay	Max delay	Throughput(%)
64	48	228	41.7
256	46	284	47.6
1024	111	926	21.3

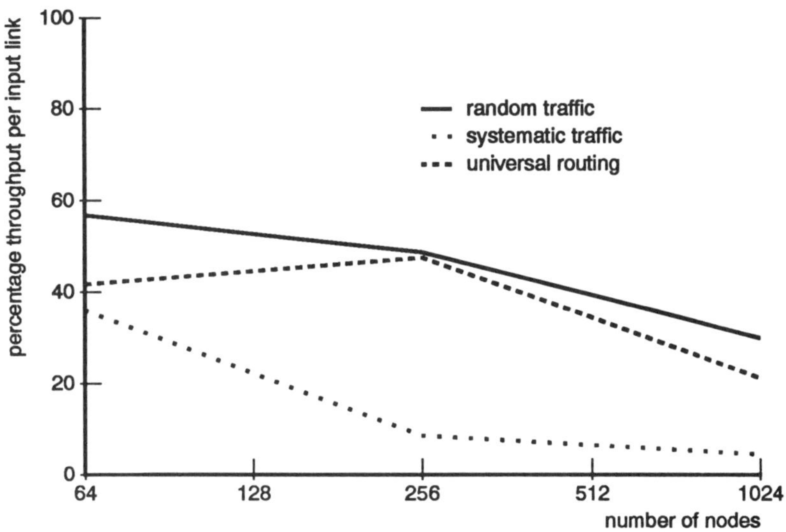

Figure 7.7 Throughput varying with network size on the indirect multistage networks

Discussion

Random traffic on the indirect multistage network shows that in the low-cost networks considered the throughput per node degrades with network size. However, the number of input links per switch can be altered, and the "centre" of the network made a lot more richly connected. This will improve the scalability characteristics.

Systematic traffic patterns show that the indirect networks have traffic patterns which can severely affect bandwidth and delay, and once again universal routing will overcome these problems. The universal routing graphs do not look smooth because the structure of the networks varies.

7.6.4 Scalability

The networks examined are all appealing for varying reasons, theoretical or practical. The hypercube satisfies the requirement for constant throughput from a node as the network size increases, whereas the grid and indirect multistage networks tail-off in throughput as the network size increases. For the grid, using up to 4 such networks in parallel would not give the throughput of a single link to a cube structure, for networks over 256 nodes. The indirect multistage networks could be replicated to provide this throughput. Note that 4-way replication of the 1024-node network gives a total throughput from the processor similar to the throughput from a single link which is available from a cube. These approximate calculations assume that traffic is split optimally over the parallel networks.

On all of the networks, universal routing removes the varying delays due to traffic pattern contention. In each case, it provides a means of taking advantage of the bandwidth inherent in the network structure.

7.6.5 Is this good use of link bandwidth?

One of the disadvantages of universal routing is the additional link bandwidth which is required. For instance, on the n-cube, the number of links required is doubled. This raises the issue as to whether these extra links are being well used. If they were used instead to 'fatten' the original cube structure, would deterministic routing provide a better solution?

If the links were doubled then the throughput could be doubled for deterministic routing which used both available paths optimally. However, even doubling the throughput on the cubes does not bring the systematic traffic throughput close to that of universal routing. This suggests that universal routing does not only give scalability, but also makes good use of link bandwidth.

For the indirect networks no extra links are used, and on the grid 1.5 times as many links are used. These factors also show that using the links for universal routing is preferable to extra links and deterministic routing on these structures.

7.7 Performance Predictability

The previous results show that universal routing can improve the throughput and bandwidth scalability of a network. In this section, universal routing is shown to improve the predictability of the network also.

We investigate the 8-cube. Each node in the network sends to a distinct destination node, i.e. the traffic pattern is a permutation. If each node creates twenty packets to the same destination, the resulting traffic pattern is called a 20-permutation.

The underlying permutation is the perfect shuffle, which is obtained by deriving the destination node number by rotating the bits of the source node number by a particular amount. A rotation of 1 gives a 2-way shuffle, the rotate of 2 gives a 4-way shuffle, and so on. The rotation was varied from 0 to the cube dimension and the time measured for a 20-permutation to complete using both deterministic and universal routing.

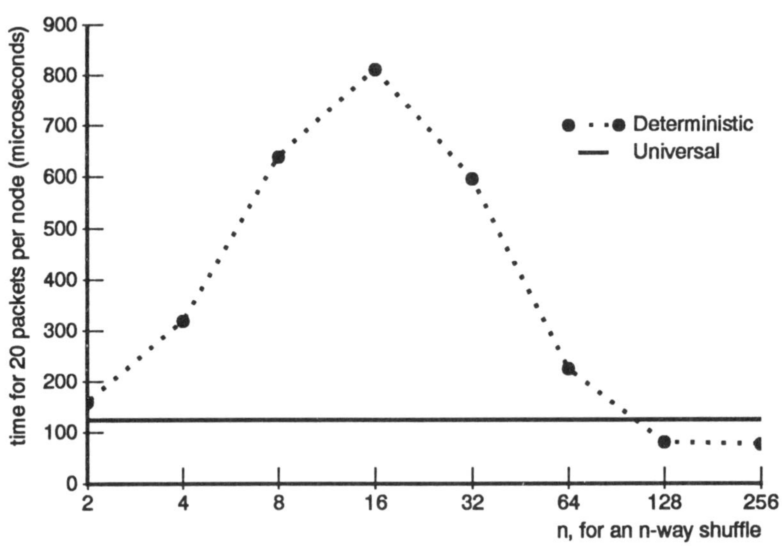

Figure 7.8 The variation of time taken to finish with the degree of shuffle

The results for the 8–cube are shown in figure 7.8. This shows that the deterministic routing gives a wide variation in run-time. For instance, changing to an 8-way shuffle rather than a 4-way shuffle increases the network delivery time by a factor of 2. With universal routing the time taken remains approximately constant (a representative value is shown). This is a major advantage, since calculating a bound on the run-time requires the worst case to be taken into account.

Again, the extra links for universal routing could be used for deterministic routing and provide extra bandwidth to allow the permutation to finish in about half of the time. However, the variability remains, and most of the deterministic routing cases would still be worse than the universal routing.

7.8 Conclusions

In this chapter we have examined communication networks which can now be built from state-of-the-art VLSI technology. Each of the networks investigated has been shown to have a systematic traffic pattern which severely effects its performance. The detrimental effect of this pattern grows with increasing network size.

The inherent scalability of the networks have been illustrated by the use of random traffic patterns. The use of universal routing provides scalability similar to that of random traffic patterns, for the systematic traffic patterns. Results have highlighted the unpredictable nature of deterministic routing, and shown that the use of links for universal routing restores predictability and the scalability inherent to the network structure.

8 General Purpose Parallel Computers

8.1 Introduction

Over the last decade, many different parallel computers have been developed, which have been used in a wide range of applications. Increasing levels of component integration, coupled with difficulties in further increasing clock speed, make parallel processing technically attractive. By the late 1990s, chips with 10^8 transistors will be in use, but design and production will continue to be most effective when applied to volume manufacture. A "universal" parallel architecture would allow cheap, standard multiprocessors to become pervasive, in much the same way that the von Neumann architecture has allowed standard uniprocessors to take over from specialised electronics in many application areas.

Scalable performance

One of the major challenges for universal parallel architecture is to allow performance to scale with the number of processors. There are obvious limits to scalability:

- For a given problem size, there will be a limit to the number of processors which can be used efficiently. However, we would expect it to be easy to increase the problem size to exploit more processors.
- There will in practice be technological limits to the number of processors used. These will include physical size, power consumption, thermal density and reliability. However, as we expect performance/chip to achieve 100-1000 Mflops during the 1990s, the most significant markets will be served by machines with up to 100 processors.

Software portability

Another major challenge for a universal parallel architecture is to eliminate the need to design algorithms to match the details of specific machines. Algorithms must be based on features common to a large number of machines, and which can be expected to remain common to a large number of machines as technology evolves. Both programmer and computer designer have much to gain from identifying the essential features of a universal parallel architecture:

- the programmer because his programs will work on a variety of machines - and will continue to work on future machines.
- the computer designer because he will be able to introduce new designs which make best use of technology to increase performance of the software already in use.

8.2 Universal message passing machines

A universal message passing machine consists of:

- p processing nodes with concurrent processing and communication (and preferably process scheduling).
- interconnection networks with scalable throughput (linear in p) and bounded delay (expected $log(p)$).

Programs for message passing machines normally consist of a collection of concurrent processes which compute values and periodically communicate with each other. These programs must take into account the relationship between the communication throughput and the computation throughput of the message passing machine. We will call this ratio the *grain* (*g*) of the architecture, and measure it as operations/operand. For simplicity, we will assume that a processor performs an operation in one clock *tick*, so that we can measure the grain in ticks/operands.

The importance of achieving a good balance between computation and communication can be understood by considering a simple example. Suppose that a two dimensional image is to be processed by an array of transputers. Each transputer stores and processes a portion of the image. Each step of the computation involves updating every element of the image in parallel. Assume that at every step of the computation, every element of the array `a[i,j]` is to be updated to:

```
f(a[i,j], a[i-1,j], a[i+1,j], a[i,j-1], a[i,j+1])
```

and that function `f` involves 4 operations. The following table shows the operations performed for each item communicated for four possible mappings.

elements per transputer	**operations per communication**
1	1
4	2
16	4
256	16

If we chose a mapping which allocates one element to each transputer, we would need each transputer to perform one operation in the same time that it can communicate one data item. This is often referred to as *fine grain* processing. If, on the other hand, we allocate a large number of elements to each transputer, the communications requirements are small. This is often referred to as *coarse grain* processing. It can be seen from the example that as the grain is decreased, the communications capability becomes the limiting factor. At this point, it is impossible to use more transputers to increase performance, but easy to use more transputers to process a larger image.

Specialised transputer configurations can often be used to provide fine grain processing. In the above example a two-dimensional array of transputers could be used, as communication is required only between adjacent transputers in the array. However, a general purpose machine should be able to provide fine grain processing for a wide variety of algorithms, and for software portability it should allow automatic allocation of processes to transputers. To do this it must support a high rate of *non-local* communication, which can be achieved with a suitable network of routers.

Another important factor affecting the performance of parallel computers is the *latency (l)* in communication. A transputer may idle awaiting data from another transputer even though the communication rate between the transputers is adequate. This is normally overcome by using extra parallelism in the algorithms to *hide* communication delays. Instead of executing one process on each transputer, we use the transputer process scheduler to execute several processes on each transputer.

Whenever a process is delayed as a result of a communication, it is descheduled and the transputer activates another process. This in turn will eventually become descheduled as a result of a communication. Execution proceeds in this way through several processes. Whenever a communication completes, the corresponding process is rescheduled ready for subsequent execution. Provided that there are sufficient processes, the transputer will never idle as a result of communication delays.

To understand the use of excess parallelism, consider the following simple *worker* process suitable for use in a processing farm. In a typical farm a controller process would hand out packets of work to many such worker processes.

```
local data, result
loop
{     input ? data
      result := compute (data)
      output ! result
}
```

This process performs input (?) to a local variable, computation and output (!) from a local variable sequentially. Any delay in performing communication will be directly reflected in the time taken for each iteration of the loop.

Provided that the result output at each iteration of the loop is not used (by the controller) to produce input for the next two iterations, this process could be replaced by the following version which allows input, computation and output to take place in parallel.

```
local data, result, nextdata, nextresult
loop
{     parallel
      {     input ? nextdata
            nextresult := compute (data)
            output ! result
      }
      data, result := nextdata, nextresult
}
```

Here delays in communication will affect the total time taken for the loop only if one of the communications takes longer than the computation. Even larger delays in communication can be tolerated by executing several such processes in each transputer, as in the following version. The *n* processes are all independent of each other, and each operates on its own local variables (data, nextdata, result).

```
parallel i = 1 to n
{     local data, result, nextdata, nextresult
      loop
      {     parallel
            {     input ? nextdata
                  nextresult := compute (data)
                  output ! result
            }
            data, result := nextdata, nextresult
      }
}
```

Here every communication can be delayed by up to *n* computation steps. An algorithm of this kind can be efficiently executed even in the presence of long communication delays.

8.2.1 Using Universal message passing machines

Designing a program for a particular grain (*g*) is a significant task, so we would like to keep g constant for all sizes of machine. In practice we would also like to keep *g* low, as this simplifies programming and allows fine–grained parallelism. A low and constant, *g*, allows programs to be written at a higher level using, for example,

- Array manipulation
- Big DO-PARs

- Explicit parallelism with lots of small processes

The programmer and compiler will take into account the grain g, and will construct a program as a collection of v virtual processors (processes) of grain $> g$ and cycle-time c (ticks). We assume that the processes are cyclical, and in each cycle perform c/g communications and c operations. Notice that we want to keep the grain of the software as low as possible so as to exploit all possible parallelism for a given problem size, but at least g to avoid processor idling.

The output of the compiler is a program suitable for use on all universal machines of grain g. We expect to keep the program in this form, and perhaps distribute it in this form. We note that g is fixed for a range of machines based on the same components, and further that there is likely to be little variation in g even for machines based on different components. This means that the compiled program is likely to be re-useable.

To load a compiled program for execution, we make use of a loader which takes as parameter the latency of communication: l (ticks). This will vary from machine to machine and will scale as $log(p)$ for realizable networks. The loader will allocate at least l/c virtual processors to at most $(v \times c)/l$ processors. There would be no point in attempting to use more processors than this, as this would result in processors idling some of the time. It would be better to leave some processors available for some other purpose. Thus the program will run with optimal efficiency on a p–processor machine provided $(v \times c) > (l \times p)$.

Notice that our loader ensures that there will always be enough processes on each processor to ensure that (at least) one is executable; the others will be waiting for communication to complete. This means that we will need to use at least $log(p)$ more processes than processors. Another way to think of this is that we could use a specialised machine exactly matched to the algorithm in which each processor executes only one process; this would offer $log(p)$ more performance. Specialised parallel computers will still be needed for maximizing performance where the problem size is limited!

We note that our proposal for universal message passing is closely related to Valiant's proposal for Universal PRAMs [10] in which $l = log(p)$ and $c = 1$.

8.3 Networks for Universal message passing machines

Universal message-passing machines consist of a number of concurrent processors, connected by a communication network. A suitable network is a *Universal Communication Network*, where the throughput per terminal link remains constant with varying network size, and the delay per terminal link grows slowly with increasing network size. Such a machine is *universal*, as the algorithm running on the machine (made up from the processes on the processors) does not depend on the underlying structure of the machine. This structural independence means that the program structure will not need to be altered if the underlying machine is changed, for instance if it has more or less processors. The machine may be characterized by the parameters, g and l.

Suppose that a process sends a message which will take time l to get to its destination. The communication delay may be hidden by the processor scheduling another parallel process (or other parallel processes) during the communication delay. Given the network delay, l, we can predict the number of processes which are required to hide the communication latency. It has been shown that several networks have constant throughput per terminal and latency growing with $log(p)$, where p is the number of processors. Among them is the n–cube.

8.3.1 A simulation of the n–cube

The 6-dimensional cube is examined. From the distribution of packet arrival times, the probability that a packet takes longer than a certain amount of time is derived. The probability, in turn, is used to predict the amount of parallel slack required. The results compare to the theory of Valiant [10], and follow similar arguments.

The probability that a packet delivery time is greater than time T is shown in figure 8.1.

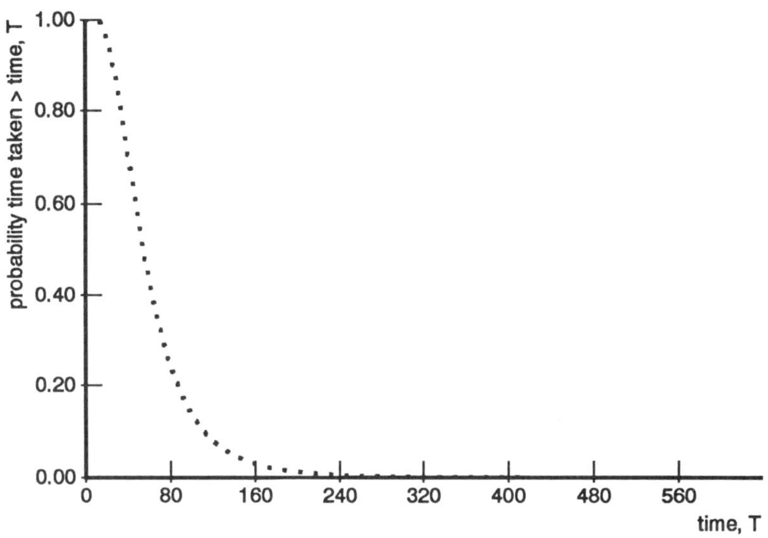

Figure 8.1 Probability that a packet takes longer than time T on a 6–cube

There are a number of processes on each processor, in this case 6, which operate one after another, for instance process 1, process 2, ..., process 6, then process 1 again. The time required between process 1 finishing and process 1 starting again is l, the latency of the communication. However, although process 1 may not have received its communication, and therefore not be ready to run again, process 2 may have received its communication, and be able to restart. This implies that the probability of no process being ready is actually the product of the probabilities that any one of the processes is not ready (assuming that these events are independent). Note that process 1 has time l, whereas process 2 has time $4l/5$, process 3 has time $3l/5$, and so on. This does not take account of the compound probabilities of many delays happening in a very short time. The probability of waiting, against the network latency l, is shown in figure 8.2.

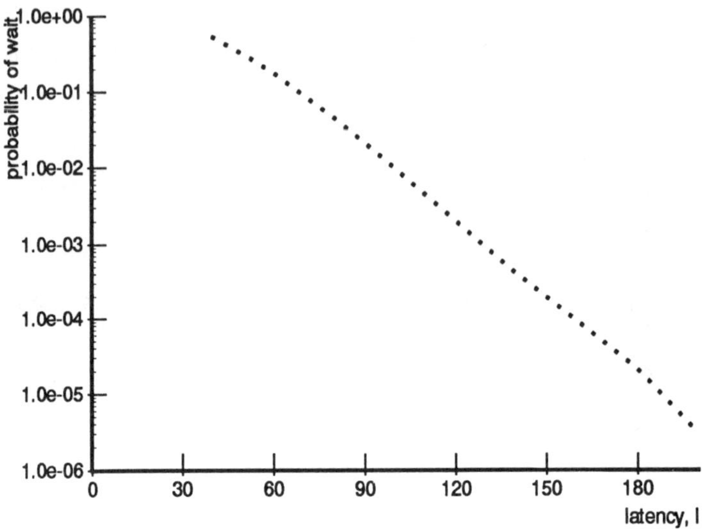

Figure 8.2 Probability that a processor will have to wait

For 6 processes, the graph shows that for a probability of waiting of 10^{-2}, we need about 100 cycles between successive executions of a process. For a probability of 10^{-3}, we need about 130 cycles. These suggest that each process needs to run for about 20 or 26 cycles respectively. This is the cycle size c, defined earlier. In the next section, the effect of the probability of waiting is shown.

The effect on program runtime

In our model, each processor has 6 processes. Each of the 64 processors run their 6 processes repeatedly. Suppose that a delay to any of the processors means that all the processors have to wait for the one which is delayed. Then there are 384 (=6 $\times$ 64) processes each of which require their packet to be delivered within time l in order to avoid a delay to the system. If the system is delayed, it waits for a further l units of time before it continues.

Because we require that all 384 packets are delivered, if the probability of any one packet being delayed is 10^{-2}, nearly all of the cycles will take time $2l$ rather than l. The time required to run the program consequently doubles.

If the probability of a delay is 10^{-3}, about one third of cycles will be delayed. If the probability is 10^{-4}, then about one in 26 cycles will be delayed. These probabilities correspond to particular values of c. The factor of increase in runtime over the case where there are no communication delays, is shown in figure 8.3.

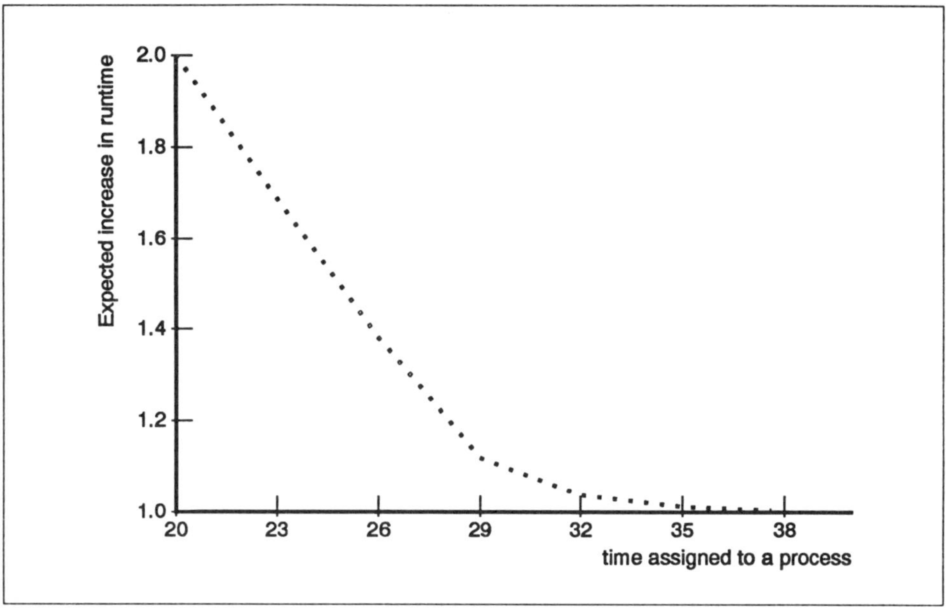

Figure 8.3 Increase in runtime due to latency as a function of cycle time *c*

8.3.2 An example

Suppose we want to run an image smoothing algorithm on a parallel machine. Then to operate where the runtime will be minimally affected, we want to hide a latency of 160 cycles. For 6 processes on each processor, this gives a cycle size, *c* of (160/5)= 32. A network throughput of about 80% (as simulated for the n–cube) means that about there will be about 25 units of output per 32 units of time.

Let the unit of time be 0.5 microseconds. This is the about time required to transmit a floating-point number using DS-Links. Floating-point values will be bundled into 4 packets, one for each of the $\pm x$, $\pm y$ directions. The header overhead is very small, so the 25 units of time corresponds to transmitting 4 groups of 6 floating-point numbers.

The image smoothing operation consists of 5 operations per pixel (4 additions and one division). This suggests that splitting a picture into 6 by 6 pixel squares will give four communications (each of six floating point numbers), and 36 calculations per process. Therefore within the 16 microseconds, a total of $36 \times 5 = 180$ floating point calculations need to be performed. The corresponding calculation rate is about 11.25 MFlops per processor. Each processor runs six such processes, giving a total of $64 \times 6 = 384$ processes in the network. This suggests that an array of such processors will process an image of $386 \times 36 = 13896$ pixels without loss of efficiency.

A corresponding calculation for a network throughput rate of 60% suggests that 5 Mflop processors could process a 6144 pixel image without loss of efficiency.

In this example we have taken an algorithm which could be executed on a dedicated two–dimensional grid and re–written it so that it can execute efficiently on universal message–passing machines of varying sizes.

8.4 Building Universal Parallel Computers from T9000s and C104s

Throughout the remainder of this chapter we assume that the basic architecture of the general–purpose parallel computer consists of T9000 processing nodes connected via C104 switches, and examine a number of practical issues in the construction of such machines.

8.4.1 Physical organization

A T9000 runs somewhat hotter than first–generation transputers; a typical T9000 processing module, with dynamic memory and drivers, might be expected to dissipate around ten watts. This power budget can, if necessary, accommodate an error correcting memory subsystem. A small mothercard, with ten T9000s and some C104 switches, might therefore dissipate about 150 watts in an area of about one tenth of a square metre. Such a board would require a cooling air flow of around twenty cubic metres per hour. This is not a huge requirement by the standards of high–performance computer design; a conventional backplane/crate implementation using forced air cooling with a 30mm card pitch is quite reasonable. Fan noise may, however, be considerable and a substantial volume will be occupied by air ducting and fans.

Higher component densities may easily be achieved using contact and/or fluid cooling. The published[1] design for the Parsytec GC supercomputer implements a sixty–four node subsystem in a total volume of about 500 by 300 by 200 mm. This *GigaCube* uses large aluminium contact plates and heatpipes to transport heat away from the active components. Two alternative cooling systems can be provided for the "cold" end of the heatpipes: a fan and fin module for forced air cooling, or a water cooling block accepting an external water supply. Either module may be accommodated within the GigaCube volume, as is a secondary power supply converting a 42V 40kHz AC power feed down to the 5V required by the modules.

We may contrast these densities with the degree of compactness required to minimize signal propagation delays. Assume that only T9000 data links travel between cards in the computer. Low level flow control[2] on such a link network is maintained on groups of eight tokens; such a group takes about 800nS to transmit at the highest 100M baud rate. An end–to–end delay of half this figure corresponds to a separation of sixty metres in free space; thus, even allowing for velocity factors, we are able to build very big machines.

Overall, it can be seen that the choice of component density is not constrained by the T9000/C104 architecture; the relatively low power requirements and long permissible cable runs allow the designer full flexibility in mechanical design.

8.4.2 Network Performance Issues

A primary part of the design of a T9000 and C104 system is the design of the data link routing network. Raw throughput and latency are two important issues that must be considered.

Early work by Dally[3] on routing networks suggested that two dimensional grids formed good routing networks for supercomputers. These results were, however, based on parameters which do not apply to C104 networks. In particular, it is desirable to use the very high valency of the C104 to real effect; connecting many links in parallel to form a low valency network wastes much of the routing capability.

There are several possible measures of network performance. One, popular with computer manufacturers, is the peak point–to–point bandwidth between a pair of processors in an otherwise unloaded network. This measure give some information about the behavior of the processor to network interface; it conveys almost nothing about the performance of the network itself. Realistic measures must quantify the behavior of the network under reasonable load conditions, taking into account contention between messages within the network. Important effects can arise as a network is loaded:

- Even if the network saturates uniformly as regards throughput, individual message latencies may become very high as the network approaches saturation; serious unfairness may also arise between different processors. Randomization, as offered by the C104, can be shown[4] to make highly delayed messages improbable.
- Certain particular patterns of communication[4] can cause a dramatic build–up of message traffic at particular intermediate nodes in the network. This is a universal property[6] of deterministic sparse routing networks. It is unfortunate that many popular networks (grid, n–cube, Clos...) show this bad behavior on traffic patterns that would be expected to arise in typical computations. Randomization can again be shown to render these systematic collisions improbable.

The use of randomization in a C104 network can be seen to offer important simplifications in the network's behavior. It can completely decouple the network topology from the algorithmic message pattern. One can then essentially characteristic a network by its throughput and average latency for randomly distributed traffic under high load. In practice, the adaptive routing offered by the C104 normally provides all the benefits of randomization, along with a useful increase in average bandwidth as will be shown below.

Throughput in a C104 network is limited by *contention*, the simultaneous presence of two or more packets requesting the same output link from a C104. Under random traffic, this may be modelled very simply as discussed in chapter 6. The formulæ derived there may be simply modified to account for restrictions on the output links. It is then straightforward to calculate approximate throughputs for networks by cascading this calculation through the various layers of the network. There are two other direct results from this formula:

- A single 100 Mbit/s link between T9000s can deliver a unidirectional throughput of 8.9M bytes/s. A perfect network could route *permutation* traffic, in which it is guaranteed that no two processors are attempting to communicate to the same destination, at the same rate. With *random* traffic, even for a perfect network, contention at the destination T9000s reduces the maximum throughput per link to 5.6 Mbyte/s.
- Consider an *indirect* network: one in which there are layers of C104 switch that are not connected directly to T9000s but only to other C104s. Then the amount of traffic on these inner layers is reduced by contention in the outer switches adjacent to the T9000s. A balanced indirect network design will thus have a density of links that is highest near to the T9000s and is reduced between the inner switches.

8.4.3 A practical Routing Network

A simple and useful routing network is the folded Clos[23]. The network provides routing between the *mn* external ports on the left side of the network, where each of the *n* switches in the left–hand column provides *m* external ports. A 512–terminal version is illustrated in figure 8.4.

23. The title is derived from an important early paper[7] on the design of telephone switching networks. The particular numbers of interconnections provided by Clos and the related Benes[8] networks are important for the establishment of telephone circuit connections without contention. These numbers have no special significance for packet routing networks such as those built using C104s.

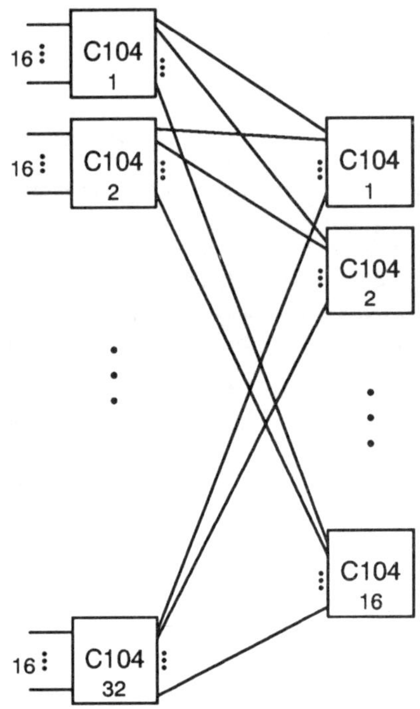

Figure 8.4 Folded Clos network

The simple model of chapter 6 can be used to evaluate the performance of the folded Clos network. If the network is programmed for random routing, then a random one of the p right hand switches is selected for each message. The probability of an output being active at the first stage is thus $P_1 = 1-e^{-m/p}$. The probability of an input being active at the second stage is also P_1 and the probability of an output being active, for random traffic, is $P_2 = 1-e^{-P_1}$. Finally, the probability of one of the external output ports being active is $P_3 = 1-e^{-pP_2/m}$, giving an average throughput per link of $8.9 \times P_3$ Mbyte/s. If grouped adaptive routing is used at the first stage, then the contention there is eliminated as long as $p >= m$. Thus, the previous formula is modified by replacing P_1 with $min(1,m/p)$. Table 8.1 below shows some calculated random traffic throughputs for typical Clos type networks.

Table 8.1 Sustained high–load throughputs for Clos–type networks

m	p	random throughput Mbytes/s	adaptive throughput Mbytes/s	random routed efficiency	adaptive routed efficiency
16	16	3.3	4.2	59%	74%
8	16	4.3	4.8	76%	86%

Note that the two networks differ only in that half the external ports are left unconnected for the $m = 8$ network. The randomization applied to folded Clos networks was effectively free; no additional links were traversed by randomized packets. Nevertheless, adaptive routing can be seen to be more efficient. Grid and n–cube networks impose more severe penalties. Random routing must be applied to all but one dimension of the grid or n–cube, almost doubling the traffic density.

Simple adaptive routing also achieves little in eliminating systematic contention from these networks.

Similar methods may be used to analyze a wide variety of networks. Homogeneous networks such as the Folded Clos and n–cube are straightforward. Inhomogeneous networks, such as two or three dimensional grids, have an unbalanced traffic pattern which peaks (linearly) in the center of the grid. Calculation of the contended throughput in the centre of the grid gives a good estimate of the overall throughput of the network.

8.4.4 Routing Network Simulations

Some detailed simulations[5] of C104 networks have been performed by Siemens as part of the Esprit PUMA project. This work was instrumental in the inclusion of grouped adaptive routing in the C104. These studies cover Clos, grid and n–cube networks. Concentrating first on the m=16, p=16 network examined above, the Siemens results find sustained throughputs on random traffic of 2.9 M byte/s for random routing and 3.1 M byte/s for adaptive routing which compare well with the crude calculations of the previous section. Interestingly, for a known bad message pattern, deterministic routing offers a throughput of only 0.3 M byte/s, random routing (of course) the same 2.9 and adaptive routing 8.8 M byte/s. It turns out that the bad pattern for deterministic routing, a block permutation, is a very good pattern for adaptive routing.

The Siemens simulations also give insight into the average packet delay in the network; for the m=16, p=16 system delivering 1M byte/s/link throughput we see an average delay of 6μS. Grids and cubes again perform worse than Clos networks in this parameter.

Overall, the Siemens results show comparable performance for n–cube and Clos networks of comparable cost, with a small advantage for the Clos designs. Two and three dimensional grids performed very badly.

There is a received wisdom that the two–dimensional nature silicon die and PCBs leads naturally to a two–dimensional network structure. There is little justification for this notion; a real system of modules in boards in crates in cabinets is more naturally tree structured. It is, however, true that the realization of good global messaging networks requires many links bisecting the system. Parsytec[1] have demonstrated a construction technique appropriate for three dimensional grids. The folded Clos network also lends itself to a natural physical implementation, with the processors and outer switched arranged on vertical boards and the inner switches on horizontals as shown in figure 8.5. Such an arrangement will require careful selection of connectors and support boards, but can easily realize a 256 processor system in a single compact rack.

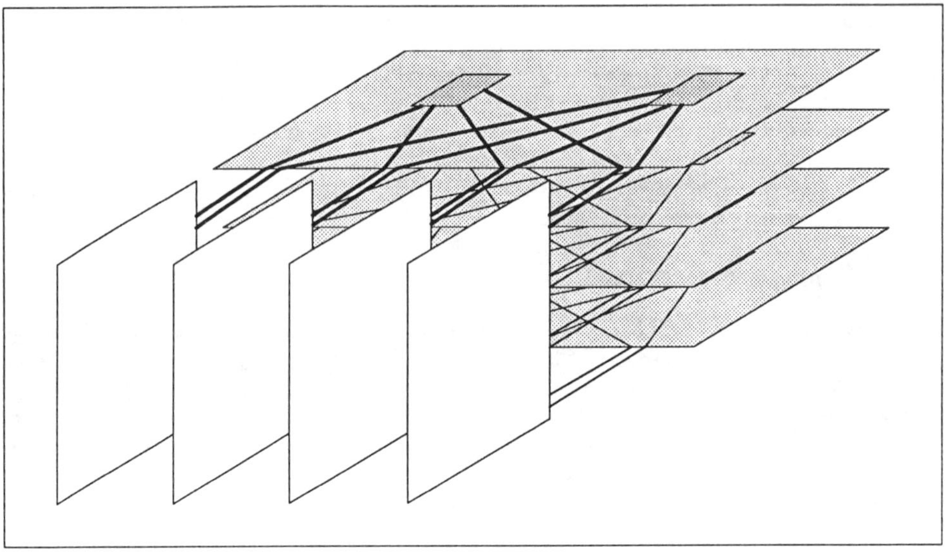

Figure 8.5 Horizontal boards containing the center stages of a Clos network

8.4.5 Security Implications of Network Topology

In some applications, secure multi–user T9000 parallel computers are required. This might be to provide conventional inter–user security in a general–purpose machine. It might also be to improve system ruggedness in the presence of some poor quality software modules. For instance, in a database system, one might hope that a client instance would be able to fail without bringing down the main database.

A simple solution to this problem would be to run all the untrusted processes in protected mode, with all communication and memory management controlled by trusted servers. Unfortunately, for a variety of reasons this is not always possible:

- Users might be using programming environments that insist on raw access to the processors, and do not support protected mode.
- The increased communication overheads of protected mode may not be acceptable.

It is possible to use a C104 routing network in order to provide some security against rogue processing nodes. The concern is that a rogue node might transmit a packet with headers that it is not authorized to use, causing corruption of a virtual channel which it should not use. The basic trick is to operate the C104s without header deletion at the boundary of the network. Thus the virtual channel number as seen by the receiving T9000 is actually used to route the packets. Careful design of the C104 network, and programming of its intervals, can ensue that individual processors can only access restricted ranges of virtual channels on the other processors. This scheme is at first sight attractive, but suffers from severe limitations:

- These schemes tend to require large numbers of C104s and an otherwise undesirable network topology.
- Large gaps are created in the range of virtual channels usable at each processor.
- Most standard programming environments[9] assume the use of header deletion at network boundaries.

- This technique offers error detection, but not error recovery. It is difficult to trace the author of bad packets, and almost impossible to protect against network flooding.

Overall, it seems wisest to accept that C104 networks are not intended to enforce protection, and to use gateway processors between trusted and untrusted subnetworks.

Most of the popular networks lend themselves naturally to rigid partitioning, but usually only in restricted ways. For example, n–cubes can realize sets of smaller n–cubes, grids can be dissected and Clos networks partitioned linearly. It is much harder to assemble closed subnetworks from arbitrary, non–adjacent sets of processors.

8.5 Summary

We have used the following result from contemporary computer science:

- the ability of certain networks together with randomized or adaptive routing to support scalable throughput and low delay (even when routing among the $p \times log(p)$ virtual processors distributed among p processors)

together with the existence of existence of message-passing hardware:

- processors with efficient process scheduling, in which processing throughput and communication throughput are balanced
- high–valency routers allowing the construction of compact communication networks with scalable throughput and low delay

and have shown that we can already construct scalable universal message passing machines. For these machines, we can write scalable, portable software exploiting message passing.

References

[1] *Technical Summary parsytec GC, version 1.0*, Parsytec Computer GmbH, Aachen, Germany, 1991.

[2] *The T9000 Transputer Products Overview Manual,* Inmos Ltd, 1991.

[3] A Klein, *Interconnection Networks for Universal Message Passing System*, Esprit '91 Conference Proceedings pp 336–351, Commission of the European Communities, 1991, ISBN 92–826–2905–8.

[4] W J Dally, *Performance Analysis of k–ary n–cube Interconnection Networks,* IEEE Trans Comput **6** pp 775–785, 1990.

[6] L Valiant, in *Handbook of Theoretical Computer Science.*

[7] C. Clos, *A Study of Non–blocking Switching Networks,* Bell Systems Technical Journal **32**, 1953

[8] V. E. Benes, *Mathematical Theory of Connecting Networks and Telephone Traffic* Academic Press 1965

[9] *Network Description Language User Manual,* Inmos Ltd, 1992.

[10] L. G. Valiant, *A Bridging Model for Parallel Computation,* Communications of the ACM, August 1990, pp 103–111

9 The Implementation of Large Parallel Database Machines on T9000 and C104 Networks

The design of large database machines requires the resulting implementation be scalable and cheap. This means that use has to be made of commodity items whenever possible. The design also has to ensure that scalability is incorporated into the machine from its inception rather than as an after–thought. Scalability manifests itself in two different ways. First, the initial size of a system when it is installed should be determined by the performance and size requirements of the desired application at that time. Secondly, the system should be scalable as processing requirements change during the life–time of the system. The T9000 and C104 provide a means of designing a large parallel database machine which can be constructed from commodity components in a manner that permits easy scalability.

9.1 Database Machines

A database machine provides a high level interface to the stored data so that the user is not aware of the access path to that data. Further, the user can specify what data is required and not how the data is to be found. In a relational database machine, the topic of this paper, the data is stored in tables. Each row of a table contains a number of columns each of which contain a single atomic value. Rows are distinguished from each other by the value of one of the columns having a distinct value. Data from one table can be combined with that from another by a process known as relational join. If we assume that in each table there is a column which holds data from the same domain, then we can join the tables on those columns. In general, the output from a join is the concatenation of one row from each of the tables where the joining columns have equal values.

A database machine allows different users to access the database at the same time for any operation. Thus different users can be accessing the database to read, write, modify and erase rows of tables. The effect of each user has to be made invisible to the other users until a user has indicated that a unit of work is complete. The database machine therefore has to ensure that different users do not interfere with each other by accessing the same rows of a table. Many users can access the same row of a table provided they are all reading the data. The maintenance of such a concurrency management system is expensive and most of the current algorithms are based upon the use of a large memory to hold locking information. The design to be presented in this paper will show how a scalable concurrency management system can be constructed.

It is vital that the data stored in the database is correct and consistent. This means that data values have to be checked whenever data is written, erased and modified. This consistency is achieved by the use of integrity constraints which can be of several different kinds. First, there is a simple check constraint to ensure that a value is contained within a simple range of values. A second more complex check constraint can be invoked which ensures that a value in a column of a table is related in some way to a value in another row of the same table, or on some function applied to the table as a whole. This can then be extended to a check which refers to another table. Finally, a referential constraint imposes relationships between tables. The column, or columns, which uniquely identify a row in a table are called the PRIMARY KEY of that table. Another table may store the same values in a column of that table. This column will not be the primary key of the second table, though it may form part of the primary key of the second table. The database system has to ensure that only values which occur in the first table are stored in the second table. The column in the second table is said to be a FOREIGN KEY which references the first table. If we insert a row into the second table then we must check that the value of the foreign key (or keys) occurring in that row already exists in the referenced table (or tables). Similarly, if a row is to be deleted from the first table then we must ensure that there are no rows in the second table which have the foreign key column with the same value as that which is to be deleted. In either case, if this referential constraint fails then the operation on the database should be terminated. It is generally agreed that if full constraint checking is imposed on existing database implementations then the performance of the system will be reduced to 25% of current performance. Thus many database systems are run without consistency checking, especially referential checking, so that the overhead is not imposed. The design to be discussed in this paper will permit the implementation of a full constraint system with a scalable performance.

A key aspect of current database technology is the ability to manipulate complex data types. This is manifested in the interest in object oriented databases. We shall describe how object oriented capabilities are captured by the design.

A final factor which is crucial to database machine performance is that of recovery from errors. Oates and Kerridge [1][2] have shown how a recovery system can be implemented in parallel with the data manipulation component of a database machine. The architecture to be described in this paper will show how these capabilities can be captured.

Many of the ideas expressed in this paper result from the highly successful IDIOMS [3][4]project which resulted in the demonstration of a database machine which could undertake both On–line Transaction Processing (OLTP) and Management Information System (MIS) queries on the same data concurrently. The IDIOMS machine demonstrated this capability for banking applications specified by the Trustees Savings Bank plc. One purpose of this demonstrator was to show that a low–cost scalable architecture could be constructed. This aspect is further enhanced with the use of T9000 and C104 technology.

9.2 Review of the T8 Design

In this section a brief overview of the IDIOMS design is presented. It demonstrates the limitations of the T8 transputer as a basis for building a system which can be scaled easily. Scalability manifests itself in two different ways. First, a system has to be scaled to match the initial size of the application, thereby dealing with different sized applications. Subsequently, the system has to be scaled to deal with changes of application. For example, the amount of data or the number of applications may increase or the response time of the system may have to be improved. Figure 9.1 shows the basic IDIOMS design. Transactions are passed to the T processors, where access is made to the disc for the required records to undertake the transaction. It is presumed that data is partitioned over the discs connected to the T processors. In this case the partitioning uses the account number. Speed of access to the account information is improved by the use of an index.

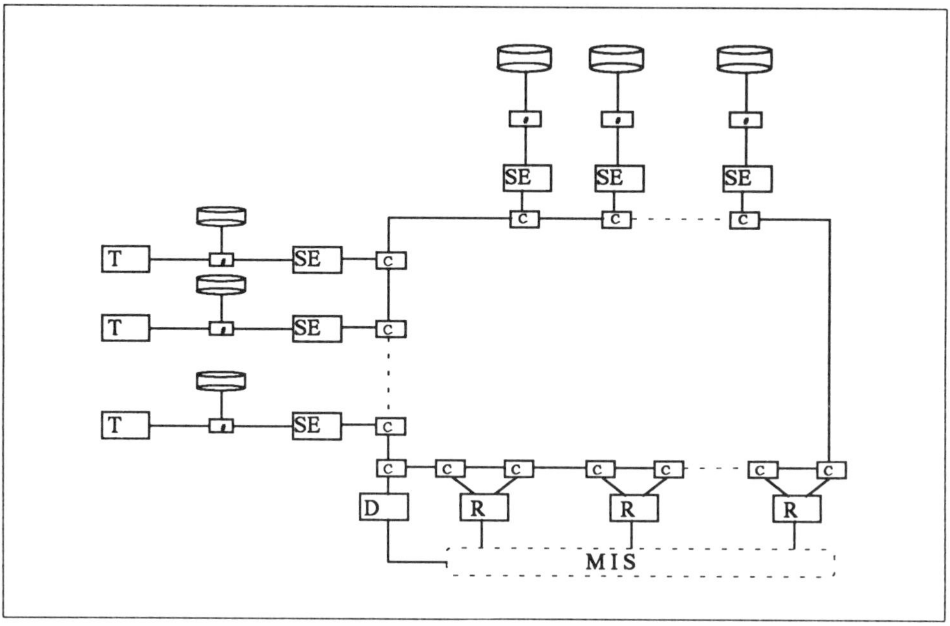

Figure 9.1 Basic IDIOMS architecture
Key:
T Transaction processor SE Storage engine D Data dictionary
R Relational processor C Communication engine # Disc controller

It is also presumed that the transaction processing time is small; that is, in general a transaction will access a single account, modify it in some simple manner and write the updated record back to disc. Conversely, it is presumed that a Management Information System (MIS) query will access many records in the database. and will thus take a long time to process. The Storage Engines connected to the Transaction processors are able to read data from the transaction data but not write data back. This means that an MIS query can be interrupted so that the T processor can access the disc, because this operation must be given priority. The IDIOMS machine design allows the transaction to access the data as if it were a traditional record structure and can thus be processed using a language such as C. The Storage Engine accesses the data as if it were SQL tables so that it can be processed in a relational manner. The machine design permits both operations concurrently on the same dataset. The overall design strategy is to ensure that the discs connected to the transaction processors (T) have sufficient spare access capacity to allow the amount of MIS activity required. The IDIOMS machine has demonstrated a transaction processing performance improvement of 45 times over the current mainframes used by TSB. The current system is incapable of providing MIS support. The demonstrator has shown that for the current mix of transactions there is sufficient disc access capacity available that the running of concurrent MIS queries results in no appreciable diminution of transaction processing performance [5].

The remaining Storage Engines are used to store data which is only accessed by the MIS system, for example summary and statistical tables. This data can be joined with the data held on the transaction discs in the relational processors R. MIS queries are input to the Data Dictionary (D) processor where they are parsed and processing resources are allocated as required. The data dictionary has sufficient information to know which parts of which tables are placed on which disc so that only those discs which hold data needed for the query actually contribute to the necessary processing. A sequence of relational operations can be constructed as a pipeline by sending the output of one Relational Engine (R) to the input of another using the communications ring of C processors. More details of relational processing techniques in such a machine can be found in

[6]. The network of C processors provides the scalability of the system because we can add extra nodes in the C processor structure as required. Thus we can add transaction nodes, MIS nodes and relational processing on an as needed basis. Compare this with a traditional mainframe solution where it is impossible to add the precise amount of extra capability required, rather the increment in performance quite often increases capability that did not need to be enlarged. In the following sections we shall discuss the changes that can be made to the IDIOMS design as a result of using T9000 and C104 technology.

9.3 An Interconnection Strategy

Networks of up to 512 processors can easily be constructed using a simple three–level CLOS network. The network is replicated for each of the links of the T9000 if full interconnection is required. In the case of a database machine we may need to have more processors than this and we may also need to ensure that the original design permits easy on–site increase in size. Applications which can justify such processing needs usually cannot be taken out of service for long periods because they are critical to an organisation's profitability. Figure 9.2 shows how a network of five–levels can be constructed which allows 1920 T9000s to be connected.

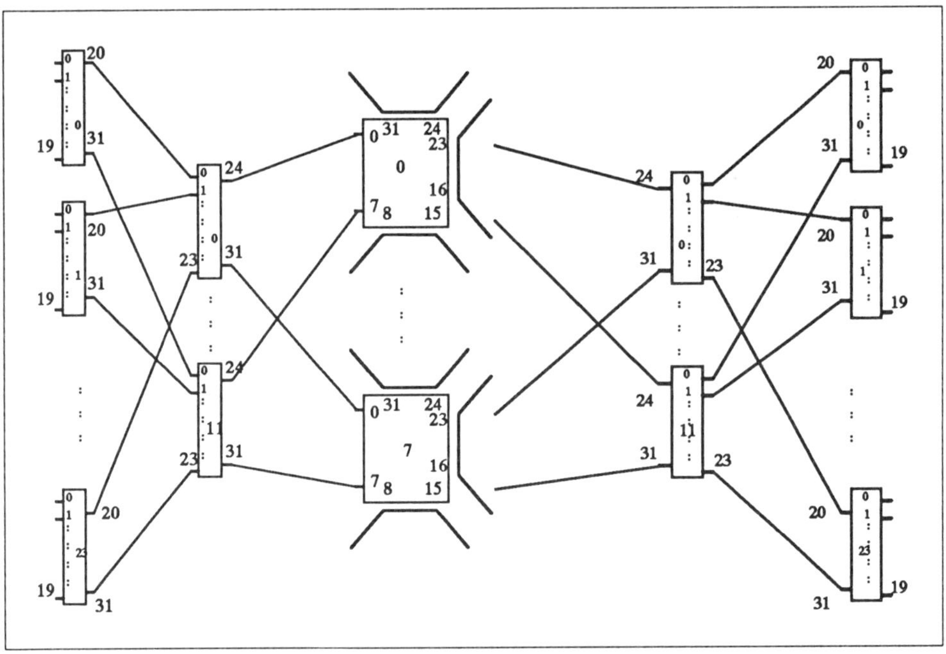

Figure 9.2 A five–level indirect network

The components in this network are all C104s. The terminal links are then connected to T9000s. The periphery of this network has sufficient capacity to hold 1920 T9000s each connected by a single link. If all four links are to be connected then the complete network has to be replicated four times. The element of the network to the right is duplicated and connected to the eight central C104s twice more, once for the lower connections and once to the upper connections. A total of 152 C104s are required to connect just one link of each transputer and thus 608 are required if all four links are to be interconnected. It should be noted that any communication between transputers on the same edge of the structure requires only three levels of communication rather than the five needed to cross from one edge to another. This structure gives sufficient capability for scalability once the database machine has been installed. The system needs initially to be set up with just one of the four quadrants and even that does not need to be fully populated. Thereafter the initial quadrant can be fully populated and subsequent quadrants filled as necessary. If only one quadrant is used then there is no need for the 8 central C104s.

9.4 Data Storage

Of crucial importance to any database machine is the provision of a high bandwidth, large volume, fault tolerant data storage sub–system. We chose to make the same design decision as was done in IDIOMS, namely that an operating system is not used to control the data storage because the file system is usually inappropriate for database operation. We therefore chose to store the data directly on the disc storage and use a Data Storage Description Language to specify the placement of the data[7]. This then permits greater and more flexible control of the database machine. Furthermore, the data dictionary process can utilize the information to make query processing more efficient.

In this design we propose to obtain fault tolerance by simply maintaining several copies of the data in a triple modular redundancy scheme. This is sometimes known as disc mirroring. We shall obtain high bandwidth by providing a large number of link connections to the disc subsystem. In some ways the design is similar to the many RAID (Redundant Array of Inexpensive Discs) products which are currently being marketed, except that we have chosen not to distribute the bits of a word over many discs. The design which is given presumes that a direct link interface to the disc unit is provided. Currently, of course, this is not the case, but the design gives compelling reasons why this should be done.

However before we can present the design a few basic facts about disc accessing are required. Disc manufacturers always quote a disc transfer speed which assumes that the read head is correctly located on the desired block before the transfer takes place. They also quote seek and latency figures which indicate the time taken to move the head to the correct track and to wait for the desired sector to rotate under the head. The figure they don't quote is the effect of these times on overall performance. In experiments we have undertaken which are confirmed in another report[8] it was shown that an effective rate of about 0.5Mbyte/sec could be achieved from a SCSI–1 disc which had a rated performance of 3 Mbytes/sec. This was the figure for sequential access. The actual rate for random reads was of the order of 0.1 Mbytes/sec. Faster disc technology may improve this overall performance but the access rate is still going to be substantially less than the figure quoted by disc manufacturers. The way that disc manufacturers overcome this performance is by constructing disc strings, that is having a number of discs on the same bus, hence the SCSI bus system which permits upto seven discs on the bus. It has been found that the optimum number of discs to have on a SCSI–1 bus is four[9]. This figure matches the 0.5 Mbytes/sec and the rated performance of SCSI–1 of 2 Mbytes/sec, for sequential access. In order to achieve good performance in a disc array it is usually suggested that consecutive data blocks are placed on separate drives so that the seek and latency time can be overlapped. This works well if most of the accesses are sequential as happens for files in traditional operating system environments. However in a database system this is not the case and there is thus little likelihood of distributing disc blocks over drives having a beneficial effect. If such disc block striping were to be undertaken it would be best to do this over a string of drives connected to a single control processor. Figure 9.3 shows the structure of a simple disc sub–unit comprising 31 drives.

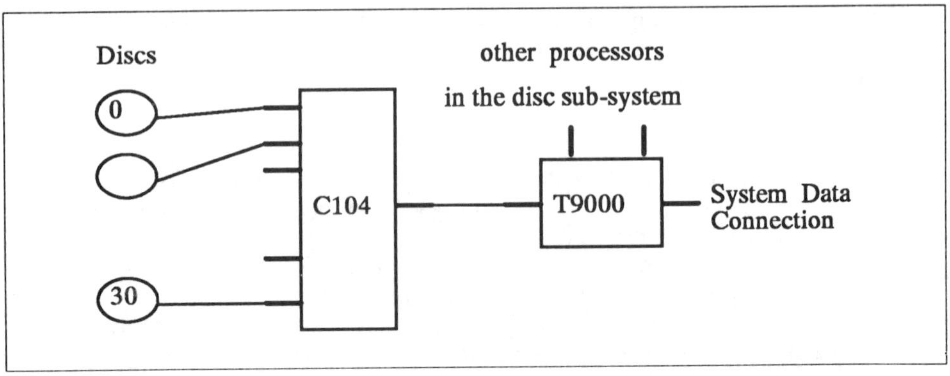

Figure 9.3 Disc sub–unit

The sub–unit chooses to have only one disc per connection to the C104. It is presumed that the disc drive contains an interface compatible with a T9000 link. In the short term this could be achieved by use of a standard disc with extra interface circuitry. The number of discs connected to a single T9000 link is justified because the bandwidth of a T9000 link is 17.48 Mbytes/sec bi–directionally. This capacity divided by the actual disc performance of 0.5Mbytes/sec result in up to 34 discs being reasonable. This sub–unit of itself has no fault tolerance and is not scalable. These aspects are achieved by making the sub–unit a component of a complete disc sub–system, as shown in figure 9.4.

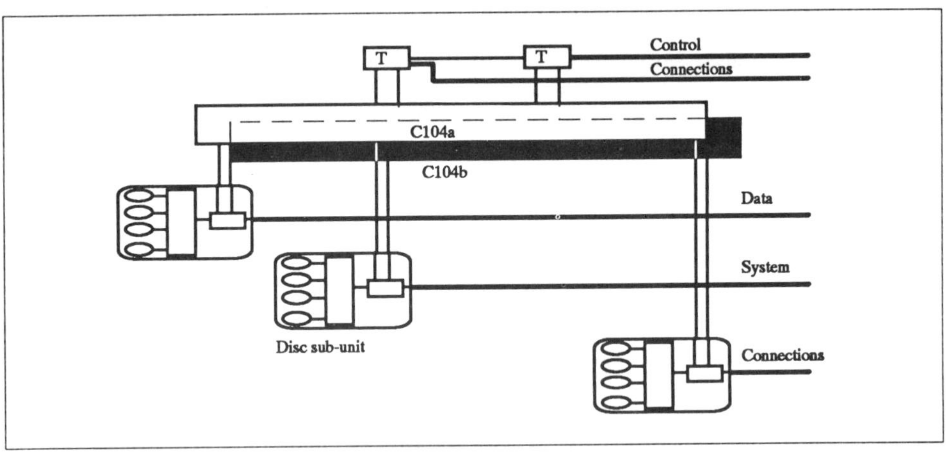

Figure 9.4 A complete disc sub–system

Each of the disc sub–units has one connection which connects it to the external environment. The other two connections are taken to a pair of C104s which provide connection between the sub–units. The two T9000's (T) which are also connected to the C104s are used to provide a fault tolerant repository of information about the data stored on the disc sub–system. The complete disc sub–system can comprise a maximum of 30 sub–units, though of course, it does not have to be fully populated initially. Assuming a fully populated system we can construct a disc sub–system which holds from 18Gbytes using 20 Mbyte capacity drives to 2325 Gbytes using 2.5 Gbyte capacity drives. In both cases, the bandwidth available is 524 Mbytes/second. As disc performance improves it will be necessary to reduce the number of discs connected to the C104 so that it matches the available link bandwidth. It should be noted that the capacity of the system will be reduced to one–third if a triple modular redundancy strategy is adopted.

Fault tolerance can be achieved by ensuring that every time data is written to the system two copies are sent via the sub–unit controlling transputer and the C104s to two other sub–units, where a copy of the data is kept. Thus we can be guaranteed that within one transfer time through a C104 data will have arrived at two other sub–units where the data can be replicated. At that point it may be necessary to wait to confirm the satisfactory writing of the data to all of the sub–units. A well understood two–phase commit protocol could be used to ensure system integrity. Read performance can be substantially improved because there are now three copies of the data. Even though a read request may be directed to a specified system connection link, there is no difference if the actual read is sent to a different sub–unit if one of the sub–units happens to be overloaded. The design could be criticized because there is only one link between the system connection and each disc. The effect of this weakness is however reduced because we have three copies of each data block, each on different disc units each having their own primary system connection. It is thus vital that we have a flexible interconnection strategy between the disc sub–system and the rest of the database machine.

9.5 Interconnection Strategy

Figure 9.5 shows the connection between the disc sub–system and the rest of the architecture when attached to an indirect network generated by 48 C104s, which permits 512 terminal connections.

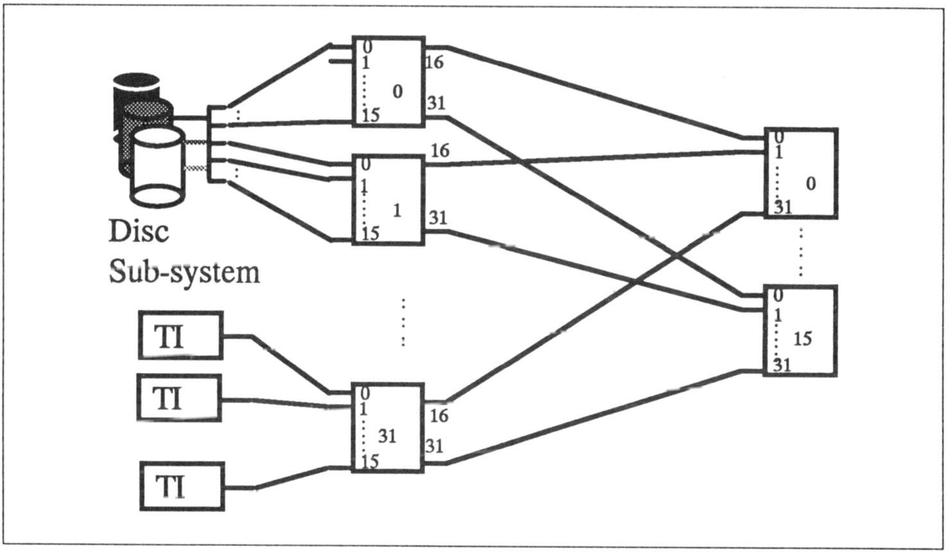

Figure 9.5 Disc sub–system interconnection

Each of the TI processors in figure 9.5 provide a generic Table Interface process to the disc sub–system. The disc sub–system is simply connected to the routing chips one link per terminal connection. This interconnection strategy permits the use of generic table handlers rather than the dedicated ones in the original IDIOMS design. Thus the table partitioning that was explicit in the IDIOMS design has become implicit in the T9000 based design. The table is allocated to the disc sub–system in such a way that the separate parts can be accessed in parallel by multiple TI processes. The TI process will usually have to manipulate the index that is used to access the part of the table that has been allocated to the particular TI process. A given query may not access the whole table and therefore only the required number of TI processes will have to be allocated to satisfy the table handling requirements of the query.

We now investigate how the remaining links on the TI process can be used given that the disc sub–system and the TI processes are on the same interconnection layer. First, we presume that the interconnection layers are replicated so that the transputers holding the TI process can be connected to other layers remembering that the disc sub–system is only connected to one layer. Thus we would end up with four layers of interconnection. We now have to allocate processes to these layers. It is not necessary in the connection system shown in figure 9.5 to consider locality of reference because all processors are equidistant from each other. In the interconnection architecture shown in figure 9.2 it would be necessary to consider which processes do communicate with each other so that those which communicate frequently are in a part of the network where there is a three level communication structure rather than one involving five levels. In the following sections we shall discuss the connections that have to be made between the processes that make up the database machine.

9.6 Relational Processing

Figure 9.6 shows the way in which the IDIOMS relational engines were constructed using three T8 transputers. This structure was required because it was necessary to provide some local buffering of data between the Storage Engine processors, which were sending data to the Relational Engine over the communication structure.

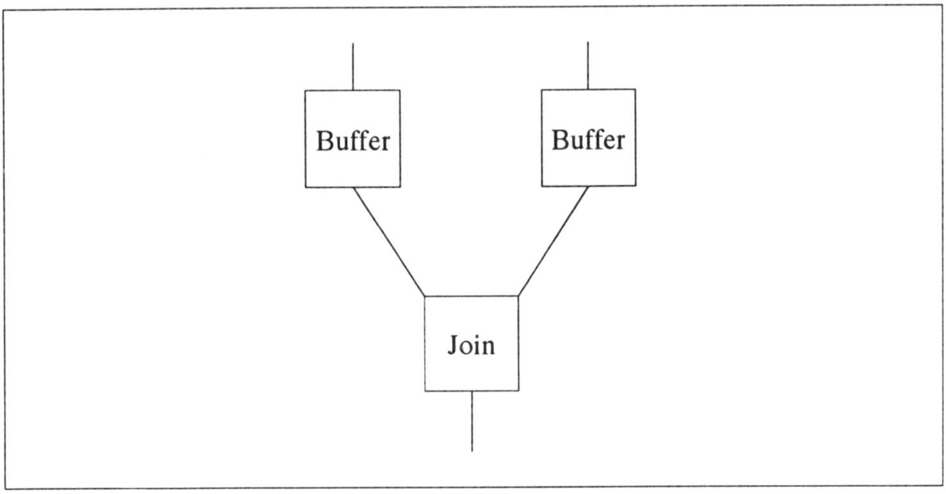

Figure 9.6 IDIOMS style relational engine

This design then imposed some software difficulties because the synchronization which normally occurs between occam processes is lost when that communication takes place between processes which are not on adjacent processors. This loss of synchronization can be overcome by having each message acknowledged by a special message which is sent from the buffer process to the storage engine which has sent the data. This extra communication results in a reduction in throughput because the sending process has to wait until it receives an acknowledgement before it can send the next block of data. The omission of the acknowledgement means that the buffer process has to be able to send messages to the storage engine, in sufficient time, so that data is not sent to the buffer process which cannot be stored in it.

This problem does not occur with the T9000/C104 solution because the hardware allows processes to communicate with each other directly. Thus the complete relational processor architecture can be implemented on a single transputer with the same process structure. However, the buffer process does not need to send wait messages to the sending process, it just does not input any more data when it becomes full, thus the sending process becomes blocked trying to output data. Provided the processes have been correctly constructed this causes no problem. The buffer processes are still required because it makes relational processing more efficient when a nested loops join has to be undertaken (every row of one table is compared with every row of a second table).

A general relational process can therefore be allocated to any one of the transputers in the architecture. In order to undertake the required processing the relational processor will need to be informed of the structure of the tables to be joined and the type of join processing to be undertaken. In addition, the relational processor will need to be told where the output from the relational processing is to be sent. This aspect of resource allocation and control of processing will be discussed in section 11.

9.7 Referential Integrity Processing

Figure 9.7 shows a typical situation that occurs in relational databases involving a many–to–many relationship between customers and their accounts. A many–to–many relationship cannot be directly represented so an intermediate linker table is introduced which implements two one–to–many relationships. The primary key of the Accounts table is the column A which contains the account number. The primary key of the Customer table is the column C which contains the customer identification number. The primary key of Account–Customer is a compound key comprising A and C, that is the combination of A and C is unique whereas individual values of A and C may be replicated. A fuller description can be found in [12]. A corollary of this structure is that in order to send letters to account holders it is necessary to join Accounts to Account–Customer on the common column A and then to join the result to Customer on the common column C.

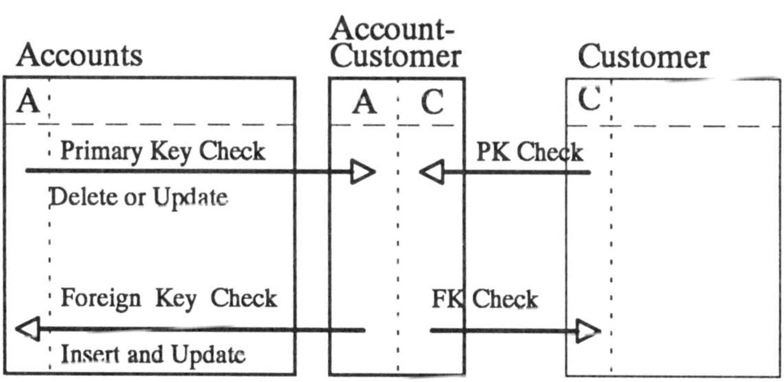

Figure 9.7 Foreign key, primary key relationships

Figure 9.7 shows the checks which have to be undertaken when undertaking insert, update and delete operations upon a database in which referential integrity processing has been specified. Thus, if it is desired to delete a row from either the Accounts or Customer tables, then it is first necessary to check that no row in the table Account–Customer has the same key value as that which is about to be deleted. That is the value of the column A or C respectively must have been deleted from Account_Customer before it is deleted from Accounts or Customer. Similarly, if a value of the primary key of Accounts A, is updated, then a check has to be made in Account–Customer to ensure that there are no rows which have the old value of A remaining.

Whenever a row is inserted into Account–Customer a check has to be made in both Accounts and Customer that a row with the same value for A and C already exist. This is known as a foreign key check. Similarly, if a row in the Account_Customer table is updated a foreign key check has to be carried out to ensure that the new values already exist in the referenced tables.

It is obvious from the foregoing description that much processing is involved in the checking of referential constraints especially in systems which involve much updating of data. It is for this reason that many existing database applications execute without referential processing enabled because the processing overhead is too great. Figure 9.8 shows how two co–operating processors can be used to implement a referential co– processing system.

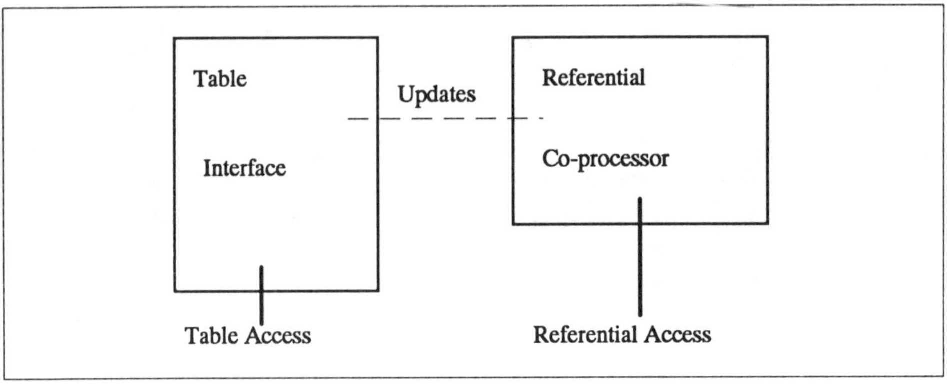

Figure 9.8 Referential co–processor architecture

The referential co–processor contains a copy, sometimes known as a concrete view, of the primary key column(s) of a table partition. This means that a particular referential co– processor is dedicated to a particular table partition and is not a general processor which can be allocated on an as needed basis like table interface processors. The referential co– processor can be accessed by any number of table interface processors because the access is read only as an existence check is being undertaken to check whether or not a value already exists in the referential co–processor. If a table interface process modifies the primary key of a table then those changes have to be communicated to the appropriate referential co–processors. This modification has to be done exclusively so that update anomalies cannot occur between table interface and referential co–processors. The referential co–processor is just a terminal transputer in the interconnect in just the same way as a table interface processor is connected. The only difference is that the referential co–processor undertakes the referential processing for a particular table partition. Thus, when a query is parsed that will invoke referential processing, access to the required referential co–processors will have to be granted.

The main advantage of this architecture is that the bulk of referential processing does not require access to the complete table, just to the columns which are referenced by other tables. It is thus sensible to provide this capability as a dedicated resource. The bulk of table accesses are, in fact, to read data from the table in response to queries, which need no referential processing. The disadvantage is that the data in the referential co–processor has to be up to date with all changes made to the database. This is closely linked with concurrency management which is discussed in the next section.

9.8 Concurrency Management

Figure 9.9 shows the architecture of the concurrency management system. Each Table Interface processor is a terminal processor in the interconnect structure as are the Transaction Manager processors (TM). The TM processors support one or more TM processes, though we shall assume this is just one for ease of explanation. There have to be as many TM processes as there are permitted concurrent transactions because we wish to ensure that the processing of one transaction is not disturbed by the processing of the other transactions which are running concurrently.

A transaction is a sequence of queries which a single user issues as an atomic piece of work. That is, either the whole transaction is successful and all modifications to the database are saved in the database, or the transaction fails and thus has no effect on the database whatsoever. A transaction may fail because a row from a table required by one transaction has already been allocated to a different concurrent transaction. It is a requirement of database management systems that they exhibit the principle of serializability. This principle ensures that the effect of a number of concurrent transactions is the same when executed concurrently as if they had been executed one after the other. In addition the effect of one transaction cannot be seen by other transactions until the transaction comes to an end and commits the changes to the database.

The design of this concurrency management system presumes that interference between transactions is low, which is reasonable for commercial style applications. For CAD/CAM applications this may not be justified and a different approach would be required because the nature of transactions is different, in particular, they tend to be much longer, which increases the likelihood of interference between transactions.

Each table is divided into a number of partitions to increase the parallel access to the table and to reduce the possibility of transactions interfering with each other. Each partition has its own, specific, Partition Manager process allocated to a dedicated processor which is connected to the interconnect in the same way as any other terminal processor. This process records which rows of the table partition have been allocated to which transaction. A Table Interface process determines whether or not it wishes to have access to a row. If it does require access to a row it sends a message to the Partition Manager associated with the table partition which the Table Interface process is accessing. At any one time many Table Interface processes may be accessing the same partition of a table. We have to ensure that these requests to access a row are received in a strict order. This can be simply achieved by using the Resource Channel mechanism provided by the T9000. This mechanism allows many processes to share a single channel which they can only access once their claim on that channel has been granted. This has a direct correspondence with the shared channel concept in occam3[10,11]. Figure 9.9 shows the individual shared channels with each Table Interface process having access to all the shared channels (indicated by the bold lines). There are as many shared Partition Control Channels as there are partitions in the database.

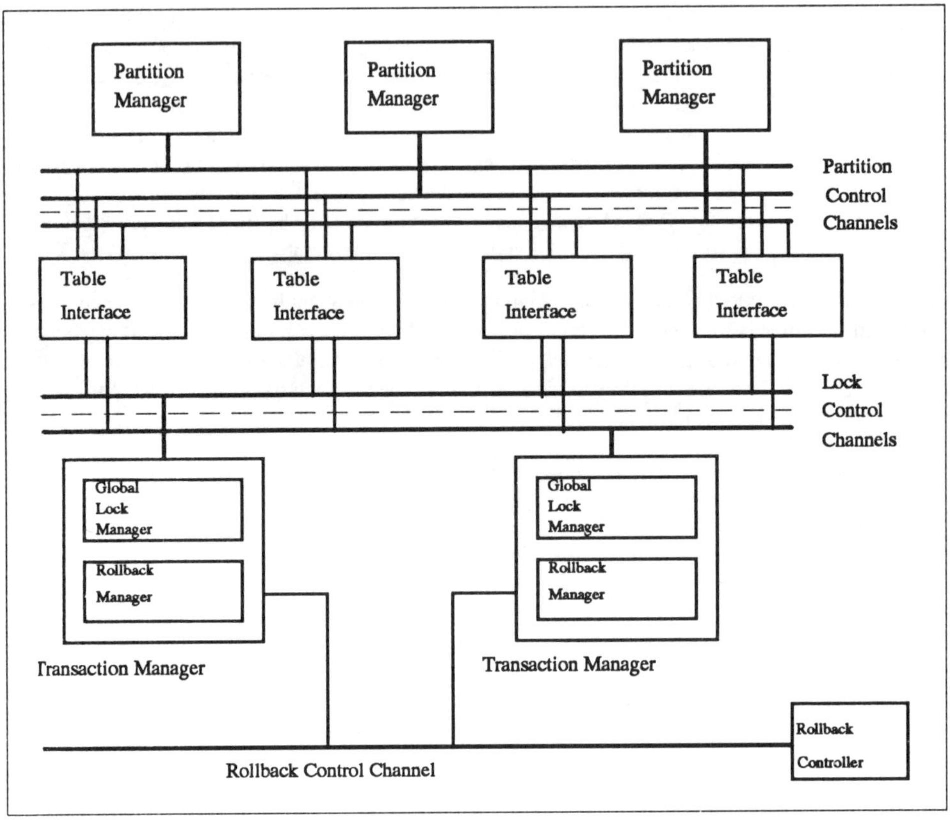

Figure 9.9 Concurrency management architecture

In addition, each Table Interface process has to indicate to one Transaction Manager process, with which it is associated, that it has gained access to a row of a table partition. If a Transaction Interface process attempts to access a row that has already been allocated to another transaction then the transaction becomes blocked and has to send a blocked message to its Transaction Manager. Yet again this mechanism has to ensure that access to the Transaction Manager is controlled and this can be simply achieved by the use of a resource channel. There are as many Lock Control Channels as there are Transaction Manager processes. Each Table Interface process can access all the Lock Control Channels.

The Partition Manager maintains a record of which rows of the associated table partition have been allocated to which transaction. The Transaction Manager maintains a record of those rows of table partitions that have been allocated to the particular transaction. In addition, the Transaction Manager needs to know with which other transactions it could interfere, so that it can determine if transaction deadlock has occurred. Two or more transactions are said to interfere with each other if they both access at least one table partition in common. In this case it possible that one transaction has already gained access to a row which the other transactions require. In this case the second transaction is made to wait until the first transaction commits its work. Transaction deadlock occurs when the transaction which is not blocked attempts to access a row which had been allocated previously to the other, now blocked, transaction. Neither transaction can make any progress because they are both waiting for each other to finish, which is impossible. This is just a simple deadlock; far more complex situations can happen in reality with many more transactions.

The traditional solution, adopted by most existing database management system implementations is to store all the lock information in a single data structure which allows the detection of such deadlock cycles. Necessarily, the access to this data structure, which is expensive to maintain becomes a bottleneck in the system. In the approach outlined above the amount of data that is saved for the normal situation, where no transaction blocking or deadlock occurs is very lightweight. It simply involves the communication of two sets of values from the Table Interface process, one set to the Partition Manager and the other to the Transaction Manager. In the normal case when the transaction completes successfully all the data structures (which are just simple lists of values containing no internal structure) will be emptied so that the memory space can be re–used for the next query.

If a transaction becomes blocked it has to determine whether or not a deadlock has occurred. This can be achieved by the Transaction Manager sending messages to other Transaction Managers with which it is known that the transaction interferes. If it is possible to construct a cycle amongst blocked transactions then it is known that deadlock has occurred and one of the transactions has to be rolled back. The cycle is created by following through each of the Transaction Manager processors looking at the row for which they are waiting. A cycle occurs when it is possible to return to the originating blocked transaction. A Transaction Manager can be informed which row it is waiting for and which transaction has accessed that row because that information is available in the Partition Manager. The decision as to which transaction to roll back is the function of the Rollback Control process. The system has been organized so that only one transaction can be rolled back at one time, hence the use of a resource channel between the Rollback Manager processes and the Rollback Controller processor, which is accessed by means of the shared channel Rollback Control.

9.9 Complex Data Types

It is becoming more important that database systems are able to support data types other than those traditionally supported by existing database management systems. Usually such systems are only capable of supporting integer, real, character and boolean data types. Some systems have supported date and time data types but in inconsistent ways. Some systems have also provided an unstructured data block into which a user can place a bit string of some length, which the user then manipulates as necessary.

The T9000 / C104 combination in conjunction with the occam3 provides a simple means of implementing complex data types through two mechanisms entitled remote call channels and library. A library allows a data type definition to be created with a functional interface to permit manipulation of structures passed to it using either ordinary channels or remote call channels. A library can be accessed by any number of concurrent user processes because it maintains no state information between calls to the library. A remote call permits the passing of parameters to a procedure using two implicit channels, one to send the parameters and the other to receive the results. It is similar in concept to the remote procedure call mechanism provided in some operating system implementations.

We can therefore construct a system in which one or more processors contain the code for a library which implements a particular complex data type. This library can then be accessed either using explicit channels or more likely by using remote call channels. The library is actually accessed using a resource channel which permits many user processes to access a single server process. The bottleneck of having a single processor to deal with a given library can be simply overcome by having many processors containing the same code and by using some form of resource sharing strategy. Resource channels can be passed as parameters so that a direct connection can be easily made by referring to a single process which allocates the resource. The complex data type processors are connected to the interconnect in the same way as any other terminal processor but once allocated are only able to process messages for a particular data type.

9.10 Recovery

In the IDIOMS environment recovery was undertaken at two different levels. The first dealt with recovery from storage media failure. This was achieved by simple disc mirroring. In the architecture described in this paper that aspect of recovery is dealt with by the disc sub–system using Triple Modular Redundancy and so can be ignored. The second type concerned recovery from transaction failure which occurs when there is some failure in the on–line transaction processing support infrastructure. Typically this occurs when there is a communication system failure. A transaction arrives at the computer system from a remote location, such as an Automatic Teller Machine, using a communications mechanism. If the communications media fails before the results of the transaction can be returned to the originating point, then the effect of the transaction has to be undone. There are a number of techniques which can be used to overcome this problem e.g. before images, shadow copies and transaction logs[12], which all require the saving of information on a stable storage media such as disc during the course of transaction processing. From the saved information it is possible to undo the effect of a particular transaction without having to re–instate the whole database. The architecture proposed in this paper can use these same techniques. Simply, a separate disc sub–system can be used to store transaction recovery information, automatically providing media failure recovery. A set of processors can be provided which can undertake the necessary processing to undo the effect of an incomplete transaction

9.11 Resource Allocation and Scalability

9.11.1 Resource Allocation

The IDIOMS architecture relied upon a single Data Dictionary / Parser processor which parsed incoming queries and allocated resources as necessary. As such it could become a bottleneck if the system was subject to a large number of small queries. The parsing of queries does not need to be restricted to a single processor. The parsing process entails the decomposition of a query into its component parts which can be allocated to separate processors for each query. A number of different processing strategies can then be identified which will depend upon the number of processors that are actually available when the query is resourced. The generation of these strategies can be undertaken without knowing what actual resources are available. In addition the strategies can be evaluated against each other to determine the most cost effective against some system defined cost function.

Once the strategies have been identified, the actual resources required can be communicated to a single processor which knows what resources are available. If one of the strategies can be accommodated then the resources can be allocated and the parser process can be sent information about the resources it can use so that it can send appropriate messages to the processors which will enable query processing to begin. When a query terminates a message can be sent from one of the processors to the single processor which holds resource availability information. If more than one strategy can be resourced, then the resource allocator processor can decide which strategy to use. The resource allocator processor could contain constraints which have to be met in order that a query can be started. It may be that at specific times of the day it would not be feasible to start a query which consumes most of the processing resource. For example, in banking systems it is known that there is a peak in transactions around lunch–time, hence it would be sensible to deny access to a large query which would use most of the processing resource just before midday.

Figure 9.10 shows a processor structure which will implement such a resource allocation strategy. We presume that queries arrive from the users into a User processor. The User processor then accesses the Resource Allocator process using the shared channel to determine which Parser process to use. If none are available the User process will be made to wait until one becomes available. The query is then sent to the indicated Parser process. It should be noted that all User processes are connected to all Parser processes. The Parser process then decomposes the query and determines the different strategies which are possible. The Parser process then accesses the Resource Allocator process using the shared channel Resource Request, which ensures that only one request for resources is dealt with at one time and thus it is not possible for the same resource to be allocated to more than one query. The Parser process will send information to the allocated resources, using channels not shown in the diagram, indicating the processing to be undertaken. Generally results will be returned to the User process from the Relational processors (R), hence it is necessary to connect all the R processors to all the User processors. When the query is complete the User process will send a message using the shared channel which accesses the Resource Allocator process to indicate that the resources used by the query are no longer required and can be allocated to another query.

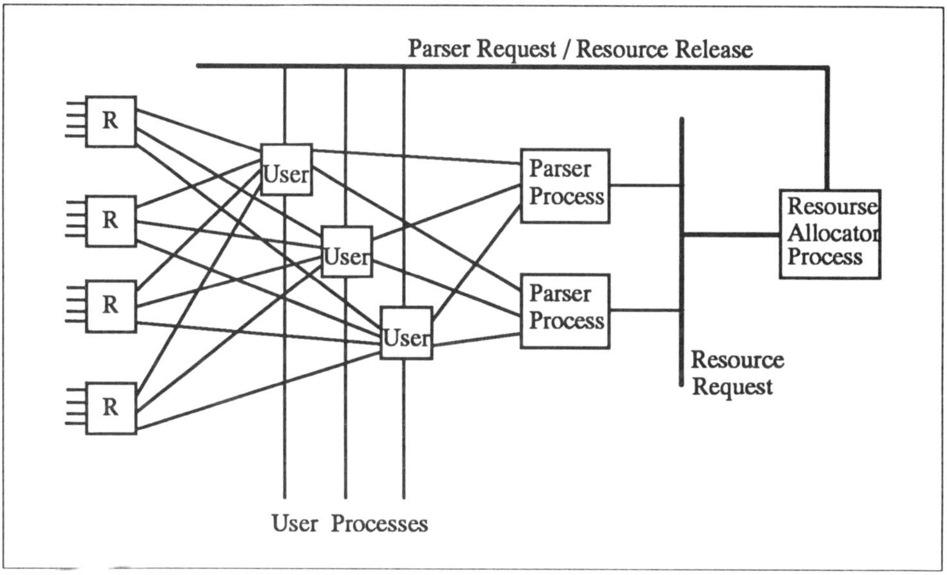

Figure 9.10 Resource allocation processor structure

9.11.2 Scalability

The system described in this paper is scalable in the two ways identified previously. First, the installed size of a system can be matched with the initial system requirements. In coming to this initial size the system designer must be aware of the likely increases in storage and performance that will ensue. For example, it is not uncommon for system to double in storage requirements over the first two years with a consequent increase in processing requirements. Thus it is vital that the system interconnect is designed so that the perceived increases can be accommodated. It is thus not sensible to build an interconnect that is limited to 512 terminal connection points if it can be anticipated that more will be needed in the future.

Secondly, the system can be scaled after installation by simply adding further resources. These resources can be added wherever they are required within the functional components in the machine because there is a uniform interconnect mechanism with a known cost. The only constraint would be in the five–level indirect structure, shown in figure 9.2, where it may be preferable to add some facilities within a three–level interconnect regime to ensure the required performance. In adding extra resources the only part which has to be changed is the resource allocator process discussed previously. Each component in the architecture that has been described is essentially a generic component, even if in use it is made specific to a particular task, such as the referential co–processors. This means that no new software has to be constructed. Thus the implementation of the system as a highly parallel system has afforded an easy mechanism for scalability.

A key factor in the operation of the database machine will be the collection of statistics so that optimal data storage can be achieved. A vital component of the collection of statistics is the monitoring of the changes in queries with time as the use of the database develops. We have already started work on such an automated system[13].

9.12 Conclusions

This paper has presented the outline for the design of a highly parallel database machine which is solely dedicated to that single task. The use of a general purpose processor has been avoided thereby ensuring that the design has had to make few compromises concerning the implementation. The advantage bestowed by the T9000/C104 combination is that we can design each individual software component as a stand–alone entity which makes the system inherently scalable. A further advantage of the use of these hardware components is that the resulting interconnect is uniform in the latency that it imposes upon the system thus the system designer does not have to take any special precautions to place closely coupled processes on adjoining processors. The paper has also shown how it is possible to build a highly parallel disc sub–system. It is a subject for further research to best determine how data should be allocated in such a system in order to maximize parallel access to the data stored in the disc sub–system. Undoubtedly, the use of a Data Storage Description Language[14], such as that developed for the IDIOMS project will be required.

Acknowledgements

The ideas expressed in this chapter are those of the author but necessarily they result from discussions with a large number of people and are also due to interaction with real users of large commercial database systems. The author is indebted to the discussions held with Bill Edisbury and Keith Bagnall of TSB Bank plc and Bob Catt, Alan Sparkes and John Guast of Data Sciences Ltd. The co–workers within the University of Sheffield include; Siobhan North, Dave Walter , Romola Guiton, Roger England, Paul Thompson, Sammy Waithe, Mike Unwalla, Niall McCarroll, Paul Murray and Richard Oates. The work discussed in this paper has been supported in part with funds from the UK Science and Engineering Research Council (through CASE Awards) and the UK Department of Trade and Industry.

References

1. RJ Oates and JM Kerridge, Adding Fault Tolerance to a Transputer–based Parallel Database Machine, in Transputing '91, PH Welch et al (eds), IOS Press, Amsterdam 1991.

2. RJ Oates and JM Kerridge, Improving the Fault Tolerance of the Recovery Ring, in Transputer Applications '91, T Duranni et al (eds), IOS Press, Amsterdam, 1991.

3. JM Kerridge, The Design of the IDIOMS Parallel Database Machine, in Aspects of Databases, MS Jackson and AE Robinson (eds), Butterworth–Heinemann, 1991.

4. R England et al, The Performance of the IDIOMS Parallel Database Machine, in Parallel Computing and Transputer Applications, M Valero et al (eds), IOS Press, Amsterdam, 1992.

5. JM Kerridge, IDIOMS: A Multi–transputer Database Machine, in Emerging Trends in Database and Knowledge–base Machines, M Abdelguerfi and SH Lavington (eds), to be published by IEEE Computer Science Press, 1993

6. JM Kerridge, Transputer Topologies for Data Management, in Commercial Parallel Processing and Data Management, P Valduriez (ed), Chapman and Hall, 1992.

7. JM Kerridge, SD North, M Unwalla and R Guiton, Table Placement in a Large Massively Parallel Database Machine, submitted for publication.

8. AE Eberle, A Gem of a Disc Drive, Digital Review, Cahners–Ziff Publishing, January 14 1991,

9. V Avaghade, A Degwekar and D Rande, BFS – A High Performance Back–end File System, in Advanced Computing, VP Bhatkar et al (eds), Tata McGraw Hill, 1991.

10. G Barrett, occam3 Reference Manual Draft (31/3/92), Inmos Ltd, 1992

11. JM Kerridge, Using occam3 to Build Large Parallel Systems : Part1; occam3 Features, submitted for publication

12. R Elmasri and SB Navathe, Fundamentals of Database Systems, Addison–Wesley, 1989.

13. M Unwalla and JM Kerridge, Control of a Large Massively Parallel Database Machine Using SQL Catalogue Extensions and a DSDL in Preference to an Operating System, in Advanced Database Systems, PMD Gray and RJ Lucas (eds), Springer–Verlag, LNCS 618, 1992.

14. JM Kerridge et al, A Data Storage Description Language for Database Language SQL, Sheffield University, Department of Computer Science, Internal Report, CS–91–05, 1991.

10 A Generic Architecture for ATM Systems

10.1 Introduction

The rapid growth in the use of personal computers and high–performance workstations over the last ten years has fueled an enormous expansion in the data communications market. The desire to connect computers together to share information, common databases and applications led to the development of Local Area Networks and the emergence of ***distributed computing.*** At the same time, the geographical limitations of LANs and the desire to provide corporate–wide networks stimulated the development towards faster, more reliable telecommunications networks for LAN interconnection, with the need to support data as well as traditional voice traffic. The resulting increase in the use of digital technology and complex protocols has resulted in the need for enormous computing capability within the telecommunications network itself, with the consequent emergence of the concept of the ***Intelligent Network***. With new, higher bandwidth applications such as video and multimedia on the horizon and user pressure for better, more seamless connection between computer networks, this convergence of computing and communications systems looks set to accelerate during the nineties.

A key step in this convergence is the development by the CCITT of standards for the ***Broadband Integrated Services Digital Network (B–ISDN)***. B–ISDN seeks to provide a common infrastructure on which a wide variety of voice, data and video services can be provided, thereby eliminating (hopefully) the final barriers between the world of computer networks and the world of telecommunications. The technological basis for B–ISDN chosen by the CCITT is the ***Asynchronous Transfer Mode (ATM)***, a fast–packet switching technique using small, self–routing packets called ***cells***.

The single most important element which has driven the development of both distributed computing and the intelligent network is the microprocessor. Indeed, as systems such as telecommunications networks have come to look more like distributed computers, so microprocessor architectures which support distributed multi–processing have come to look like communications networks. A message–passing computer architecture, such as that of the transputer, shares much in common with a packet switching system and thus provides a natural architecture from which to build communication systems. The communications architecture of the latest generation transputer, the T9000, shares much in common with ATM and is thus a natural choice for the implementation of ATM systems.

In this Chapter we describe the application of the transputer, in particular the serial links and packet routing capabilities of the communications architecture, to the design of ATM switching systems. We discuss their use in public switching systems and present a generic architecture for the implementation of private ATM switches and internetworking applications. We look at terminal adaption requirements and develop some ideas for interfacing transputers, routers and serial links to ATM networks. Finally, we consider various aspects of the performance of this architecture.

10.2 An Introduction to Asynchronous Transfer Mode

10.2.1 Background

Current communications systems split roughly into two basic categories:–

a) The existing telephone network, a ***Wide Area Network (WAN)***, predominantly designed around the requirements to transmit voice traffic around the globe

b) Existing ***Local Area Networks (LANs)***, designed to transmit digital data between computers over relatively short distances

As the idea of distributed computing and corporate–wide networks has gained acceptance, so has the desire to connect computers (predominantly PC's and workstations) across larger and larger distances. Unfortunately, seamless transmission of data from computer to computer across the globe using either of the existing types of networks is severely limited by the constraints inherent in each system:–

a) The telephone network is optimised for low–bandwidth, low latency point–to–point voice traffic (this traffic is relatively insensitive to noise and data errors)

b) Local area networks are optimised for high bandwidth computer data (which is not generally sensitive to latency, but is intolerant of data errors and usually uses some form of shared medium)

In summary, the telephone network is unreliable and too slow and LANs can't carry voice easily and don't go far enough. This split has led to communications networks developing from two directions over the past decade or so; one trying to make the telephone network faster and the other to make LANs go further.

Attempts to make the telephone network faster and more useful to data communications has resulted in a plethora of communications techniques and standards to transmit data between otherwise isolated computers. First came analogue modems (maximum 19kbits/s), then digital networks like X.25 (generally 64kbits/s), and latterly higher bandwidth access via basic/primary rate ISDN, frame relay, etc. However, the fastest access rates in common use are still no more than 1.5 – 2 Mbits/s, compared with 10–16 Mbits/s on LANs such as ethernet and token ring. Of more concern has been the need to use 'heavyweight' protocols to protect computer data as it travels over the existing, relatively unreliable, telephone network. The processing overhead of these protocols has a significant impact on the useable bandwidth available.

Progress on extending LANs has resulted in the development of ***Metropolitan Area Networks (MANs)*** designed to offer high bandwidth connections between computers over an area the size of, say, a reasonable city. An example is the ***Fibre Distributed Data Interface (FDDI)***, which can offer 100 Mbits/s connection over several kilometres. FDDI, however, is still a shared medium, is relatively expensive, requires new fibre cabling (although copper standards for short distances have been developed) and still requires expensive internetworking equipment to connect to WANs. In addition it cannot support voice traffic very easily. Another standard, ***IEEE 802.6***, shows greater promise in the longer term since it is designed to be 'media independent' and also to integrate more easily with WANs.

However, the situation has become exacerbated in recent years with the arrival of higher and higher bandwidth users (large CAD design databases, for example) and the expected growth of ***multimedia***, with its requirement to support voice, video and computer data applications (multimedia applications are described in more detail in Chapter 11 of this book). So, into the picture comes the CCITT with its efforts to provide the basis for the ***Broadband–ISDN***, a telecommunications infrastructure capable of supporting any type of traffic anywhere across the globe. The

CCITT has based this infrastructure on ***Asynchronous Transfer Mode (ATM)*** technology, which is described in the next section.

10.2.2 Basic ATM Concepts

ATM Cells

ATM is based on the concept of a universal ***cell*** (a very small packet) 53 bytes in length, of which the first 5 bytes are used for a routing header and the remaining 48 bytes are for carrying data. Each ATM cell is a self–contained entity which can be routed individually through each switching node in the network from source to destination. This cell has no awareness of the type of data it is carrying and can be considered to be a universal carrier of data, a sort of communications 'truck' (or 'lorry', for those of us in the UK) into which you can put voice, video, data, etc. The term 'asynchronous' is used since no clocking or timing relationship is maintained between the ATM cells.

DATA FIELD	HEADER
48 bytes	5 bytes

Figure 10.1 ATM Cell

The CCITT Recommendations for the public networks have so far defined ATM to run at a nominal 155 Mbits/s to fit in with the *Synchronous* (framed) bit rates used in the transmission systems between exchanges. In these systems, the ATM cells are packed in like bricks into a two–dimensional frame for transport to the next switch (described later). In reality the bit rate available for the ATM cells is about 149 Mbits/s once the framing overhead has been allowed for. It is expected that a 622 Mbits/s standard will follow (4 x 155 Mbit/s plus some extra overhead) with eventual data rates up to 2.4 Gbits/s being anticipated.

The situation for private networks is not yet clear, since the standards have not yet been set. 155 Mbits/s seems likely, but since ATM cells can be transmitted either framed (synchronously) or unframed (asynchronously) lower data rates (< 155 Mbits/s) for unframed cells may also be adopted. It is important to remember that this is the point–to–point bandwidth available to each connection, not the bandwidth of the network as a whole, which is the case of conventional shared–medium LANs/MANs like ethernet and FDDI.

ATM Connections

Any user who wishes to gain access to an ATM network must first establish a connection with the local switch. In the diagram below, our subscriber picks up a (very sophisticated) ATM telephone in order to send data across the network. During call set–up, the user negotiates with the network for the call and service characteristics desired. For example, the number dialled, bandwidth and service quality (error rates, etc) required may be sent to the local switch. This is important, since different types of traffic require different performance from the network and the user will be charged accordingly. The local switch then negotiates with all the other switches necessary to connect to the desired destination. Assuming the connection is possible and that the user requested bandwidth and quality of service can be supported, the local switch confirms the connection to the user and allocates an ATM cell routing header from those available. If the requirements are not met and a lower standard of service is offered, it is up to the user to either accept this or terminate the call. Otherwise, the user equipment can now start sending data into the network using ATM cells and the routing header specified by the switch.

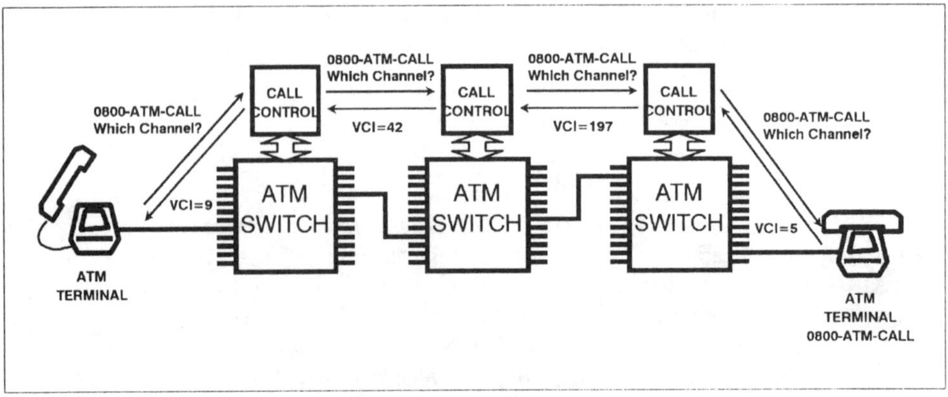

Figure 10.2 ATM call connections

Cell Header Policing

During the call set–up, the user negotiates with the network for certain service characteristics such as bandwidth. This may be specified in terms of the peak and average bandwidth required from the network (other parameters are under discussion). Since the user will be charged (on the public network) for his/her use of the system, and this charge will be dependent on the bandwidth negotiated, it is clearly necessary to monitor the actual use made to ensure nobody is cheating. It is proposed that this be done by monitoring the instantaneous and average bandwidth (or any other parameters) used by each cell on the network. This is referred to as ***Cell Header Policing*** and is done on a cell–by–cell basis on input by the network interface (ATM line card) at each ATM switch. Various algorithms have been proposed to perform this bandwidth policing, the most common of which is the ***Leaky Bucket*** algorithm. Depending on the type of service negotiated, transgressors of the negotiated policing limits may either be charged more (according to their use) or find their cells being discarded if they threaten the quality–of–service of other users.

Another important aspect of header policing arises due to the nature of ATM itself. On entering each ATM switch, each ATM cell is routed asynchronously (hence the name) from input to the appropriate output across the ATM switching fabric. Since cells may suffer delay in crossing this fabric due to internal traffic congestion, they may arrive at the output in 'clusters', resulting in a larger instantaneous bandwidth through no fault of the user (this is analogous to the behavior of buses in cities...). In extremis, if no flow control is provided across the switch fabric, cells may arrive at the output out of order. It would clearly be unreasonable to charge the user more or, worse, start discarding cells because of this behavior, so it is therefore necessary for the ATM switch itself to re–time the cells on output to the next switching node in order to meet the original user requirements. There is, therefore, a requirement to use header policing on output, as well as on input, and the system must ensure that cell order is maintained across the switch.

Cell Header Translation

The route that an ATM cell takes through the B–ISDN *network* is determined by the routing values in the cell header. Only a very limited routing 'space' is provided for each ATM cell since the header is only 5 bytes long and the bit–fields available are necessarily limited. To overcome this, the routing value is re–used (re–mapped) at each ATM switching point in the B–ISDN network. That is, the routing value only applies locally to one switching node and changes as the cell progresses through the network from one switching node to another. This constant re–mapping of the cell header is called ***Cell Header Translation*** and is performed when the cell is received by the ATM switch. Cell header translation is performed on a cell–by–cell basis by the network interface, or ATM 'line card', and with ATM operating at 155 or 620 Mbits/s, this requires either very fast processing, custom hardware, or preferably an intelligent combination of the two.

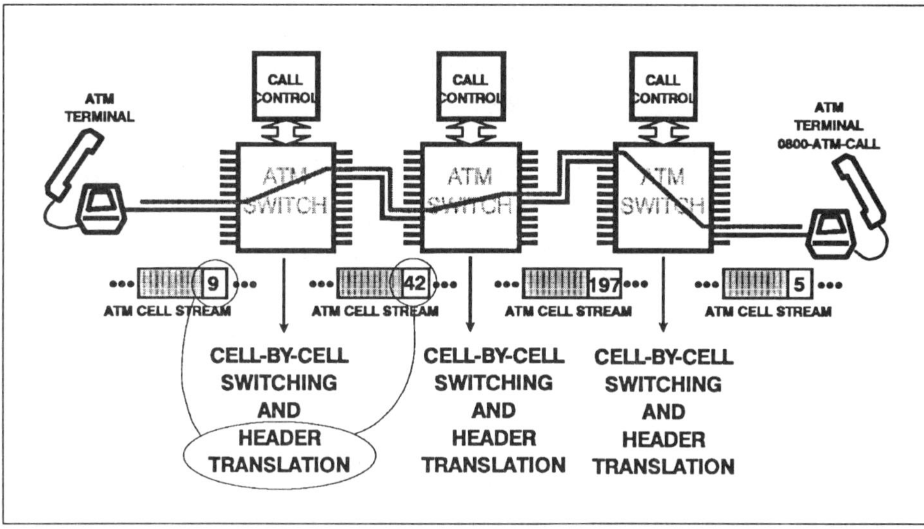

Figure 10.3 ATM Cell Header Translation

Within the ATM switch itself, routing decisions from network input to network output across the internal switching fabric also need to be made on a cell–by–cell basis. It may be necessary to perform another translation of the ATM cell header, to an internal format for routing purposes within the ATM fabric itself.

10.2.3 ATM Protocols and Standards

Having explained the basic principles it is now worth considering a few of the details. A good place to start is the CCITT Recommendations which apply to ATM. These are part of the I.xxx series of Recommendations which form the standards for ISDN networks.

ATM Protocol Reference Model

Like all good protocols, the ATM standard is defined as a series of layers. There are 3 basic layers which, from the top down, are:–

AAL: The '*ATM Adaption Layer*' defines various 'mapping' mechanisms from existing protocols (ISDN, voice, video, LAN data, etc) onto ATM and vice versa.

ATM: This defines the *ATM cell*, routing techniques and error mechanisms

PHY: This is the *Physical* layer and defines media (for example fibre/copper, connectors, etc), bit timings, framing standards, etc.

In addition, the ATM standards describe Management and Control functions for each of the layers, such as call set–up and maintenance functions within the network. These layers constitute the ATM *Protocol Reference Model (PRM)* and are shown pictorially in Figure 10.4. The details of each layer are shown in Figure 10.5.

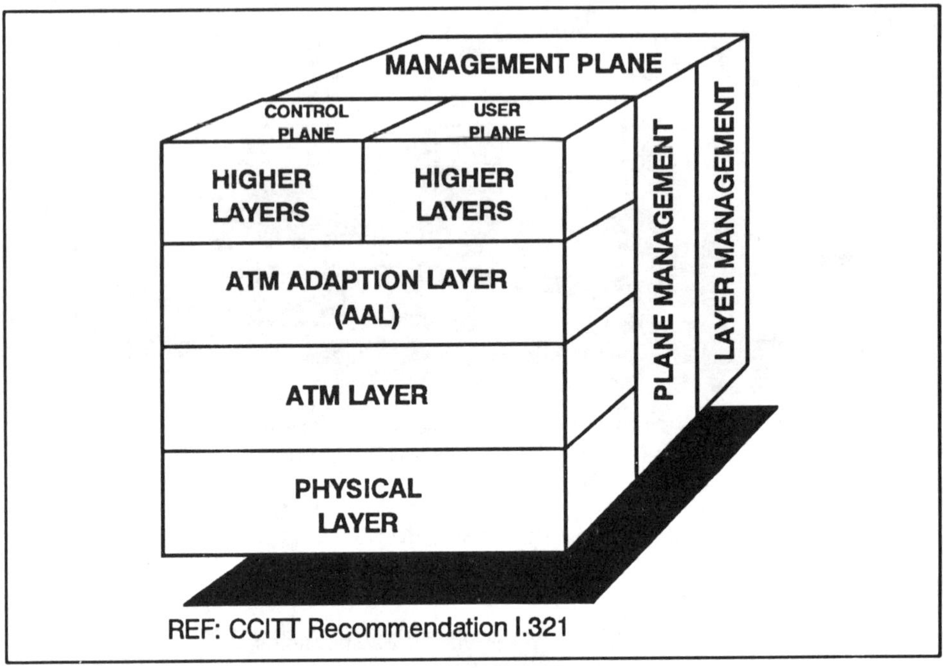

Figure 10.4 ATM Protocol Reference Model (PRM) [1]

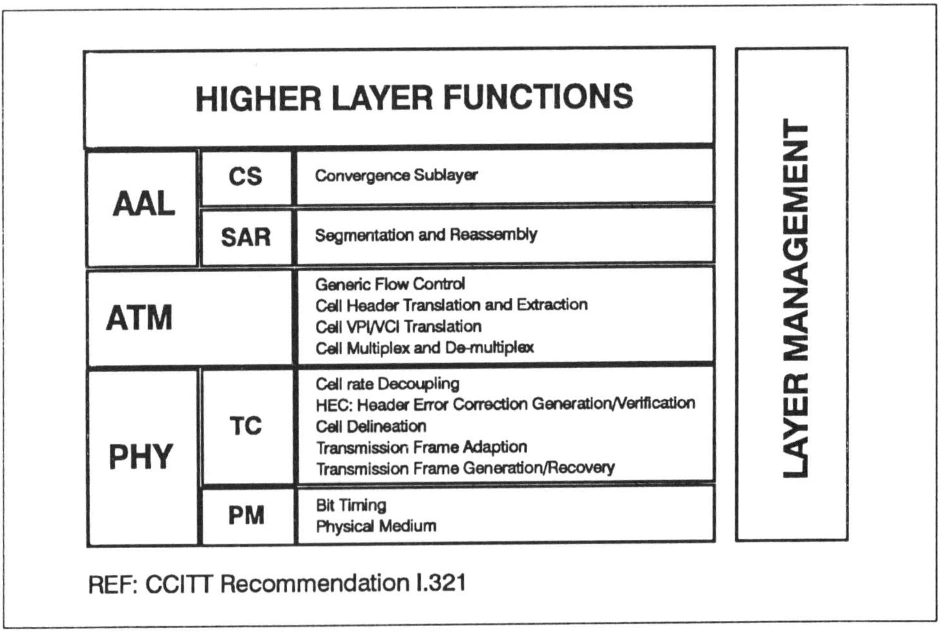

Figure 10.5 ATM PRM Layer Functions [1]

It is important to point out that many of the details in the ATM standards are still not yet finalised, particularly many of the management functions. However, a simplified diagram showing what all 3 layers do is given below and this may be referred to in the discussion of each layer in the following sections.

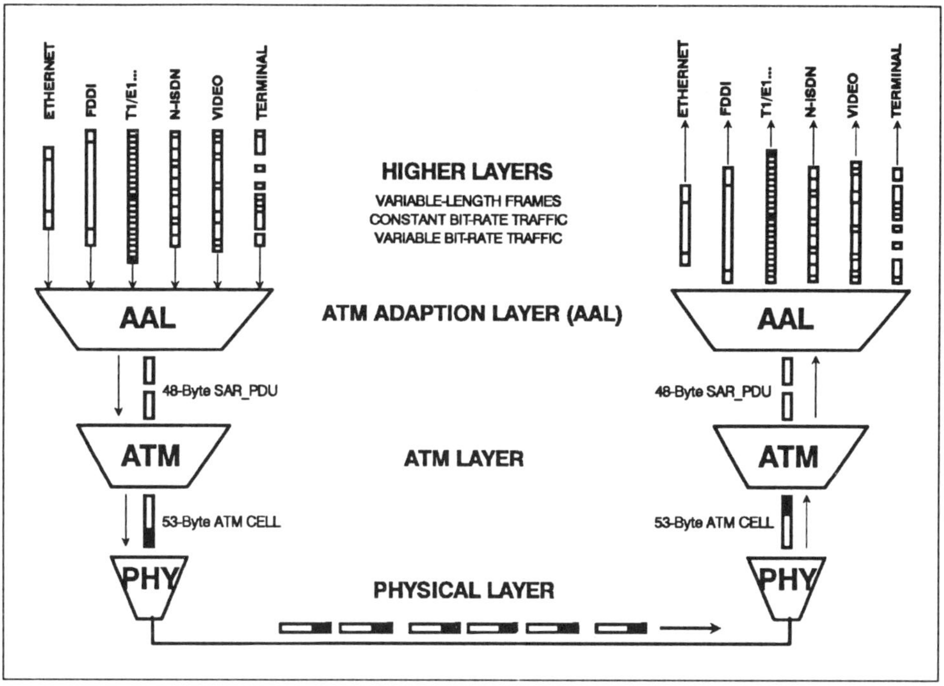

Figure 10.6 ATM Summary

The AAL Layer

The 'ATM Adaption Layer' is responsible for mapping other protocols onto the ATM cell format for transmission and switching. Examples of this would be to carry data traffic (in the form of ethernet, token ring or FDDI frames), voice traffic (64 kbit/s ISDN, for instance) or video traffic. Of necessity, the AAL layer comes in several varieties to suit the nature of the protocols being mapped. Data traffic is typically 'bursty' in nature and needs to be handled on a frame–by–frame basis. Voice traffic ia referred to as 'constant bit rate' traffic, that is, it is a constant flow of bits with no pause. Video traffic is referred to as 'variable bit–rate', since video coding algorithms typically generate an output which varies in bit–rate according to the contents of the picture being transmitted. The AAL layer provides functions to map all of these different types of traffic onto a flow of ATM cells. shown in the previous diagram.

There are four types of AAL specified in the CCITT standards, denoted as AAL1 to AAL4. Recently, a proposal for a fifth, AAL5, has been made with a view to providing a 'lightweight' AAL for frame (packet) based computer data (currently provided by AAL3). In each case, the AAL layer is responsible for ***Segmentation*** of the outgoing data, whatever it is, into small chunks of 48 bytes which then form the data field of the ATM cell. This 48–byte field will also contain overheads, such as CRC and payload type information which depend on which type of AAL is in use. For example, the actual user data field in AAL3 is only 44 bytes, with 2 bytes of header and 2 bytes of trailer added by the AAL to form the 48–byte field. Incoming data received from the ATM layer undergoes ***Reassembly*** by the AAL to provide an appropriate output stream, i.e. it undergoes the reverse of the segmentation process. An example is given in Figure 10.7, showing the AAL3 operation.

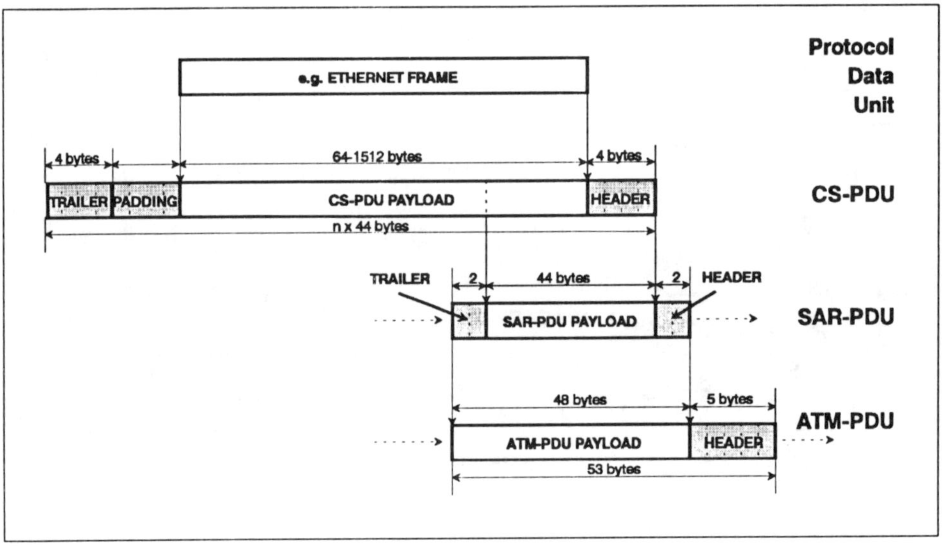

Figure 10.7 AAL3 Example

The use of each layer of the ATM protocol standard is illustrated in a simple form in Figure 10.8. ATM and PHY layer protocols are imnplemented everywhere in our simple network, but an AAL is only invoked at the termination points of the ATM network; that is, an AAL function is needed at:–

- the endpoints of the network (the user terminals)
- points where the ATM network meets another type of network (connecting to an ethernet network, for example)
- certain control nodes within the ATM network itself (passing signalling, management and control information between the control processors in the ATM exchanges, for instance).

The AAL layer is not needed as part of the switching function of an ATM network; this is handled entirely by the ATM layer.

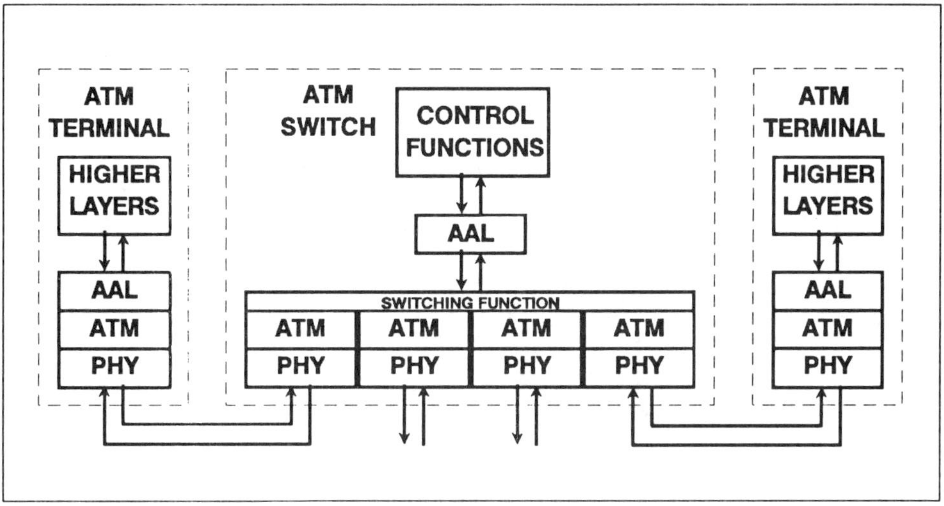

Figure 10.8 PRM Illustration in a simple Network

There is insufficient space here to cover the AAL layer in detail so the reader is referred to the many papers on the subject for more detailed information, for example in [1] and [2]

ATM Layer

There are two versions of the ATM cell format, one for the ***User–Network Interface (UNI)*** and another for the ***Network Node Interface (NNI)***. The basic structure of the ATM cell is shown in Figure 10.9.

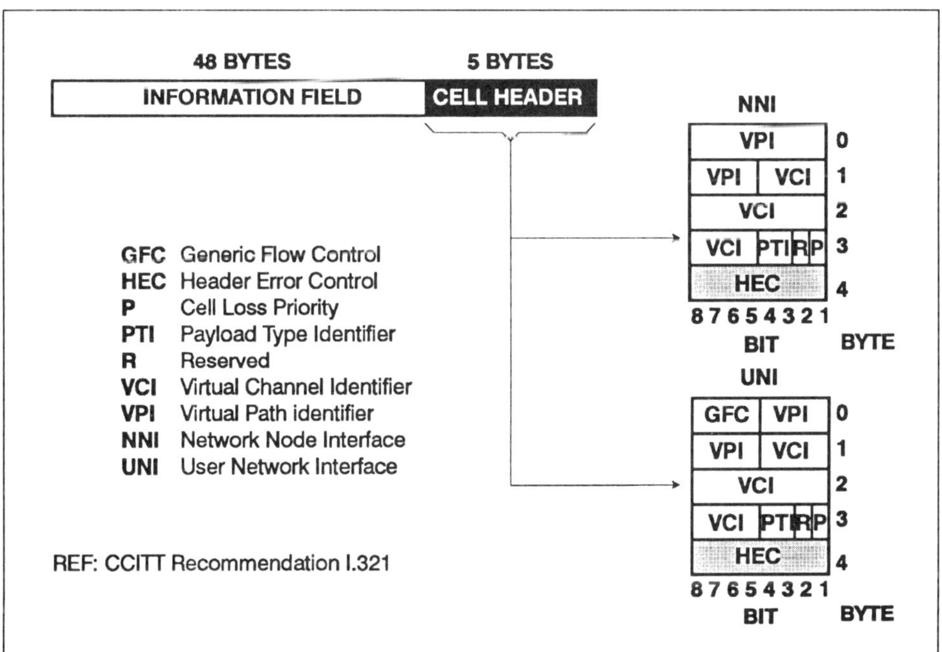

Figure 10.9 ATM Cell Structure

The cell header contains routing information, control bits and error detection features. Two methods of routing are provided; one is via the ***'Virtual Channel Identifier'*** and the other the ***'Virtual Path Identifier'*** (VCI and VPI respectively).

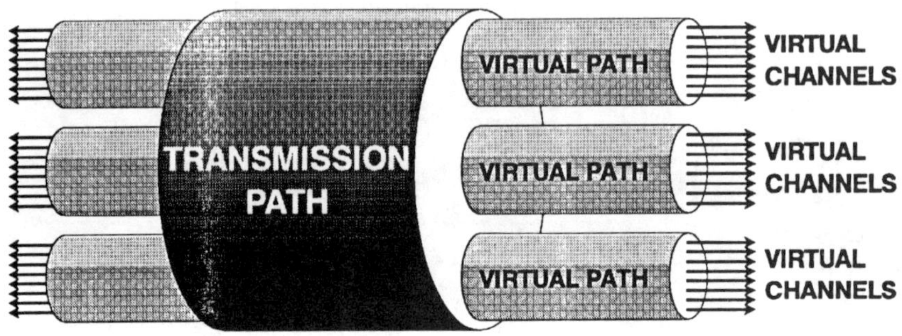

REF: CCITT Recommendation I.321

Figure 10.10 ATM VCI–VPI Relationships

Virtual Paths may be considered to be 'bundles' of Virtual Channels and may therefore be used to route a common group of cells together. An analogy would be that the VPI represents a virtual 'leased line' between two sites, with the VCI's being used to carry individual calls, as shown in Figure 10.11 below.

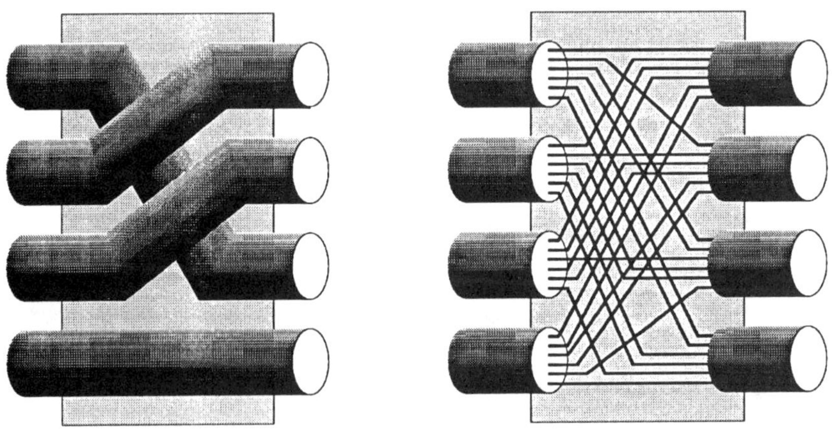

REF: CCITT Recommendation I.321

Figure 10.11 ATM Cell Routing

The ***Header Error Correction (HEC)*** byte is an error detection/correction mechanism for the cell header contents only to avoid mis–routing of cells. The definition of the HEC code and its intended use is actually part of the PHY layer standards, but is included here briefly for convenience. Protection of the data field is left to higher layer protocols. The HEC byte can detect and correct single–bit errors in the header and detect (only) multi–bit errors. It is up to the network to decide what to do with multi–bit errors, although the most likely course of action is to discard the cell and report the error. Another use of the HEC byte is for ***Cell Delineation***. The HEC is continually evaluated on a bit–by–bit basis in order to provide a synchronisation mechanism at the receiver –an ATM cell HEC has been identified when the HEC output is 0, so the location of the rest of the cell can be easily determined.

The ***Generic Flow Control (GFC)*** bits are not, currently, fully defined but are provided in order to support future flow control mechanisms within the network.

The ***Priority*** bit is used to indicate whether the cell can be discarded by the network in times of extreme congestion. For example, discarding a cell containing video data may result in a brief but acceptable sparkle on a monitor, whereas discarding maintenance and call set–up information may result in (an unacceptable) loss of service

The PHY Layer

This layer defines how cells are transported from terminal to network, between switching nodes within the network and then from the network to the destination terminal. The medium used in public networks is most likely to be optical fibre at 155 Mbits/s and above. As mentioned previously, ATM cells can be transmitted in a framed, synchronous format or in an unframed asynchronous format. For the public networks, a synchronous mechanism has been defined based on the bit rates defined in the CCITT ***Synchronous Data Hierarchy (SDH)*** and the ***SONET*** (Synchronous Optical NETwork) frame structure developed in the US. This mechanism allows the packing of ATM cells into the SONET/SDH 2–D frame format, rather like bricks or tiles (the use of a synchronous transmission medium is sometimes referred to as ***Synchronous Transfer Mode (STM)***)

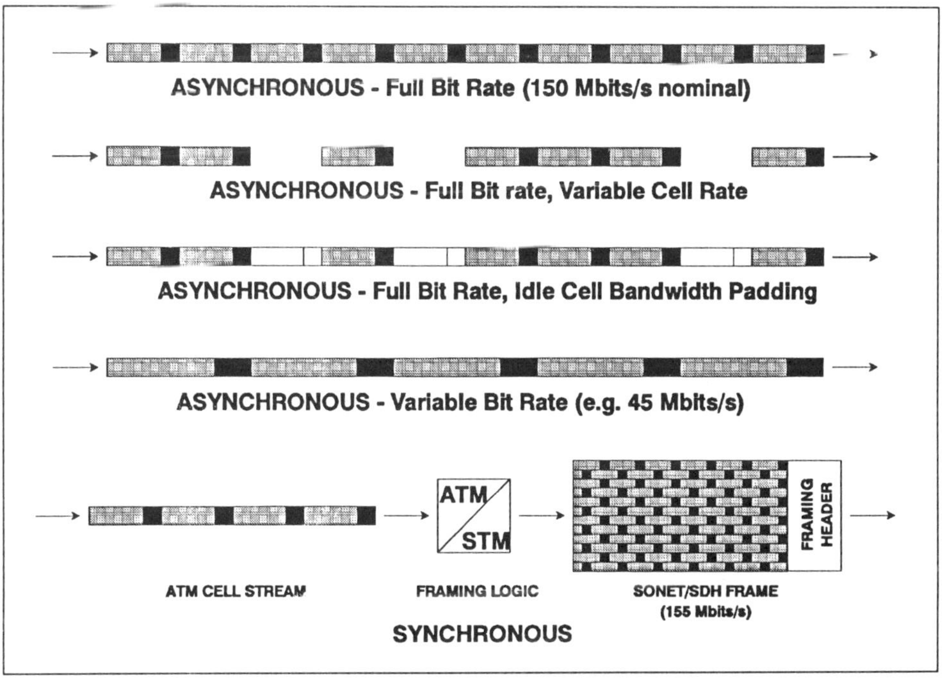

Figure 10.12 Transmission variations for ATM Cells

Various proposals have been made for PHY layer standards for private networks, including the use of Fibrechannel. In private networks, however, there is an incentive to use existing, installed twisted pair cable where possible and this is likely to constrain the data rate available. Cost issues at the user terminal end are also likely to work against a full SONET/SDH implementation, at least initially. AT INMOS in Bristol we have been using transputer links as a physical medium for carrying ATM cells in our demonstrators, since they come free with every transputer. Work is in progress to develop drivers for ***DSLinks*** to copper and fibre, since they offer a cheap and attractive physical interconnect and could form the basis for low–cost ATM connections over distances of 10–100 metres, or even further, to a local ATM switch (further information on physical drivers for DSLinks can be found in Chapter 4 of this book and some of the issues surrounding their use to carry ATM cells are discussed later in this Chapter).

10.3 ATM Systems

In describing the use of DSLinks, routers and transputers in the construction of ATM systems we need to consider the types of equipment needed to build an ATM network. We make here a relatively naive split between ***Public*** Switching Equipment, ***Private*** Switching Equipment and ***Terminal*** Equipment, as shown in the diagram below, and then describe ways of applying the communications and processor architecture of the transputer to this equipment.

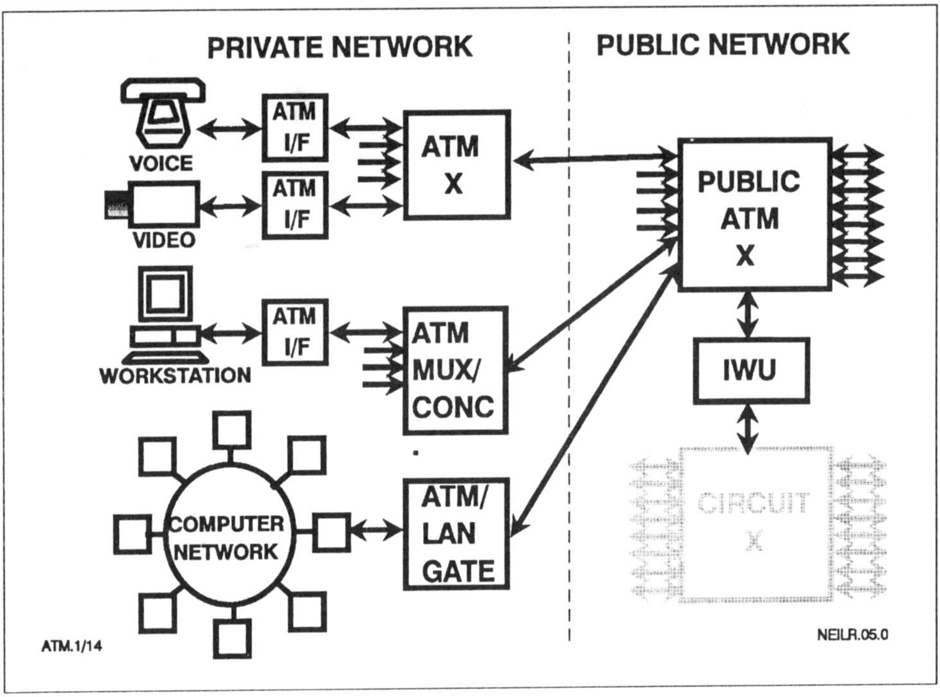

Figure 10.13 Possible ATM Network Equipment Environment

The first efforts in ATM date back to the early 1980's and until about 1991 the bulk of ATM development was focused on ***Public Switching*** systems, particularly in Europe. Field trials of public switching equipment have already started in some areas, but most public activity is expected to begin in late 1993/1994 with more widespread field trials of CCITT compliant equipment in the US, Europe and Japan. How long it will take for the general availability of 155 Mbits/s services on the public network is anyones guess. As with any major infrastructure investment like this it must be expected to be a 10–20 year program. During this period, the developing ATM network must coexist with existing networks [5], hence the requirement for ***Interworking Units (IWU)*** between the two.

Since late 1991/1992, there has been an enormous surge of interest in ATM for private use, mainly driven by computer manufacturers and users predominantly in the US. The creation of the 'ATM Forum' and the release of draft standards by Bellcore/Apple/Sun/Xerox for the use of ATM as a sort of local area network has spurred interest considerably. The initial use of ATM in this area is clearly as an interconnect fabric for existing ethernet/token ring/FDDI networks (there is considerable debate as to whether this interconnection will be done by 'pure' ATM or a MAN, such as IEEE 802.6). This would require ***Internetworking*** equipment capable of converting from LANs/MANs to ATM and then connecting into the public network. Ultimately, the possibility of building small, cheap, high–bandwidth ***Private ATM Switches*** for use in an office or building extends the idea closer to the user and offers the possibility of a seamless communication system, with the distinction between Local and Wide Area Networks finally disappearing.

If the cost of providing a physical ATM connection can be driven low enough, it becomes attractive to take ATM right to the desktop. An ATM ***Terminal Adapter*** in each workstation or PC would provide a fast communications medium capable of supporting voice, video and data traffic and would form the basis for widespread multimedia applications. Coupled with cheap ATM switches, mixed data could be sent or received from anywhere on the planet extremely quickly. First generation adapters would be board–level solutions, but there is plenty of scope to integrate this into a single–chip ATM terminal adapter later, when standards are firmer and the silicon technology more mature.

It seems reasonable to suppose that not all of these private terminals would necessarily require a full 155 Mbits/s ATM connection each. Lower speeds between the terminals and the local switch would be sufficient, at least in the early years of use and an ATM ***Concentrator*** could be provided to make efficient use of the connections to the local public switch. Operating at lower speeds, say sub 50 Mbits/s, also opens up the possibility of using existing cabling plant within buildings and offices.

So, having considered a possible environment for ATM equipment, let's now consider where the communications and processing architecture of the transputer can make a contribution towards realising this network.

10.3.1 Public Switching Systems

Various fast packet switching architectures suitable for the implementation of ATM switches have been described. Indeed, this has been and still is the basis for an enormous amount of research and development activity around the world. Martyn De Pryckers book [2] gives a thorough description of most (if not all) of these architectures, as well as providing an excellent introduction to ATM principles and concepts.

Fast Packet Switch Model

In [4] a generic model of a fast packet switch is presented and we make use of such a simple model in order to illustrate where the DS–Link communications architecture and the transputer processor family contribute.

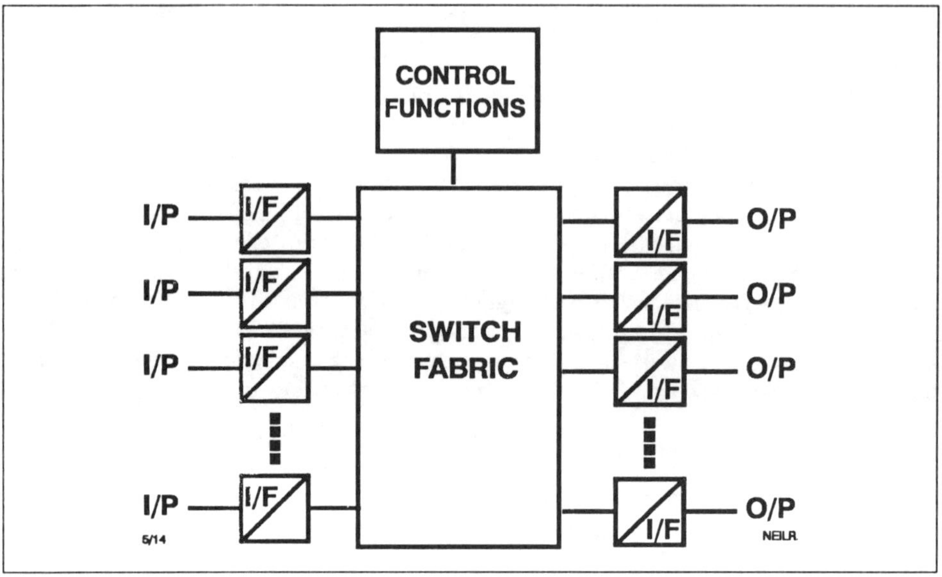

Figure 10.14 Generic Fast Packet Switching Architecture.

This basic architectural model has three main components:–

- Central Control functions (for signalling, control of the switch fabric and operations and maintenance)
- Input/output ports to and from the network
- A switching fabric

In a real switch each of these components will be a complex subsystem in its own right and each will require varying degrees of embedded computing and control. The usefulness of the transputer architecture is in providing the basis for the *control* of these complex subsystems and in particular as a ***distributed control system*** for the exchange as a whole.

Central Control Functions

Probably the most computationally intensive areas of the switch are the ***call–control computer*** and the ***billing*** (or ***call accounting) computer***, which form the central control and maintenance functions within the switch. The call control computer handles all of the signalling, call set–up/ clearance and resource allocation for the exchange. It is a real–time function which, on a large exchange, has to handle hundreds of thousands or even millions of transactions per hour. It goes without saying that it needs to be reliable, since the allowable downtime for a main exchange is 2 hours every 40 years or so. Different manufacturers have different preferences as to whether a centralised or distributed architecture is used, but increasing processing requirements and the development of modular switches means that even centralised architectures are usually multi–processor in nature.

The billing computer tracks the use of the system by individual users in order, naturally, to provide billing information to the network operator. This is also a demanding task if millions of transactions per hour are involved and requires considerable processing power to handle the large transaction rate and database requirements. There is probably more emphasis on the fault–tolerant aspects of this part of the exchange than anywhere else; to the network operator, losing the billing computer means losing money!

Both the billing and call–control computer represent the major software investment in a public switch. The software maintenance effort is huge; hundreds, even thousands, of software engineers are needed to maintain the software on these systems in each of the major manufacturers. At a colloquim at the Royal Society in London called 'Telecommunications Beyond 2000', one of the senior executives at AT&T in the US pointed out that they have 6 million lines of code on their main switch, which grows at about 1/2 million lines a year. Supporting this sort of investment **and** adding new features and functionality for new services becomes increasingly difficult, especially when in time a mature, single–processor or shared–memory multiprocessor computer approaches the limits of its processing performance.

The advantage of the transputer architecture here is purely as a ***scaleable, multiprocessing computer***, which is capable of being used in machines with up to many thousands of processors. The communications architecture of the T9000, for instance, is designed to provide a means of building such large computers free of the performance constraints experienced by shared–memory machines. This same architecture also supports various redundancy models economically (via the serial links), so ***fault–tolerant*** computer systems can be built in a straightforward fashion.

On existing (non–ATM) switches it should be possible to migrate towards such a parallel architecture for these computers, rather than outright replacement of existing machines, in order to preserve as much as possible of this existing software investment. A network of transputers could be provided as an ***accelerator*** to an existing billing computer, for example, to take some of the more intensive load off the existing machine. On new ATM switches, however, there is an opportunity to build a new architecture for these functions right from the beginning, one which is capable of growing with the demands of the application.

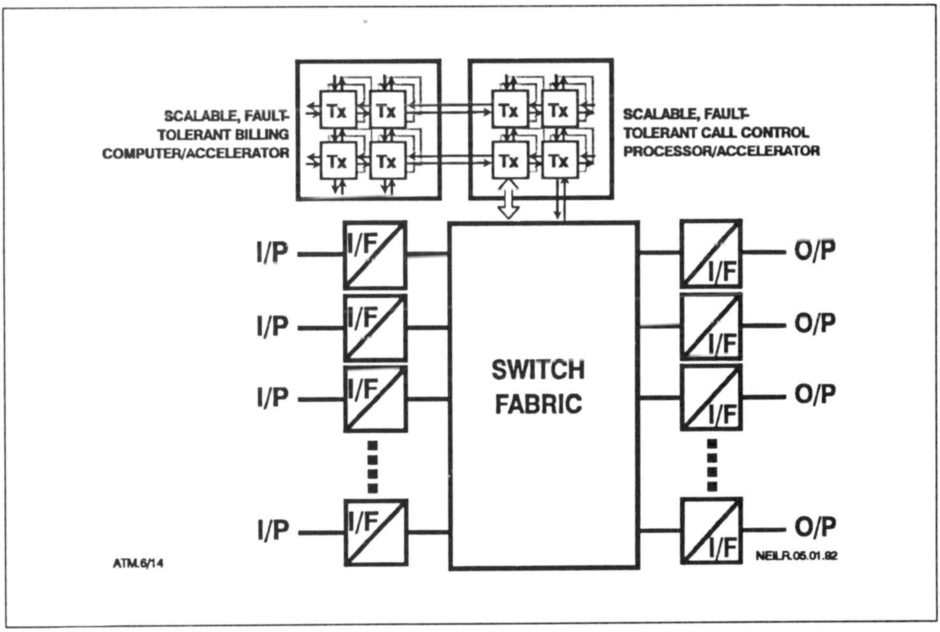

Figure 10.15 Billing/Call Control Application

If a transputer–based multiprocessor is used for the call–control functions, it will be necessary for it to communicate with the ATM traffic carrying the signalling and maintenance information around the network. This traffic is transmitted using ATM cells (naturally) with reserved values for the cell header, so that they can be detected, decoded and acted upon by the control functions in the exchange. This maintenance traffic rate is actually quite low (less than 5% of the total ATM bandwidth) so carrying it around directly on the DSLinks within the control computer is no problem, even if the actual ATM traffic rates rise to 622 Mbits/s and beyond. A simple ASIC to interface between DSLinks and the ATM cell stream is all that would be required, with an AAL function provided in software on the transputer to extract the signalling data.

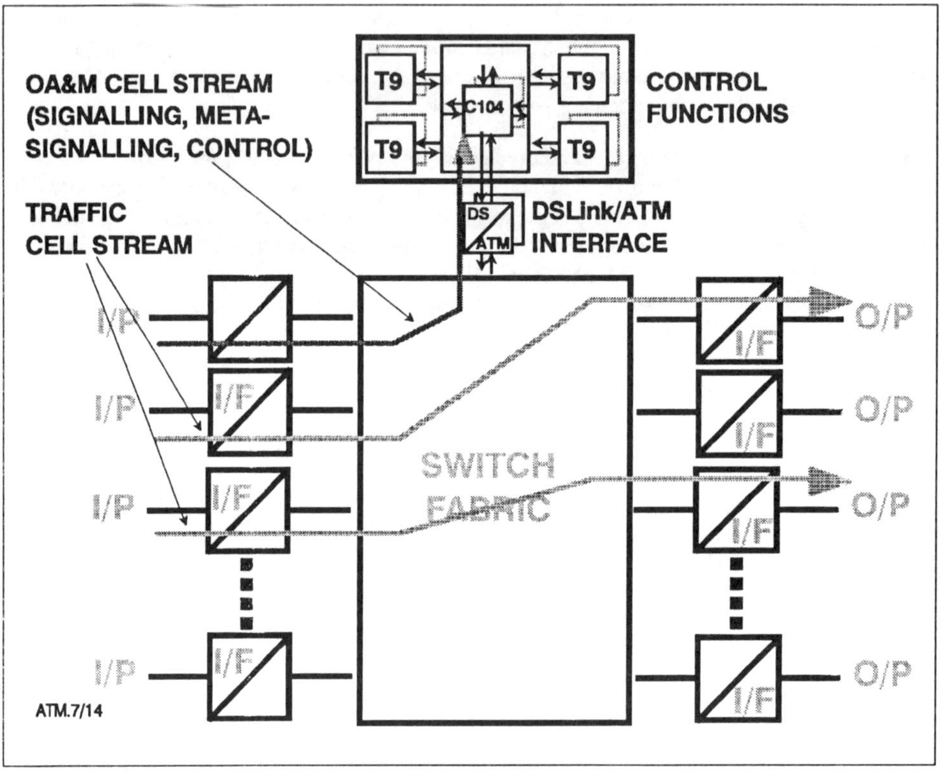

Figure 10.16 Interfacing to ATM Maintenance Traffic

Network Interfaces

ATM 'line cards' on a public switch need to be fast and reasonably intelligent. ATM cells arrive at the line card about every 3 us and header translation, policing functions and error checks all need to be made on each cell on the fly. It isn't possible to do all of this in software (certainly not economically) and a full hardware solution is expensive and inflexible. The combination of a fast, inexpensive micro like the transputer and some dedicated hardware functions is a good compromise that provides a balance between performance and flexibility. The context switch time of the T4 transputer of 600–950 ns means that some useful processing time is still available even if it is interrupted on every cell, although in most instances the hardware could be designed to interrupt the processor on exceptions only. It would be possible, for example, to perform the header translation operation using a direct table look–up, but use hardware for the HEC verification. However, the real value in having a fast but inexpensive micro on the card is the ability to track statistical information for use by the operations and maintenance functions, report faults and take recovery action where necessary.

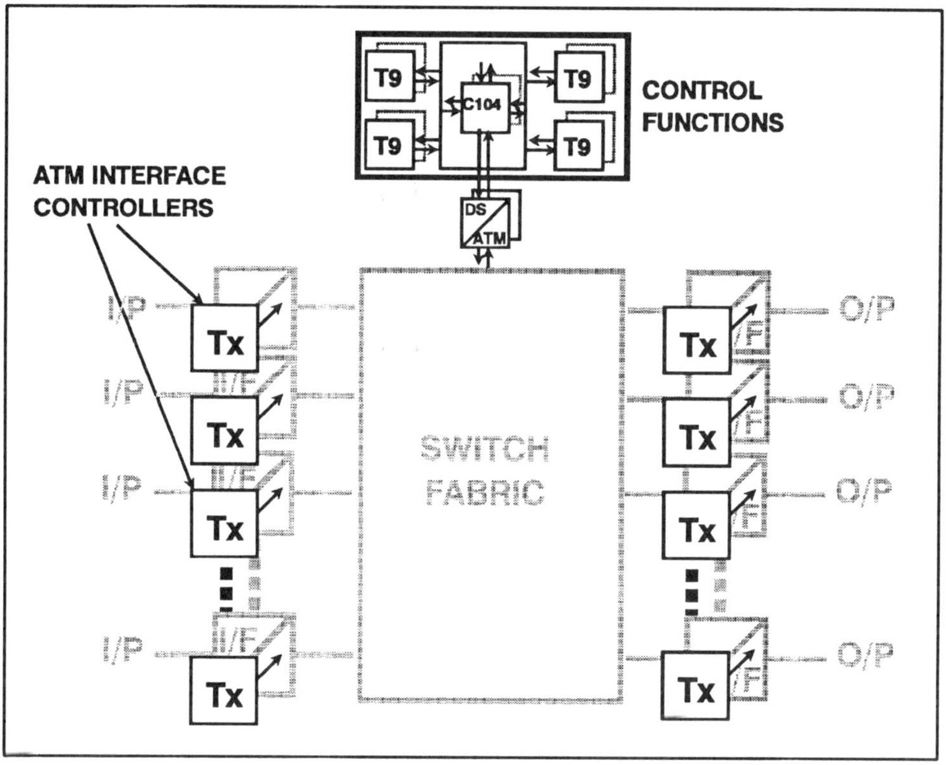

Figure 10.17 Transputers as Embedded ATM Interface Controllers

These line cards will typically consist of a hardware interface to the ATM/STM line, some logic to handle HEC checking, etc, an internal interface to the switching fabric and access to the transputer, via interrupts and memory. RAM will be required for program and data (translation look–up tables, etc). The basic idea is shown below in Figure 10.18. The dotted line indicates where future integration is possible using semi–custom technology.

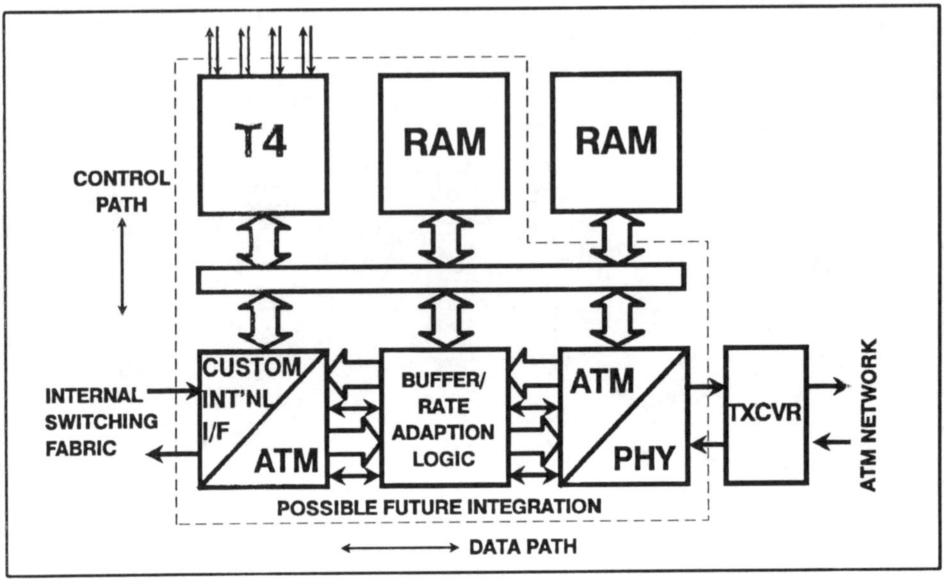

Figure 10.18 Possible ATM 'Line Card'

Such a line card is essentially a uniprocessor application, so the use of the transputer serial links for multiprocessing is not required. However, the serial links are very useful in other ways; for program download and debugging, test and diagnostics.

Putting software in ROM on the line card is undesirable from an upgrade and maintenance point of view. It would be better to be able to download code from some central point within the exchange. This could be achieved either by sending code via the switch fabric (possibly using a small boot ROM for cold–starts only) or by sending it down the transputer serial links (performing cold starts via the ***boot–from–link*** capability).

If the serial links are brought to the edge of the line card they can be used for testing in one of two ways. First, they can be used as part of the production test of the card by integrating them with an ATE system. Test code can be downloaded into the transputer (via the links) which runs entirely in the internal RAM. This code can exercise, at full speed, the external interfaces of the transputer as part of the test functions of the ATE system. Secondly, if the serial links are accessible while the card is in service in the exchange, it is a useful 'entry point' for a test engineer to interrogate the system. Better yet, if the serial links are internally interconnected, the switch control computer itself can use them to interrogate the system.

Switching Fabric

In a large public switch the data rates and requirements of the switching fabric are such that it is most likely to be built out of dedicated hardware and will in itself be a very complex subsystem. It is **not** appropriate to consider the use of the C104 for this fabric directly, nor to consider that the (non–maintenance) ATM traffic could be carried via transputers. However, like the network interfaces, there is considerable benefit in embedding processors within the hardware to provide intelligent control of the fabric. Maintenance and statistical measures can be provided, routing tables updated (if applicable) and the fabric monitored and reconfigured under fault or congestion conditions.

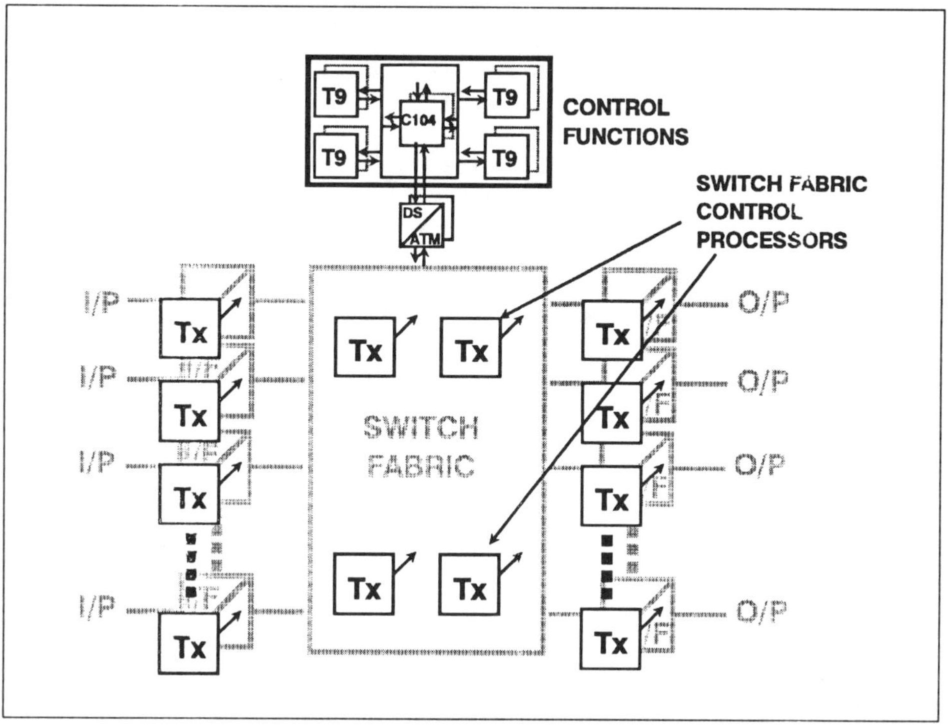

Figure 10.19 Embedded Switch Fabric Control

If desired, the links available from the control transputers can themselves be interconnected via a C104 network to provide a distributed control plane which is quite independent of the main ATM switch fabric.

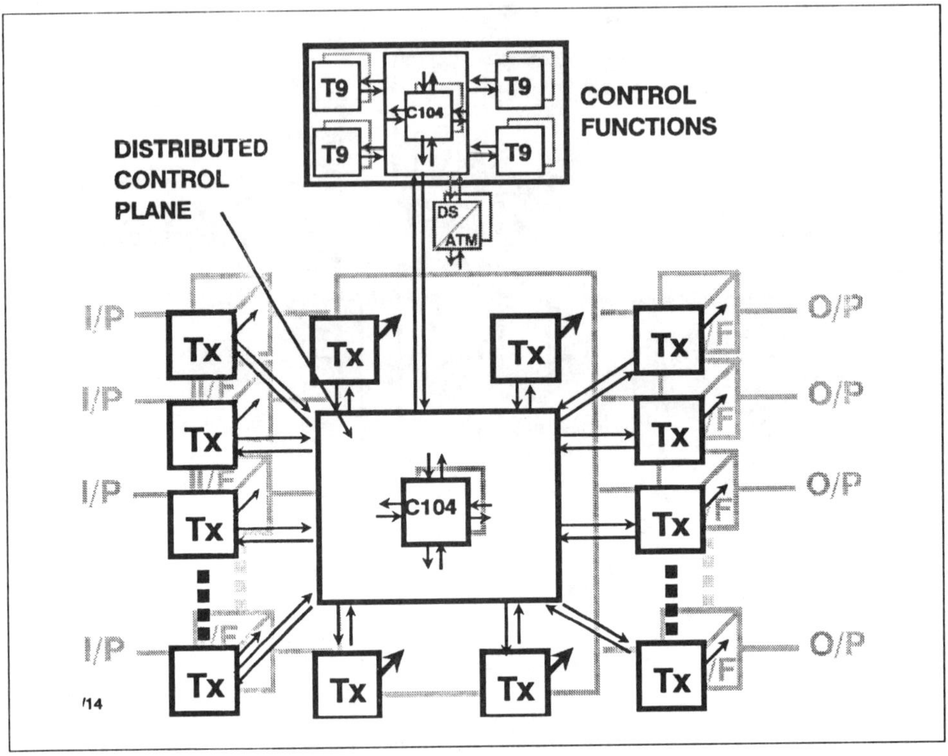

Figure 10.20 Distributed Control Plane

There are many other possibilities for mixed processor/hardware intelligent switching fabrics that remain to be investigated, and it is hoped that further ideas will be presented in future papers.

10.3.2 Private Switching Systems

All of the preceding discussion on public ATM switches also applies to private systems. However, there are some important differences:–

- the machines are not as large
- the bandwidth requirements are likely to be lower
- they are far more cost sensitive.

The nature of the ***Customer Premises Equipment (CPE)*** market is also likely to require much faster design cycles for the equipment, probably 1–2 years as the technology becomes established. The dynamics of the market are likely to place manufacturers under pressure to provide modular, flexible designs which can be upgraded, either in terms of performance, services or number of connections. Greater emphasis than in the past will be placed on network reliability, so the fault–tolerance aspects of the equipment will come under closer and closer scrutiny.

A Generic Private ATM Switch

The main difference from the point of view of applying the transputer architecture is that in private systems it is now possible to consider to use of the C104/DSlink as the basis for an inexpensive switching fabric. Many current 'campus' ATM switches have been derived from existing bridge/router technology and are based on shared bus interconnect schemes. These do not provide scaleable performance, as the common bus quickly becomes a bandwidth bottleneck. However, using the communications architecture of the transputer we can construct a scaleable ***Generic ATM Switch*** for private applications [6].

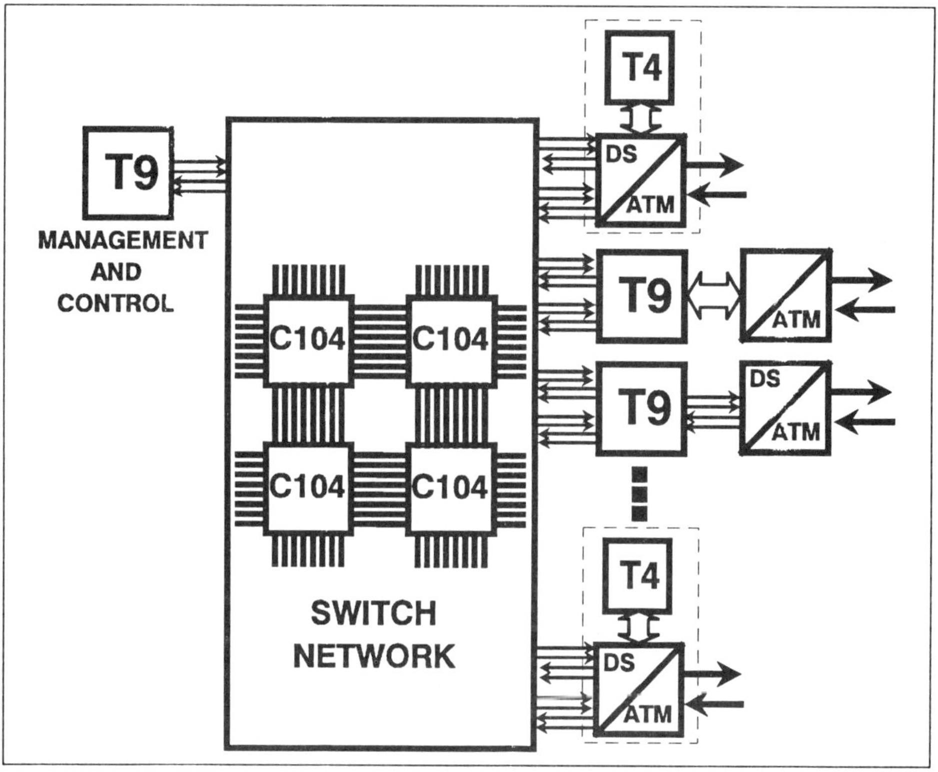

Figure 10.21 Generic Private ATM Switch

At its simplets, this switch may be considered to be a no more than a 'black box' multiprocessor computer running an ATM program. It has interfaces around the periphery to allow it to talk to the transmission network outside, but in essence it exploits the architectural similarity of message–passing/fast–packet–switching machines discussed earlier. Figure 10.21 shows illustrates several ways in which ATM interfaces can be built for such a switch, depending on cost/performance trade–offs required.

There are some important features of the DSLink/C104 communications architecture which apply in its use as a fast packet switch:–

- DSLinks are ***cheap***
- The C104 can be used to build ***Scaleable*** networks
- The in–built ***Flow Control*** mechanisms at the Token layer of the DSLink protocol mean that the fabric is ***Lossless***, that is, no data packets/cells are ever lost internally due to buffer overflow within the fabric itself. Buffer dimensioning/overflow issues are moved outside the switch fabric to the network interfaces at the edge.
- DSLinks may be ***Grouped*** to provide high bandwidth connections within the fabric. This can be used to:–
  - o minimise congestion for a given desired bandwidth

- o carry high-bandwidth traffic (for example, to 622 Mbit/s ATM).
- o provide redundant paths in the fabric for fault–tolerance reasons

- Link grouping on input can be used to avoid ***Head–Of–Line Blocking*** (congestion at the input to the switch fabric) by statistically increasing the chances of accessing the fabric (this is illustated in the previous diagram)
- Universal (randomised) Routing can be used to avoid the 'hot–spot' congestion which can sometimes occur with certain systematic traffic patterns (for a full examiniation of this see Chapter 7).
- Traffic of ***any packet length*** may be carried by the C104 fabric. Only traffic intended directly for the (current) T9000 needs to be segmented into 32–byte packets, although longer packets may affect the congestion characteristics of the fabric.

Since the C104 fabric is simply an interconnect mechanism for a multi–processor computer, it is trivial to add further processors to this architecture to perform the Management and Control functions. As many as necessary can be attached to the switching fabric and they can communicate with the 'line cards' directly using the same fabric.

Multiple switching planes could also be used to provide either:–

- Separate control/data traffic planes
- Different planes to handle different traffic priorities
- Redundant Fault–tolerance within the overall switching fabric

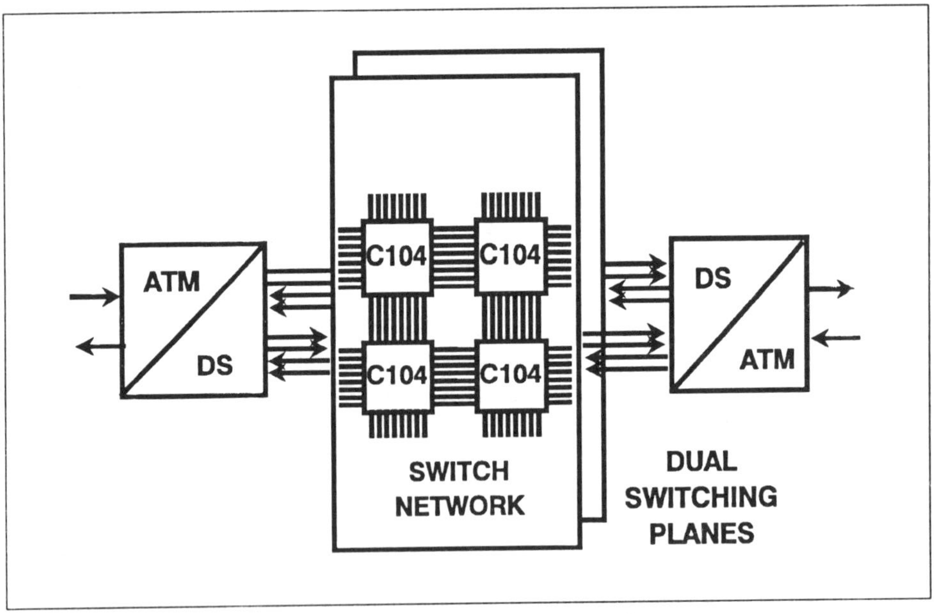

Figure 10.22 Multiple Switching Planes

Generic Internetworking Unit

One of the attractive aspects of this architecture is that interfaces to other networks, for example ethernet, token ring, FDDI, frame relay, etc., can be added very easily and so provide a ***Generic Internetworking*** architecture:–

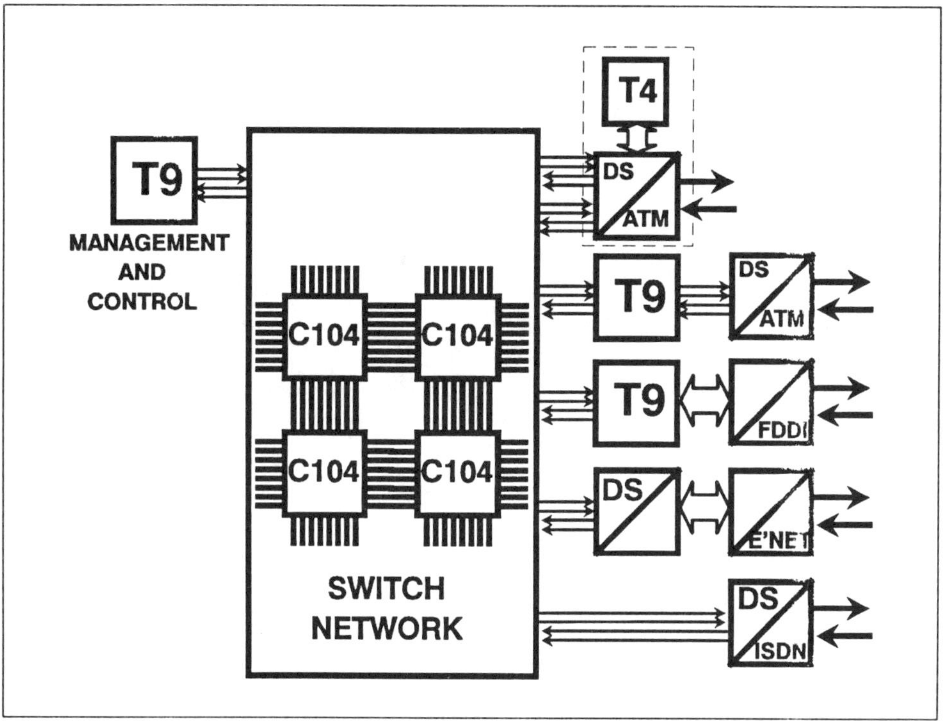

Figure 10.23 Generic Internetworking Architecture

Since we have simply built a computer (and one which is scaleable in performance at that) we can add additional computing performance where required. A "pool" of processors can be added to this system to provide high–performance protocol processing between the various networks. Indeed, "***Parallel Protocol Processing***" techniques may be applied. For example, a 'farm' of T9000 processors may be made available to perform frame–by–frame AAL conversion from ethernet to ATM.

ATM Concentrator

We can extend the internal serial interconnect beyond the confines of our 'black box' ATM computer to provide a low–cost, lower speed entry point from an ATM terminal into the network, a sort of broadband serial concentrator.. By using appropriate physical drivers, we can use the DSLinks directly to carry ATM cells asynchronously over local distances into the switch. Apart from cost advantages (since the DSLinks are inexpensive and the complication of full STM framing is not required) the DSLinks also provide an in–built ***flow–control mechanism*** which would provide an automatic means of 'throttling' the traffic flow back to the source. This is something which is currently missing from the ATM standards (GFC bits notwithstanding) and which could be added without requiring any alterations to the ATM standards by using the DSLinks. The availability of flow control to the source would considerably ease the buffering/performance design issues within the local switch as well as reducing the hardware/software costs associated with header policing on input.

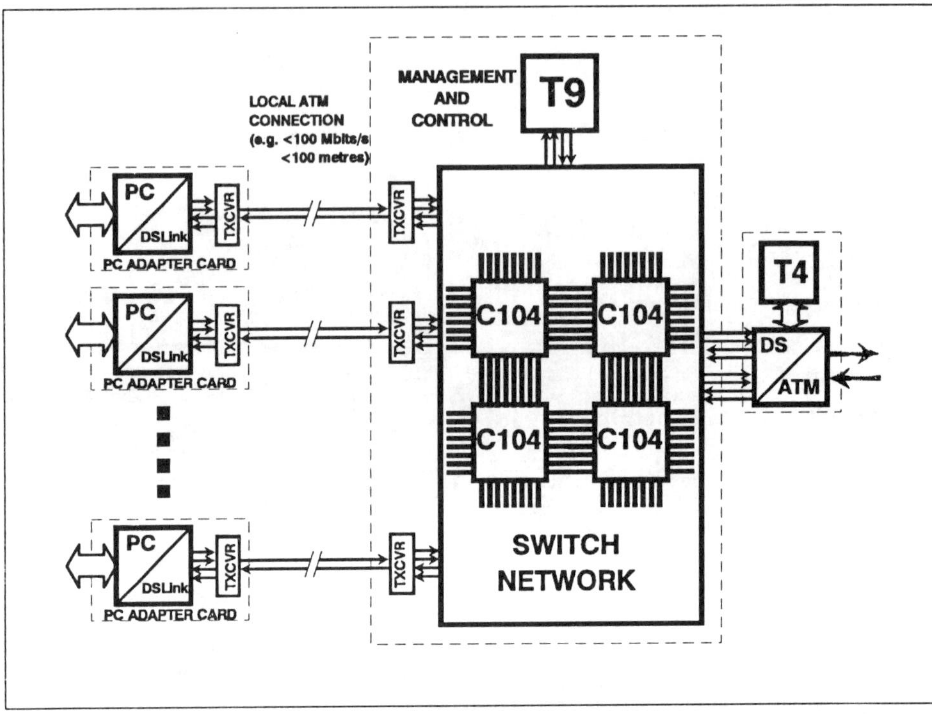

Figure 10.24 Low Cost ATM Concentrator

Issues and techniques for using DSLinks at a distance have been covered in Chapter 4 and such an interconnect could probably provide a very low cost entry–point into an ATM network for end user terminal equipment.

Private ATM Network Interface

The basic issue concerning the network interfaces for our private C104–based ATM switch is how to get ATM cells from the transmission system onto the DSLinks. Later in this Chapter a discussion is presented of the various ATM–DSlink mappings that are possible and the performance issues that arise. Here, we consider the functional aspects of such interfacing for the moment.

The ATM line card must perform:–

1 **Rate adaption:**

- The need for rate adaption will vary depending on the speed and number of DSLinks provided at the line interface. In any case, some FIFO buffering will be needed to cope with slight rate mismatches caused by cell header processing, etc. More exotic methods may be added if the DSlinks are to run at a substantially different rate to the ATM line. Rate adaption between the DSLink network and ATM can be provided by supporting one or more of the following:–
  - FIFO's to cope with traffic bursts
  - Inserting and deleting ATM 'Idle cells' (null cells for bandwidth padding) into a full–rate 155 Mbit/s ATM cell stream
  - Allowing the ATM clock rate to be varied (for example 1.5/2/34/45/155 Mbits/s. This may be allowable for private networks, but not on the public side).

2 **ATM Cell Header Processing:**

- HEC checking and generation for the ATM header
- Policing functions
- Header translation

3 **Packetisation:**

- Encapsulation of ATM cells into DSLink packets for transmission via the DSLinks to the switching/processor network

4 **STM/ATM Interfacing:**

- Interfacing the ATM cell output stream to the synchronous, framed transmission system, where required on the public network. This will typically be done in hardware.

5 **Management and Control:**

- HEC error counts
- Policing parameters/algorithms
- Translation table updates, etc

There is a hardware/software 'threshold' to be determined here which is the subject of further investigation. Some functions are obviously suited for hardware implementation, others for software. There is a grey area in between for functions such as policing and header translation, where the exact split between hardware and software could vary. A simple block diagram of a proposed network line card is given in the diagram below. The dotted line indicates where scope exists for a semi–custom integration of the card onto a single device in future.

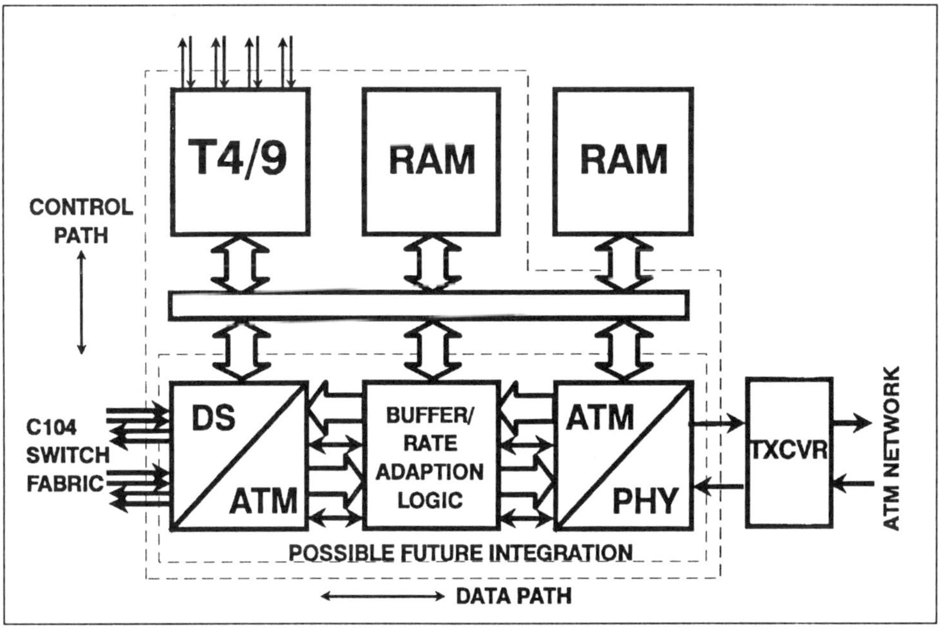

Figure 10.25 Simple ATM–DSLink Network Interface Card.

10.3.3 ATM Terminal Adapters

Current PC's and workstations typically provide a fairly 'dumb' interface to a network in the form of a simple card to memory map an ethernet or token ring chip set into the hosts address space.

All interfe control and higher layer protocol processing then falls on the host machine. It is becoming increasingly attractive to add a fairly powerful processor directly onto the network adapter cards in order to offload more of the protocol processing overhead from the host machine. As the bit–rate of the physical layer has increased in recent years, so the performance bottleneck in network access has moved to the higher layers of the protocol stack, which are more software/processor performance bound than the lower layers.

As 32–bit micro costs fall, we can apply many of the arguments for intelligent ATM line cards to an ATM Terminal Adapter and it becomes sensible to consider 'smart' rather than 'dumb' adapters. However, instead of providing an interface to a switching fabric (proprietary or DSLink) we need a shared memory interface to one of the standard PC/workstation buses. A terminal adapter will also have to run one or more of the AAL standards and this is another reason for having a fast micro on the card – the AAL layer can be quite complex, the standards are changing and it may be necessary to run multiple AAL's to support, say, multimedia applications. This tends to mitigate against a hardware–only implementation and, like the line card, a hardware/software 'threshold' needs to be determined. Also, an ATM terminal adapter may not need to run at a sustained 155 Mbits/s rate, so it may be possible to sacrifice some performance in order to save cost by using software functions. In the end, the application requirements will decide.

A simple block diagram for a shared–memory PC Adapter card is shown below. A suitable ATM/PHY interface chip is assumed (these are now becoming available) and some appropriate system interfacing logic to load and store ATM cells in memory. Again, the dotted line shows the integration possibilities.

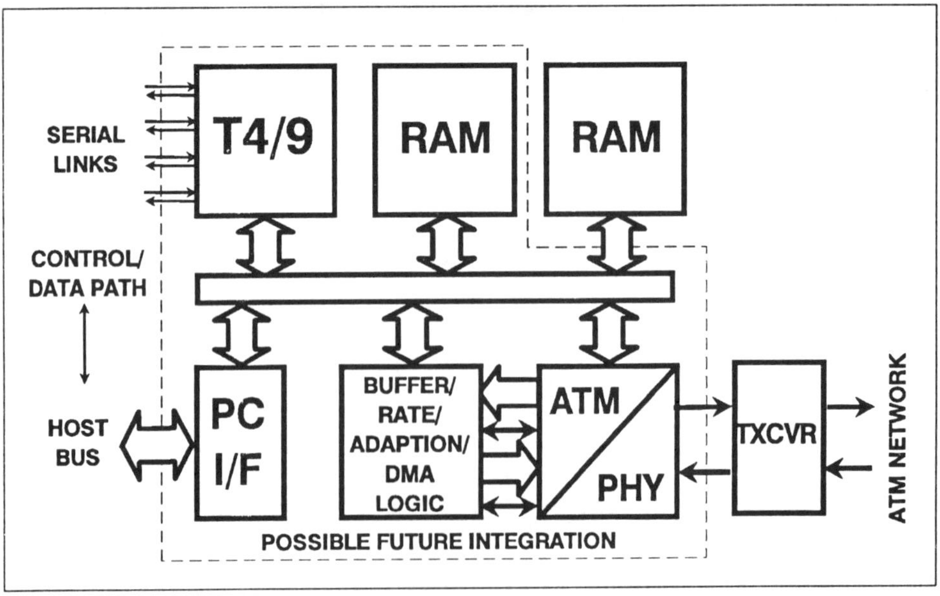

Figure 10.26 ATM–PC Terminal Adapter Card

In this example it is assumed that the AAL layer is handled in software by the transputer. A version of the AAL3 is currently being written for the transputer at INMOS in order to evalute performance trade–offs and whether a software–only implementation is fast enough for modest applications. Details of this will form the basis of future papers.

An alternative form of Terminal Adapter can be envisaged for the control functions in a public or private switch. If a T9000 or multiple T9000's are being used for the control then it may be necessary to interface the DSLinks of the T9000 straight to ATM. A relatively simple ASIC would be required in order to do this and which would perform the rate adaption, ATM cell timing, packetisation and HEC functions described above. All other functions could potentially be performed in software, since the Maintenance and Control cell rate is very low.

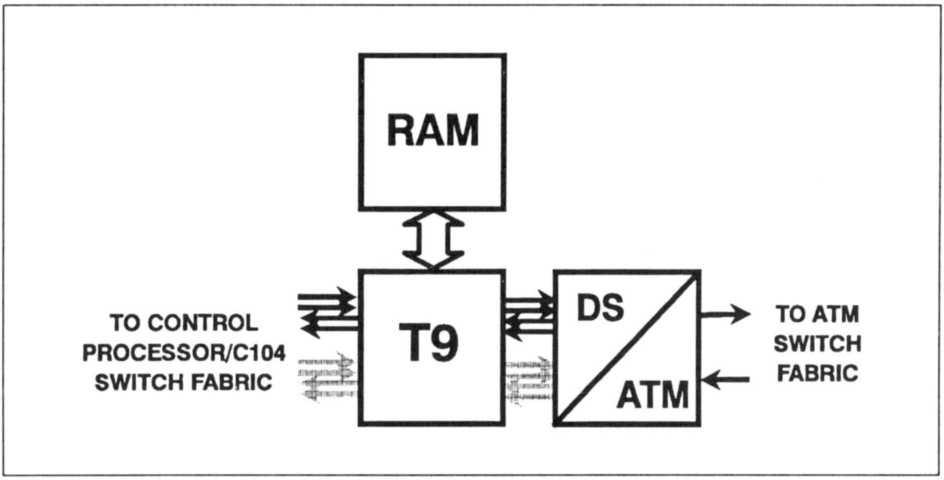

Figure 10.27 ATM–DSLink Adapter Application

10.4 Mapping ATM onto DS–Links

In this section the issues associated with carrying ATM traffic over a DSLink are considered. The DS–Link and the C104 do not require packets to be of a specified size, although the performance of the C104 chip has been optimised for use with small packets. This optimisation is for parameters such as the amount of buffering on the chip and so variations in packet length will affect the blocking characteristics, although no packet data will ever be lost because the buffers cannot actually overflow. The current T9000 implementation, however, does place a constraint on packet length, presently of 32–bytes, and this means there are at least two ways of carrying ATM cells using DS–Links, depending on whether a T9000 is in the data path or not (this constraint could disappear in later T9000 versions if commercial issues justify a variant).

10.4.1 ATM on a DS–Link

In this section we consider the raw bandwidth the DS–Link can provide in order to carry ATM cells. We can consider 2 possible ways of using the DS–Links:–

- In a 'T9000' system with a full T9000 packet layer protocol implemention i.e. acknowledged packets of 32–byte maximum length
- In a 'hardware' system (built with no T9000's in the data path) where the packet layer protocol implementation may be different, i.e. different packet length (and possibly without support for packet acknowledges).

A general performance model of the DS–Link is given in Chapter 6. This describes the data throughput of the DS–Link, given a specified message and packet size. It takes account of packet overheads, flow control and unidirectional and bidirectional use of the links. This basic model is extended here to show the throughput of the DS–Link carrying ATM cells, both with and without the full T9000 packet layer protocol. That is:–

- One ATM cell in single packet:–

  - One 53–byte packet on the DS–Link
- One ATM cell in 2 T9000 packets:–
  - One 32–byte data packet
  - One 21–byte data packet

Both unidirectional and bidirectional use of the DSlinks is considered in the folllowing analysis. Data rates and throughput are calculated for DS–Links operating at 100 and 200 Mbits/s to give a representative performance spread.

10.4.2 Unidirectional Link Use

Single 53–byte packet

Suppose that the 53–byte ATM cell is sent as a single 53–byte packet. The packet has a one byte packet header and a four bit packet terminator. The flow control overhead is rounded up to one flow–control token, of four bits, per ATM cell. The total number of bits transmitted is the sum of the data bits, the header bits, the terminator bits, and the flow control bits, with the DS–Link transferring a byte of information as 10 bits.

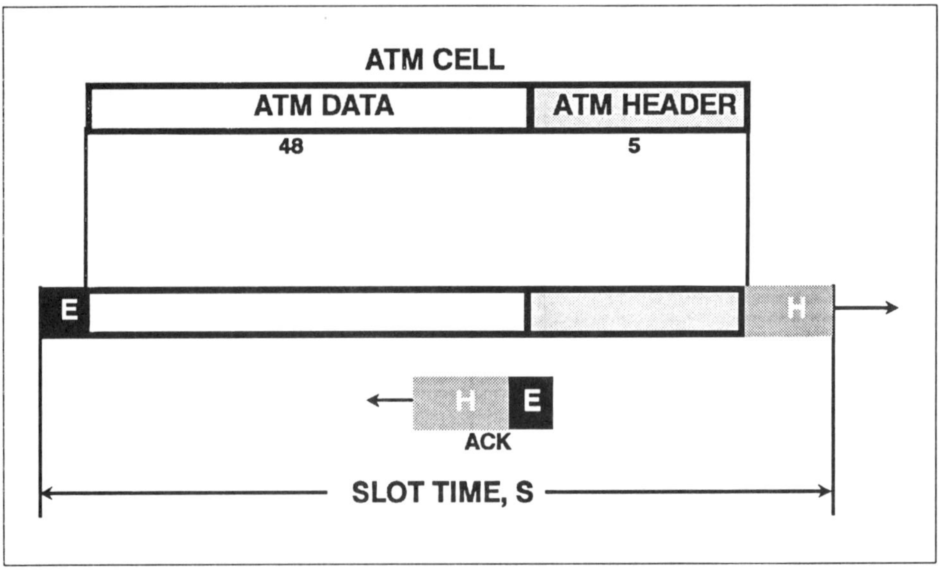

Figure 10.28 Unidirectional Single–Packet ATM–DSLink Mapping

The net bandwidth available for the ATM traffic in this configuration has been calculated and is presented in Table 10.1 at the end of this section.

Double Packets

Now suppose that the largest packet contains 32 bytes of data, as is the case for a T9000. The 53–byte ATM cell will be transmitted as 2 packets, one 32–bytes long, the other 21–bytes. Each packet has a one–byte header and a 4 bit terminator. Again the overhead of flow control tokens is less than one token per ATM cell, and is rounded up to one token per ATM cell. This is an extra 4 bits.

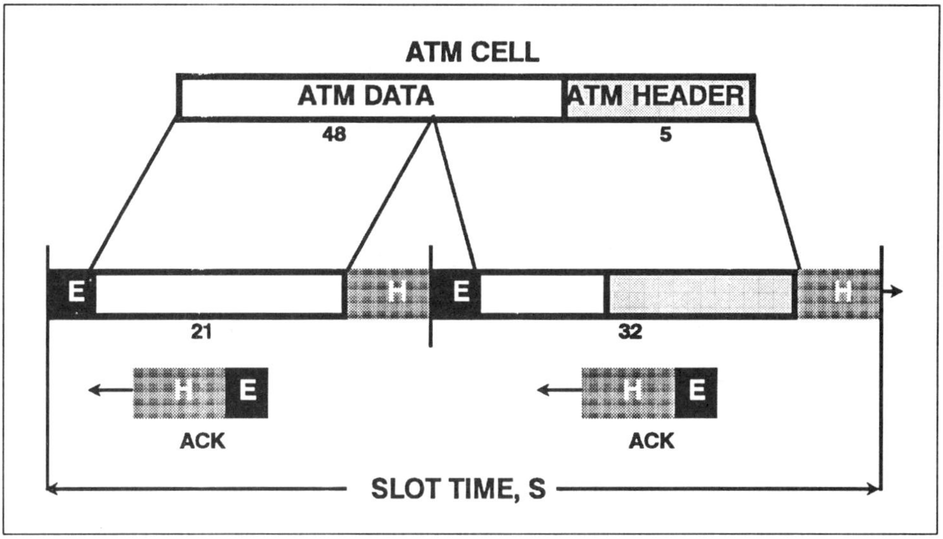

Figure 10.29 Unidirectional Double–packet ATM–DSLink Mapping

Again, the bandwidth results are presented in Table 10.1 at the end of this section.

10.4.3 Bidirectional Link Use

When considering the effect of bidirectional operation, it is assumed that the inbound link carries a similar traffic load to the outbound link.

For bidirectional link use, the link overheads are greater. The link carrying the outbound data must now carry the acknowledge packets for the data on the inbound link, and vice versa. An acknowledge packet consists of a one–byte packet header, and a four–bit packet terminator. The outbound link must also carry flow control information for the inbound link.

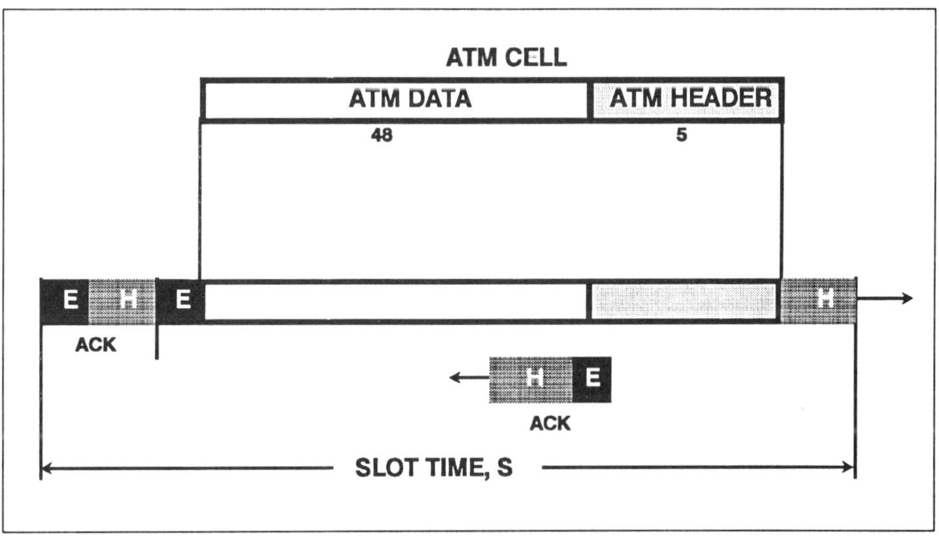

Figure 10.30 Bidirectional Single–Packet ATM–DSLink Mapping

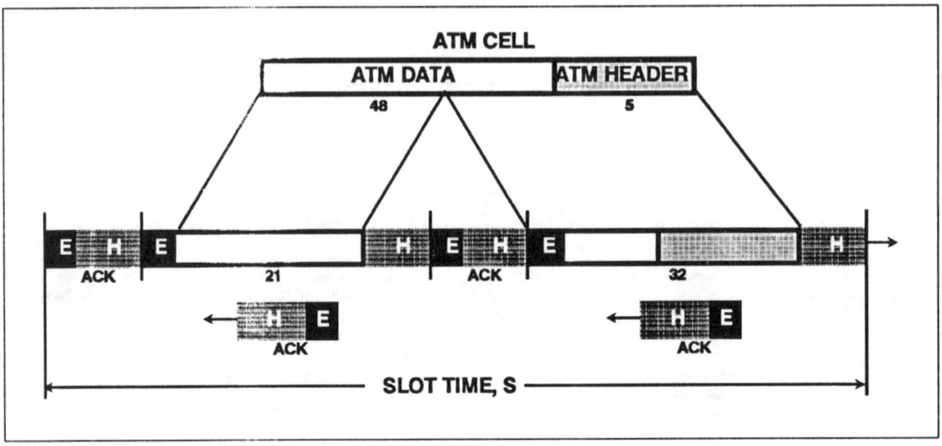

Figure 10.31 Bidirectional Double–Packet ATM–DSLink Mappings

The results are presented in Table 10.1.

10.4.4 Summary of DS–Link Results

The performance results of the above configurations are summarised in the following table. The bidirectional throughput is available simultaneously in both directions on the link.

Link Speed (Mbits/s)	Max Packet Size (bytes)	ATM Cell Throughput (Mbits/s)		ATM Cell Rate (Cells/s)	
		Unidirectional	Bidirectional	Unidirectional	Bidirectional
100	32	75	69	177k	163k
	53	77	72	182k	175k
200	32	150	138	354k	325k
	53	154	144	363k	340k

Table 10.1 ATM Performance over DSLinks

The results indicate that 100 Mbits/s links would be more than sufficient to carry ATM at T3 rates, say sub–50 Mbits/s, so could be used to provide an economical point–to–point local connection from a terminal into an ATM concentrator. The DSLink speed can be varied anywhere from 10 Mbits/s upwards in 5 Mbit/s increments, so the bit rate could be set appropriate to the physical medium used (only the transmit speed needs to be set, the receiver is asynchronous).

At 200 Mbits/s the DSLinks could provide a full–rate ATM connection unidirectionally and an only marginally slower (144 Mbit/s) bidirectional one, although if the traffic flow was asymmetrical this rate could be improved.

For interconnect use within a C104 switching fabric, single 200 Mbits/s DSLinks could provide full performance. However, traffic congestion issues would be far more significant than the marginal DSLink bandwidth, so the use of 2 grouped links would be beneficial for blocking/congestion reasons. Assuming the fabric could support at best only 80% per–link throughput (based on the simulation models for a hypercube with Universal routing), this would mean that any DSLink pair running at a bit–rate from about 120 Mbits/s up would support full–rate ATM traffic through the switch fabric (for a more complete treatise, see Chapter 7).

10.5 Conclusions

In this paper the use of the transputer architecture, its multiprocessing capability, its communication links and its packet switching interconnect capability, has been described in terms of applications within the emerging ATM systems market. Applications within public switching, private switching/internetworking and terminal adaption equipment have been considered. The main motivation in these discussions has been the convergence of architectures necessary to support message–passing multiprocessing computers (such as the transputer) and fast–packet switching systems (such as ATM). As each technology evolves and matures it is reasonable to expect an even closer relationship between the two.

A distinction has been drawn between the use of the transputer architecture in public versus private switching systems. In high–speed public switches the T9/C104 architecture is offered as a multiprocessing architecture for the *control plane* of the switch, with ATM traffic carried by a separate, dedicated (usually proprietary) switching fabric. Lower–speed private customer premises equipment has the potential to use a C104–based switching fabric directly, which could be used to carry both control **and** data traffic.

The use of transputers as uniprocessors, as opposed to multiprocessors, for building network termination and terminal adapter cards has also been considered. This area has a different set of constraints, mainly driven by cost, since ATM adapters and line cards will represent the volume end of the market. Silicon integration is the key, and the move to semi–custom techniques for transputer technology is an important factor here.

Given economical drivers for fibre and twisted pair, the DS-Links themselves offer their potential as a low–cost physical interconnect between terminals (PC's and workstations) and a local C104–based ATM concentrator. Transporting ATM cells and protocols across a DS-Link physical medium is very straightforward and provides relatively cheap office–scale connections with the added advantage of a built–in flow–control mechanism back to the source.

ATM is an exciting field and the transputer architecture offers a multitude of possibilities for building ATM systems. There are numerous combinations of ideas possible and no doubt in time many unique and interesting variations will emerge.

REFERENCES

[1] CCITT Draught Recommendations. Technical Reports I.150, I.321, I.327, I.361, I.362, I.363, I.413 and I.432. CCITT

[2] Martin De Prycker: 'Asynchronous Transfer Mode: Solution for Broadband–ISDN', Ellis Horwood, UK, 1991, ISBN 0–13–053513–3

[3] A.L.Fox and A.K.Joy: 'ATM–based Switching for the Integrated Broadband Network', Electronics and Communications Engineering Journal, 2(4), August 1990

[4] C. Hughes and A. Waters: 'Packet Power: B–ISDN and the Asynchronous Transfer Mode', IEE Review, October 1991

[5] Karl Anton Lutz: 'ATM Integrates Different Bit–Rates', Technical Report, Siemens AG, 1989

[6] C. Barnaby and N. Richards: 'A Generic Architecture for Private ATM Systems', Proceedings of the International Switching Symposium 1992, Session A8.4

11 An Enabling Infrastructure for a Distributed Multimedia Industry

11.1 Introduction

Advances in technology for telecommunication and new methods for handling media such as voice and video have made possible the creation of a new type of information system. Information systems have become an essential part of the modern world and they need to be made accessible to a very high proportion of the working population. It is therefore important to exploit all the means available for making the transfer of information effective and accurate. In fields such as computer assisted training, multimedia presentation is already well established as a tool for conveying complex ideas. So far, however, the application of multimedia solutions to information retrieval has been limited to single isolated systems, because the bulk of the information required has needed specialized storage techniques and has exceeded the capacity of present day network infrastructure. There do exist special purpose multimedia communication systems, such as those used for video–conferencing, but their cost and complexity separates them from the common mass of computing support.

If, however, *distributed* multimedia systems can be realized, many possibilities for enhanced communication and more effective access to information exist. The key to this new generation of information systems is *integration*, bringing the power of multimedia display to the users in their normal working environment and effectively breaking down many of the barriers implicit in geographical distribution. Now that significant computing power is available on the desktop, integration of voice and video is the next major step forward.

These integrated systems represent a very large market for components and for integrating expertise. It will probably be the largest single growth area for new IT applications over the next ten years. A coordinated set of components, conforming to a common architectural model with agreed interface standards, is required to allow the research and development of prototypes for new applications and to progress smoothly to the delivery of complete multimedia distributed systems. T9000 transputers, DS-Links and C104 routers provide a cost–effective platform on which this infrastructure can be built.

11.2 Network Requirements for Multimedia

11.2.1 Audio Signals

Digital techniques for encoding audio data are well established, and now lie at the heart of the telephone system and the domestic compact disc (CD) player. A number of encoding schemes exist, giving different trades–off between quality, bandwidth and processing costs. Audio support for applications can draw on these techniques and does not pose a major communications problem. However, use of conferencing involving large groups between sites may require a surprisingly high quality of microphone and speaker system to give an acceptable level of reproduction; such environments are often noisy and acoustically complex.

For many purposes, such as remote participation in seminars or discussions, telephone quality speech will be satisfactory. The normal standard for telephony is Pulse Coded Modulation (PCM) [1]. PCM speech will handle frequencies up to 3.4kHz, and is provided as 8k samples of 8bits each per second, or 64kbps. For long distance use, an almost equivalent service can be provided at 32kbps using the more sophisticated algorithm Adaptively Quantized and Differentially Encoded PCM (ADPCM) [2, 3, 4]. Modern algorithms such as Code Excited Linear Prediction (CELP) can even produce reasonable results at 4.8kbps, but there is no justification for such techniques when communicating with fixed locations on a single site.

Application of ADPCM at 64kbps yields a higher quality speech service, conveying frequencies of up to about 7kHz, which will cover almost all the current requirements. Where higher quality is required (for example, for music or comparative linguistics), one might as well opt directly for a single high quality service, using, for example, CD encoding, in about 0.34 Mbps (stereo). Again, compression will reduce this bandwidth significantly.

The simple PCM encoding is very robust against network loss. The compressed schemes are less so, and the economic balance is probably in favour of compressed data on a moderately reliable network.

11.2.2 Video Signals

The techniques for video transmission are evolving rapidly, with more powerful coding devices giving steadily lower bandwidth requirements. If uncompressed, video information is very bulky, running up to hundreds of Mbps if high quality color is required. Proposed high definition standards, already in use within studios, are even more demanding, with an increase of analogue bandwidth from 15 MHz to 70 MHz and a correspondingly increased digital requirement. However, the information to be sent is highly redundant and great savings can be achieved by compression. Indeed, compressed still images are sufficiently compact to be treated as normal computer data and this section restricts itself to moving images.

There is a significant design choice to be made here: is a moving image to be sent as a sequence of independent still images, or as a progressive representation in which the similarity of successive images is exploited? The latter offers considerably higher compression factors, particularly when motion of objects in the image is detected and exploited. However, this high compression rate is at the expense of greatly increased complexity, particularly if access to the video is to start at arbitrary points.

There are at present three major video compression standards: JPEG [5, 6], MPEG [7, 8] and the CCITT Recommendation H.261 [9, 10].

JPEG (produced by the Joint Photographic Experts Group – an ISO/CCITT committee) provides compression of single images, with compression factors of between 10 and 30, depending on the quality required. There are hardware implementations of JPEG using large scale integration, which give good perceived quality at normal video rates (25 frames per second). A typical PC[24]–based JPEG card costs about £2,000 at present.

MPEG (produced by the corresponding committee for moving pictures) and H.261 (from CCITT) both exploit interframe coding and can achieve compression ratios of up to 100 or better, depending on the programme material (static material is obviously much more suitable for compression, but quite small scale movements have a large effect on the compression efficiency). However, current implementations are much more complex and expensive, and interfaces with filing systems require research. Current H.261 Codecs cost about £20,000, but much cheaper VLSI implementations are under development.

There also exist other highly effective compression schemes, such as that used in DVI (Digital Video Interactive [11] – a format from Intel) and various fractal–based proposals. However, these suffer from the disadvantage of requiring an expensive compression phase which is slower than real time, ruling them out for many of the intended network applications.

24. PC is a trademark of the IBM Corporation.

All the above encoding techniques have parameters which allow the selection of various qualities of service, the primary parameters being number of points in the image, frame rate and degree of information discarded during encoding. These parameters allow the cost trades–off to be adjusted to meet different quality requirements, so that higher compression might be applied in a general interview, say, than a detailed fine art study. At the bottom end of the range of qualities, there is some competition from rough video provided entirely by software on existing platforms, such as the PC or the Macintosh (Quicktime[25]), but this low quality material is not a serious competitor for most purposes.

In summary, the most flexible and cost effective technology currently available is that based on motion JPEG. This requires between 2 and 5 Mbps to achieve good quality video from most programme material, although up to 15 Mbps may be needed for guaranteed studio quality. The compressed material is not tolerant of errors, the only effective recovery mechanisms being frame discard and repetition of the previous frame. Future system development based on MPEG or its relatives will offer higher compression ratios at similar costs within five years, but will require low error rate channels.

11.2.3 Performance

Multimedia systems need to be able to capture and present a wide range of media. Some of the media are very bulky, and so present a considerable challenge to network and operating system designers. The most demanding requirements come from isochronous media, such as audio and video, since they have fixed timing deadlines.

The network requirements can be characterized in terms of the necessary bandwidth and end–to–end delay, and by the acceptable variation, or jitter, in the delay. Media transmitted in their raw form also show different tolerance to loss of data samples, but as increasing use is made of powerful compression techniques, data loss becomes correspondingly less acceptable.

To a considerable extent, the demands can be matched to the available network resources by adjusting the quality of reproduction offered. Both audio and video remain usable for many applications through a wide range of qualities. Low bandwidth allows understanding, but higher bandwidth increases quality, pleasure and impact of the presentation. The particular demands from a range of media are summarized in Table 11.1.

25. Macintosh and Quicktime are trademarks of Apple Corp.

Table 11.1 Bandwidth Requirements

Medium	sample size (bytes)	repetition rate/ duration	uncompressed rate	compressed rate
Text Page (A4)	5k	1 sec	40k bps	10k bps
Colour image (640 x 512 pixel)	320k	3 sec	800k bps	90kbps
Audio (3.4kHz)	1	8k/sec	64k bps	4.8k bps
Audio (7 kHz)	1.5	16k/sec	200k bps	64k bps
Video (high resolution)	320k	25/sec	65M bps	7.5M bps
Video (low resolution)	20k	15/sec	2.5M bps	200k bps
Videophone (static subject)	20k	15/sec	2.5M bps	64k bps

11.3 Integration and Scaling

In addition to the requirements of the media themselves, the need to integrate them into a single system must be considered. In multimedia applications, presentation of a number of different media needs to be coordinated. Typically, this implies a need for some form of general distributed platform, providing efficient and flexible communication for control and synchronization mechanisms. Modern object–based platforms can meet these requirements in a flexible manner.

Until recently, most multimedia computer systems were constructed on the basis of computer control of essentially analogue systems. For example, interactive video systems generally consisted of analogue videodisk equipment controlled by, and sharing display facilities with, a personal computer. Such analogue systems do not scale well. Analogue video networks are difficult to maintain, manage, and share between different applications.

Developments in the technology available have now made possible the construction of equivalent digital networks, and digitally–based multimedia systems can now be constructed. This opens up the possibility of multi–service networks (both local and wide area) which can convey a range of multimedia information types on a single network, giving economies of scale, flexibility and ease of management. In this environment, site–wide distribution of audio and video information, integrated with traditional computer data and control, becomes a realistic proposition.

11.4 Directions in networking technology

From the computer user's perspective, network developments over the past ten years have been dominated by the increasing coverage and performance of the local area network; there now need be few barriers to the sharing of text, data and program within a site. For the more demanding media, particularly for video, current networks can support single user demonstrations, but not the activities of a realistically sized user community.

For example, the bandwidth requirements listed in Table 11.1 indicate that a number of existing technologies would be able to support the requirements of a single multimedia station (e.g. servicing a small office or conference room). Such requirements probably do not exceed 20 Mbps each way in total and current ring and bus technologies (such as Fibre Distributed Digital Interface (FDDI) [12], FDDI–II and Distributed Queue Dual Bus (DQDB)) all have the necessary raw capacity – although the capabilities of their routers and the ability to reserve bandwidth are more questionable.

In reality, however, a building (or group of buildings) will require the parallel operation of many such stations. The University of Kent, for example, has some 125 teaching rooms registered for AVA provision. Even if only 20% of these were using multimedia at one time, the total bandwidth requirement would be almost a Gigabit per second, beyond the capabilities of any of the current ring or bus networks. Something with an order of magnitude greater capacity is needed.

Fortunately, a quiet revolution has been taking place in the wide area networks, exploiting the power of fibre optic transmission and providing the basis for a telecommunication infrastructure of enormous capacity. The aim is to produce a truly integrated network that is able to carry all types of traffic, from the isochronous data of digital voice and video to the bursty packet traffic produced by computer applications, using a single underlying network technology.

The approach being taken is based technically on the CCITT Recommendations for the so–called Asynchronous Transfer Mode and the resulting networks are called ATM networks. They use the efficient switching of small fixed–size (53 byte) packets to provide a combination of high speed to any individual user and simultaneous service to large numbers of customers. The small fixed–size packets are called cells and their use facilitates the multiplexing of traffic that is sensitive to delay jitter with traffic that is not. ATM systems designed for telephony are expected to operate at speeds of 155Mbps and above. This implies a packet switching rate of over a quarter of a million packets per second from each link into a single switch. The distribution of the switching function means that the total switching and transmission capacity is not limited to that of any individual link or switch; the system scales up naturally like the telephone system and does not suffer from size limits like a LAN.

11.5 Convergence of Applications, Communications and Parallel Processing

11.5.1 Multimedia and ATM

The capabilities of the new ATM networks are well matched to the requirements of distributed multimedia systems. ATM networks operate at a high enough speed to support all the types of information wanted, and give the flexibility needed to share information between many users.

Recent advances in compression technology also affect the situation by reducing the peak requirements of audio and video to the point where they can be handled and stored in conventional desktop systems. The ATM networks cope well with the varying load presented by compressed data streams.

The future therefore seems clear:

- there will be an increasing penetration of ATM technology as the networking solution of choice, both in the wide area and as the local infrastructure;
- there will be a major expansion in the use of multimedia technologies for integrated communication and information retrieval both within and between organizations.

As an example, the UK academic sector has recently initiated the SuperJanet project to provide a new generation of wide area infrastructure capable of supporting multimedia applications, and a number of multimedia research groups are planning to make use of it to extend their local facilities.

11.5.2 ATM on your Desk

However, the currently available ATM equipment is primarily aimed at the telecommunication carriers. The real benefits of an integrated ATM network become apparent when the flexibility of the mixture of ATM based services is delivered to the end user's desk [14]. This implies a need for local area ATM solutions, and for ATM compatible end user equipment.

In the multimedia architecture described in this chapter, the further step of using ATM cells for communication within the workstation is proposed. Multimedia activities produce a great deal of movement of data and the same considerations regarding the transmission and switching of this data pertain within the workstation as in the local and wide area. It therefore seems sensible that a similar solution should be applied.

At present, however, ATM switches on offer commercially are disappointingly expensive. Prices of £75,000 for a small switch are typical and this renders – for the time being – their use uneconomic for supporting the above scenario.

11.5.3 Transputers and ATM

Starting from the need for the flexible interconnection of parallel processing elements that is required to produce parallel computers, a style of architecture has emerged in which separate processing elements are interconnected by communication links. Some of these designs are packet based, and the best known is the INMOS transputer. In the T9000 range of transputers, INMOS have chosen a style of communication which is similar both in general philosophy and in technical capability to the ATM networks. The rationale behind this decision is broadly similar to that which led the CCITT to choose ATM for the Broadband Integrated Services Digital Network (B–ISDN).

The INMOS choice has the happy consequence that it will be possible to construct systems which, with a minor amount of technical 'glue' to make the necessary detailed adaptations, carries the same high level view of ATM based communication from the wide area into the local processing component within multimedia devices. Integrated multimedia networking becomes possible at reasonable cost (with the cost of an ATM switch being reduced by at least one order of magnitude, probably more).

11.5.4 Convergence ... and an Opportunity

This three–way convergence of application requirements, telecommunications standards and parallel processing technology represents a real opportunity for progress; all the important pieces are becoming available now (1993). It is therefore the right time to seek to define standards so that the necessary components can come together from different vendors to form a single family of compatible products.

11.6 A Multimedia Industry – the Need for Standard Interfaces

The development of multimedia applications depends on the availability of suitable products. Broadly based applications can only be constructed easily if the necessary components are offered by a number of suppliers in a form which is simple to integrate and to configure to meet the specific needs of the user. The detail of the configurations needed on a desktop and in a meeting room will be different; so will the configurations needed by the author of training material and users of that material.

The solution to this problem lies in a modular approach, based on the definition of a small set of key interfaces between components. The interfaces are crucial because the exact packaging of functions and the power of the components themselves will evolve as the technologies develop. The interfaces between components, however, are relatively stable and allow the construction of systems using components from different sources and with different levels of technical sophistication.

Some interfaces need to be common to all components; others are more specialized. Universal interfaces are needed for the control and management of the components – particularly for:

- the control of communication and information storage and retrieval, so that common tools and common user paradigms can be applied across the full range of media;
- those enquiry functions which allow each component to determine the capabilities of any others with which it interacts and so take account of the changes and limitations of the configuration in which it is placed.

At a more specific level, agreed interfaces are needed for each of the media types so that, for example, all audio or all video components can interwork successfully.

To a large extent, these interfaces can be based on internationally accepted standards, but in some of the areas being addressed such standards do not yet exist, or the way they are to be combined is not fully defined. There is an urgent need, therefore, for the involvement of a broad range of potential component suppliers and system or application developers. What is required is the minimum of technical work for the definition of a profile for multimedia use of ATM standards. It would provide both an architectural framework which identifies the interfaces needed and a portfolio of references to related interface specifications covering the full range of multimedia requirements.

The agreement by the Industry to such a profile would provide a firm basis for the development of new applications using distributed multimedia systems and would be a major input of practical experience into future formal standardization.

11.7 Outline of a Multimedia Architecture

11.7.1 Components, Stations and Sites

The basic building block of the architecture is the 'component'. Components will either handle a piece of equipment (such as a microphone, video camera, display, disk, ...) and/or carry out a function such as encryption or compression. Each component will contain one or more processors. The most important feature of the architecture is that the components will communicate with each other in a single universal fashion by the transmission and reception of ATM cells. ATM cells will be used to carry the media, to carry control information and to carry signalling information (i.e. the commands for organizing the pattern of interconnection between the components). Components are viewed under this architecture as atomic devices – i.e. communication mechanisms *within* a multi–processor component are specific for that component and would not follow ATM standards.

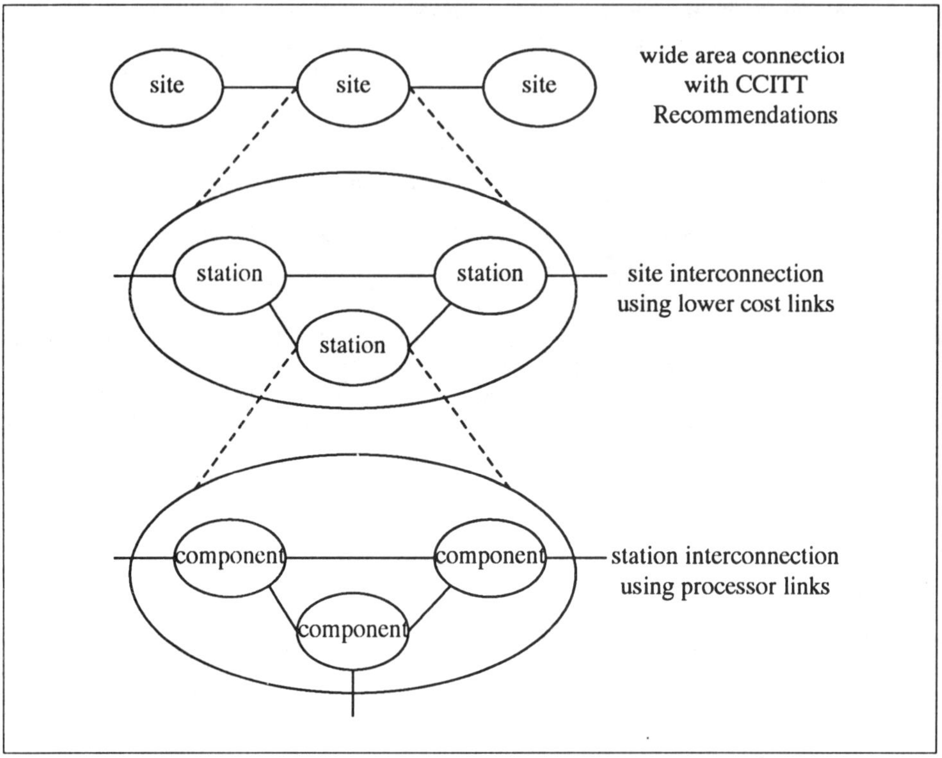

Figure 11.1 Hierarchy of interconnections

Three regimes of ATM interconnection between components are envisaged (see Figure 11.1). The first regime is that of a 'station'. A station is a set of one or more components that can be considered to act together – i.e. they are either all switched–on or all switched–off, and the transmission of cells between them can be considered to be error–free. The second regime is the local interconnection of stations – a 'site'. This is a regime in which transmission delays will be short, and error–rates will normally be very low. It must cope with stations varying their status between inactive and active. Such a regime may use synchronous or asynchronous transmission. The third regime is that of the 'wide–area', in which it is assumed that the full application of CCITT standards will be the norm – i.e. quality of service, policing, tariffing, etc.. In this regime, synchronous transmission will be used. Within all three regimes there will be components that are used for switching cells.

The architecture has three main areas that require agreement on standardization:

- specifications of how different types of media are to be carried in cells. As far as possible this will follow international standards – i.e. use of ATM adaptation layer, use of standard encoding for voice (CCITT G.series Recommendations) and video (JPEG, MPEG, H.261), etc.;

- specifications of how components are to be controlled. This will have two parts: a general scheme of control and realization of this scheme for particular components;

- specifications of the manner in which signalling is to be carried out – i.e. how connections are to be created and removed within the three ATM regimes. Clearly in the wide–area regime this will be determined by outside authority.

11.7.2 Example Components

The hardware requirements to support audio and video revolve around a family of interfacing components delivering and controlling the media. In each case, the information flows from the network as a stream of ATM cells. The interface decodes and decompresses the information, converts it to analogue form and passes it to the display device or audio system – see Figure 11.2. For input devices, the process is reversed.

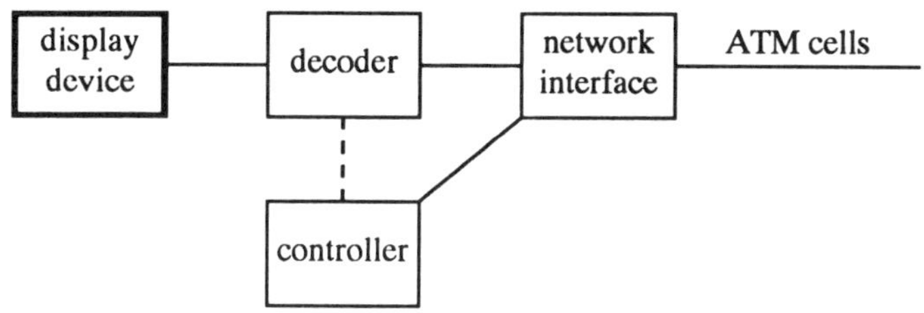

Figure 11.2 A Component

The display (or capture) can be performed by connecting existing audio–visual devices, although more integrated solutions will appear as time goes by. The controller element can be a specialization of a single design for the whole family, but the decoder (or encoder) is specific to the medium being supported. The network interface can be expected to have two variants: one for direct connection as a station to the site network for use by isolated devices and a largely vestigial one for use within a station for connecting the different components supporting multiple media.

The following components are considered to be basic to the architecture:

- video capture (still and full motion) including compression;
- display including decompression and input device handling (keyboard, mouse, etc.);
- audio input and output (including compression);
- bulk media storage;
- encryption;
- switching both within a station and in the local area;
- access to other networks and other communications technologies.

This is an initial list of areas to be covered and it will grow as the industry develops. The central component is a very small ATM switch (on a single card) to integrate a local cluster into a station – a single C104 router and a minimal controlling processor may be all that is required.

11.7.3 Example Station

Using the components outlined above, a suitable multimedia station for an office or conference room can be constructed from modular components. The size of the modules will be determined largely on economic grounds, relating to processing costs. For example, it may be attractive to provide both audio input and output in a single card, but to separate video input from output.

A typical configuration would always provide a hardened network interface for the station as a whole, an enclosure and power supply, together with a small integrating switch. The switch would be used by components specific for that station (e.g. a full–duplex audio card, a video input card, a video output card and a control terminal interface, also providing OHP tablet output) to share a single outgoing ATM link to the site multiservices network – see Figure 11.3.

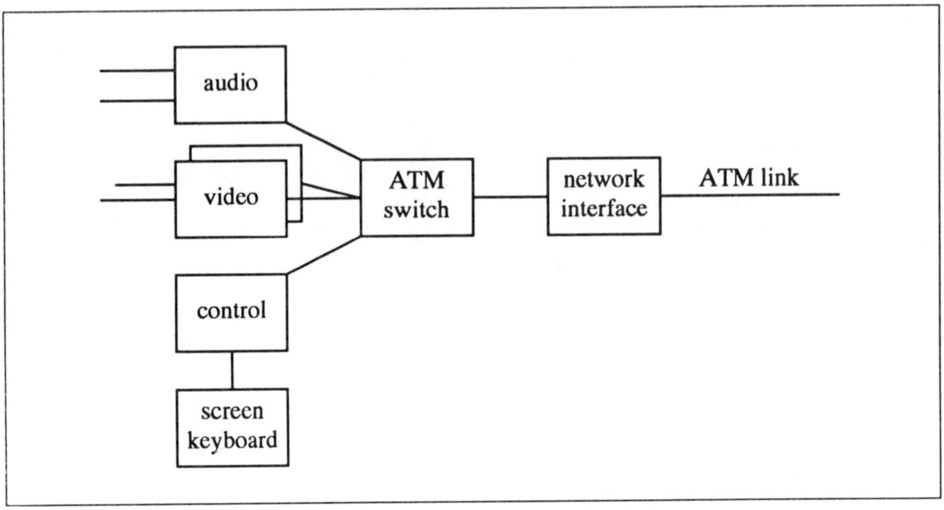

Figure 11.3 A Station

11.7.4 Example Site

The campus of the University of Kent at Canterbury provides a typical 'site' for such a multiservice network. Geographically, it is a compact single area with most of the major teaching buildings falling within a circle of 500m radius. There are some outlying locations, but none are more than 2 Km from the centre. The campus is crossed by public roads, but the University has ducting under them.

Fibre optic links have been installed throughout the campus and services are being migrated onto them. The new links provide for an FDDI–based backbone and a number of distribution links to the Ethernet segments in individual buildings. Provision varies from 12 fibres per link in the central ring to 8 or 4 fibres on the distribution spurs. The central part of the campus, together with the fibre network, is shown in Figure 11.4.

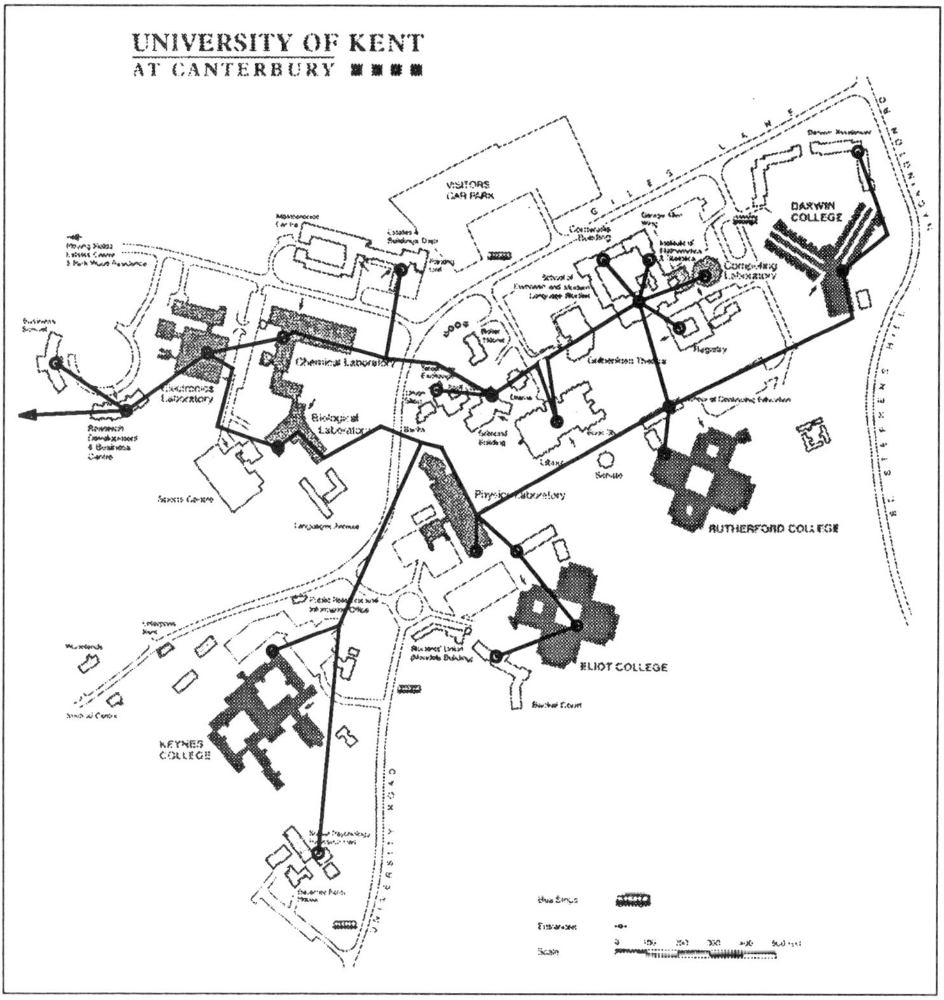

Figure 11.4 The Fibre Routes at UKC

These optic fibres (or, at least, the physical channels in which they are laid) would form the backbone for a 'site' ATM network – once the low–cost distributed multimedia industry described in this chapter and enabled by T9000/DS–link/router technology comes into place. The logical structure of a possible (initial) UKC site is shown in Figure 11.5.

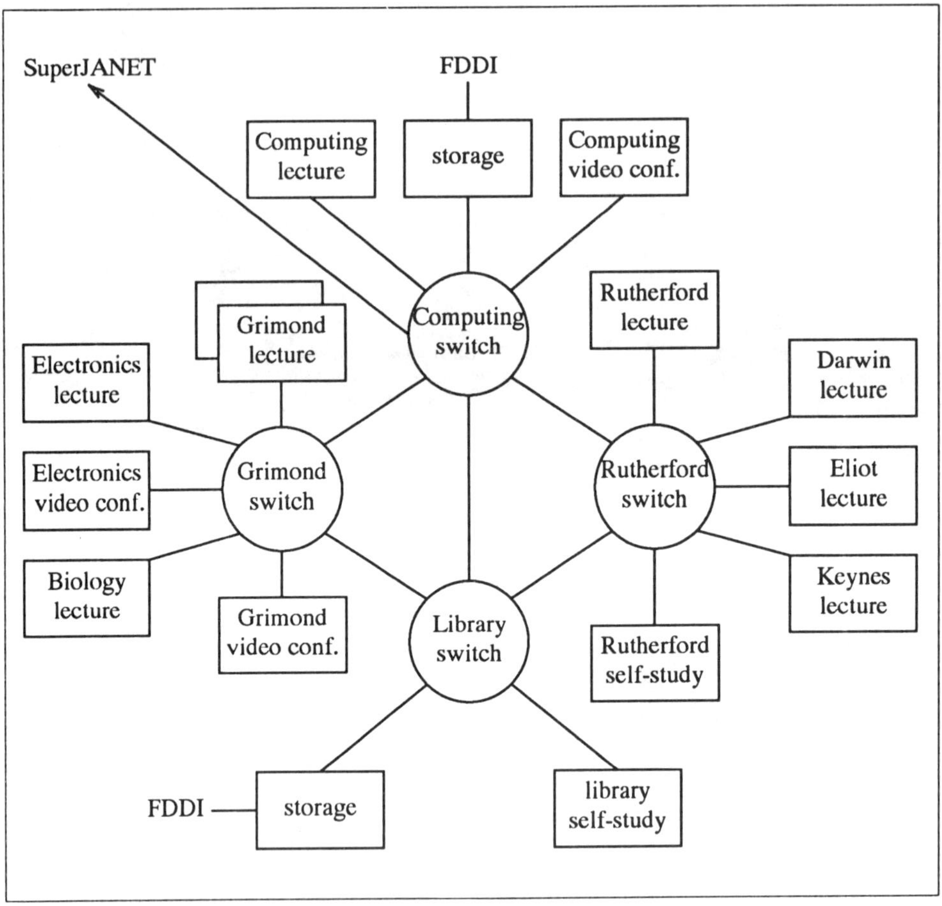

Figure 11.5 A Site

11.8 Levels of conformance

Combination of modular components can be viewed at a number of different levels. The more detailed the specification used, the lower the integration cost, but the more limited the field of application. It can therefore be worthwhile to identify different levels of conformance to the interface specifications.

One can distinguish:

- an abstract statement of the media types, the processing components and the interfaces and data flows between them. It is the essential minimum set of agreements necessary for system integration to be possible, since it includes the agreements on data types and interpretations needed to have a common understanding of how to process and represent the various media. However, it does not commit an implementor to any particular communication technology or physical packaging. Using the terminology of the international standards for Open Distributed Processing (ODP) [13], this corresponds to ODP 'information and computational specifications';
- a statement of how the various interfaces are to be realized, giving the detailed constraints on implementation in a particular environment. This corresponds to ODP

'engineering and technology specifications'. Several different solutions may be needed to support different kinds of integration. Of particular importance are solutions to:

- *network interconnection*: specifying the formats and protocols that are to apply between two systems on a wire or a fibre. This form of specification does not constrain the internal structure of the systems and is the minimum requirement for the construction of distributed applications;
- *physical packaging*: specifying the form and interconnection requirements for a system component at, for example, the card level. Widely accepted standards for particular computer families, such as the format for PC cards and buses fall into this category;
- *software interfaces*: specifying the interface to device drivers and presentation management systems at a language level. These specifications should be obtained directly by selection from established industry practice, rather than creation of new specifications. Support for specific software environments such as MS–DOS/ Windows[26] or UNIX/X–Windows[27] falls into this category.

This framework then allows integration to take place at many different levels, but within this structure all players are expected to conform to the abstract specifications. All suppliers of communication components are expected to conform to one of the agreed communication specifications. All suppliers of, for example, PC cards are expected to conform to the specifications for the physical, bus and device driver specifications for the machine range. A supplier of a video display card with an integral network interface might need to conform both to the networking and the subsystem interfaces (see Figure 11.6).

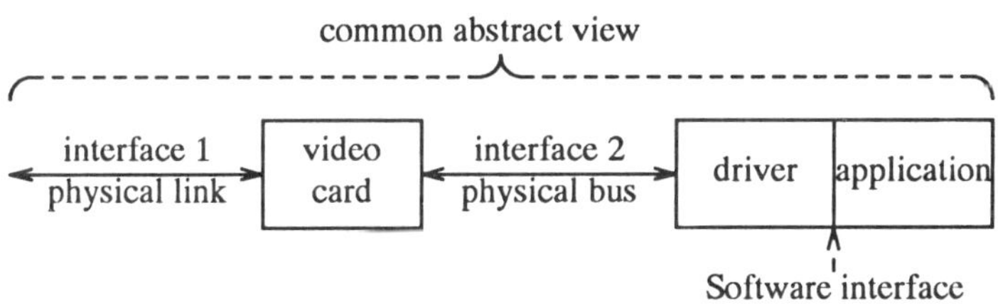

Figure 11.6 Possible conformance points

11.9 Building stations from components

As well as the abstract standard for the architecture, hardware standards such as methods of transmission of cells, particularly within the station, board standards, etc. have to be specified for the concrete realization of components.

For the transmission of cells within a station there are broadly two possibilities: use of a standard bus or use of point–to–point links in conjunction with routing between components. Use of a bus has two major disadvantages. First, it would put a non–scalable resource at the centre of the station, which would, moreover, be a shared resource whose properties would have to be taken into account when various combinations of components are integrated together in a station. Second, there are a large number of possible bus architectures that might be chosen.

Links do not suffer from these disadvantages; they are scalable and they exploit the same interconnection model between components as has already proved effective at higher levels (between stations and between sites). The approach taken is thus logically coherent.

26. MS–DOS and Windows are trademarks of the MicroSoft Corporation.

27. UNIX is a trademark of AT&T Bell Laboratories and X–Windows is a trademark of MIT.

A final question that must be addressed in the definition of the architecture is its relationship to various existing workstation architectures. The two main architectures to be considered are the Unix–based stations and the PC–based stations. The Macintosh architecture has strong claims for consideration, but certainly runs third to the others. Interfacing between workstations and the multimedia architecture is principally in the areas of the display screen, control of the multimedia components and access to files. At a minimum, interfacing through X–windows and/or MS–Windows, via a simple RPC mechanism and via ethernet, will be required.

11.10 Mapping the Architecture onto Transputer Technology

T9000 transputers, DS–links and C104 routers are well–suited for the construction of low–cost ATM networks – detailed technical analysis to support this claim is presented in chapter 10. On top of this, INMOS have defined a board technology for the construction of modules. This technology defines a board format called the H–TRAM for small boards that plug into motherboards. Thus, if most of the multi–media components are built as H– TRAMs, they could be used with different motherboards to fit a variety of situations. Motherboards dealing with switching and interfacing functions are likely to be built for all the popular bus standards.

For communication and switching between components within a station, T9000 technology provides the necessary means of integration directly – without further development. ATM cells can be conveyed directly over DS–links, routed through a small C104 network (one chip will generally be sufficient).

The use of transputer parts between stations in the local ATM regime and the interfacing to wide area ATM will require the development of specialized chips. For the local area regime, a part is required that will allow INMOS links to be carried over distances of up to a few hundred metres. This part must also provide guaranteed immunity of the component at one end from any type of failure of the component at the other end. This isolation is necessary because the different stations in the local area belong to different people and may be powered up or down (or reinitialized) independently of each other and of the switching and communication components.

To interface to the wide area, a part suitable for interfacing a T9000 processor to a synchronous link running at up to 155 Mbps is required. However, this is a peak speed and represents the loading of a multiplex of many user activities. It is therefore possible to distribute it immediately onto a number of DS–links in all but the most pathological congestion situations, where higher level recovery can be expected to take place. The initial 155 Mbps serial link interfacing requires moderately fast hardware, but is well within the capabilities of available components.

Some preliminary investigation of these requirements has been made and it is felt that both the local area and the wide area problems can be solved by an adaptor constructed using electronically reconfigurable programmed logic arrays rather than custom designed chips. However, the T9000 link engine is expected to be available as a semi–custom library component, allowing the creation of multisourced low–cost components as the market grows.

REFERENCES

[1] CCITT Recommendation G.711: Pulse Code Modulation (PCM) of Voice FRequencies.

[2] CCITT Recommendation G.721: 32kbit/s Adaptive Differential Pulse Code Modulation (ADPCM).

[3] CCITT Recommendation G.722: 7kHz Audio Coding within 64kbit/s.

[4] CCITT Recommendation G.725: System Aspects of the Use of the 7kHz Audio Codec within 64kbit/s.

[5] ISO/IEC 10918: Information Technology – Digital Compression and Coding of Continuous Tone Still Images (JPEG).

[6] Wallace, G.K., "The JPEG Still Picture Compression Standard", CACM, vol 34, pp. 30–44, April 1991.

[7] ISO/IEC 11172: Information Technology – Coding of Moving Pictures and Associated Audio for Digital Storage Media (MPEG).

[8] Le Gall, D., "MPEG: A Video Compression Standard for Multimedia Applications", CACM, vol 34, pp. 46–58, April 1991.

[9] CCITT Recommendation H.261: Video Codec for Audiovisual Services at p*64k bit/s.

[10] Liou, M., "Overview of the p*64 Kbit/s Video Coding Standard", CACM, vol 34, pp. 59–63, April 1991.

[11] Ripley, G.D., "DVI – a Digital Multimedia Technology", CACM, vol 32, pp. 811–822, July 1989.

[12] Ross, F.E., "An Overview of FDDI: The Fibre Distributed Data Interface", IEEE J. on Selec. Areas in Commun., vol 7, pp. 1043–51, Sept 1989.

[13] ISO/IEC 10746: Basic Reference Model of Open Distributed Processing, Part 2: Descriptive Model and Part 3: Prescriptive Model.

[14] Hayter, M.D., and McAuley "The Desk Area Network" Operating Systems Review vol 25, no. 4, October 1991

Appendices

Appendix A New link cable connector

A major part of any connection standard is the choice of connector. The connectors mentioned in the section on standards all have major benefits, but no connector combines these benefits. The requirements listed below have been collated from transputer users.

- Ten pins are needed per DS-Link[28]. A connector carrying more than one link should carry two, four, or eight links, with the same pinout and PCB layout for each link;
- The connector should be latched, mechanically sound and robust, but ergonomic so that the end-user finds it easy to plug and unplug;
- The connector should be EMC screened for FCC/VDE/EEC regulations; ideally this should include unused connectors which do not have cables plugged into them;
- It should be able to handle 100 MBit/s signals without introducing serious discontinuities in the transmission line impedance;
- It should be dense enough to allow a reasonable number of separate link connectors, ideally up to ten in the height of a PS2 adaptor or four in the 28mm pitch of an HTRAM;
- Cable connections should be IDC, even from round cable;
- Any mechanical stress should be taken by the mechanical panels and mounting brackets, rather than by the PCB;
- It should be Hard Metric;
- Ideally, versions should be available in the same mechanical dimensions which house a pair of coax or optical fibre connections;
- Reliability is, as always, more important than cost, but the connector should be reasonably low cost and available worldwide.

Several existing connectors come close to meeting these requirements in one or other respect. The latches used in the LEMO cable connectors and SC optical connectors are highly ergonomic and robust. The lanyard latch on some of the LEMO connectors is possibly even better for a high density connector. The modularity, metric dimensions, and high density of the METRAL family from DuPont come close to meeting some of the requirements. There are a number of good cable connectors to fit backplanes, one of the closest to the requirements being the Fujitsu FCN-9505/9506 which combines modularity, robustness and good screening.

The new connector pulls together the best features of these connectors.

This 10-way modular I/O connector system has been designed by AMP, Fujitsu, and Harting, in cooperation with INMOS/SGS-THOMSON. Pins are on 2mm pitch to give a height small enough to fit the mounting brackets of personal computer cards, and connector pitch is 6mm.

The resulting connector: is Hard Metric, in line with IEC 917; is screened, to aid compliance with EMC regulations; has a leading 0V pin for reliable 'hot-swap'; has ten pins for buffered differential DS-Links, together with pins for remote power; is exceptionally dense, with two to five times as many connectors in a given panel length compared with existing connectors; and fits all the board standards such as PC, VME, SBus as well as those based on IEC 917. A particular benefit of the connector is that it allows equipments to benefit from a large number of ports, in the same way as DS-Links make it possible to build a routing-switch-chip with a large number of ports.

28. Two differentially–buffered data/strobe pairs (8 pins), one leading ground pin, and power for remote devices.

INMOS have built the connector into prototype PCBs for the T9000, and presented the work on the connector (together with other aspects of proposed standards for DS-Links) to ESPRIT partners and to several IEEE and ANSI standards working groups.

There is now full agreement between the connector manufacturers and INMOS on all aspects of intermatability of the connector, with minor changes having been agreed as a result of building and using the prototypes. The connector's electrical and mechanical robustness, its density, modularity and ergonomics, are widely applicable to electronics which becomes ever smaller.

Without the new connector, standards are still possible. For example office equipment such as terminals, laser printers, disks, and fax machines, each of which might use from two to four of the connectors, could use one type of connector; and computers, which might use many more connectors, use a different type. But there are obvious advantages in using the same connector for all the equipments. In some respects, the links would become a 100 MBit/s RS232, with autobaud and a simple packet routing protocol built in.

The new connector is not limited, however, to use with transputer links. There are many other interfaces which use point-to-point connections, and there is a huge number of 9-way D connectors installed around the world. As electronic equipment gets smaller, connectors begin to dominate the size of the equipment. Much work has gone into increasing the density of the connectors, but usually with a view to having more ways in the same space. This proposal uses these improvements in density to fit the same small number of ways into a smaller space.

Although the new connector has been derived from the needs for transputer links, it appears therefore that such a connector would meet the generic needs of the computer and electronics industries.

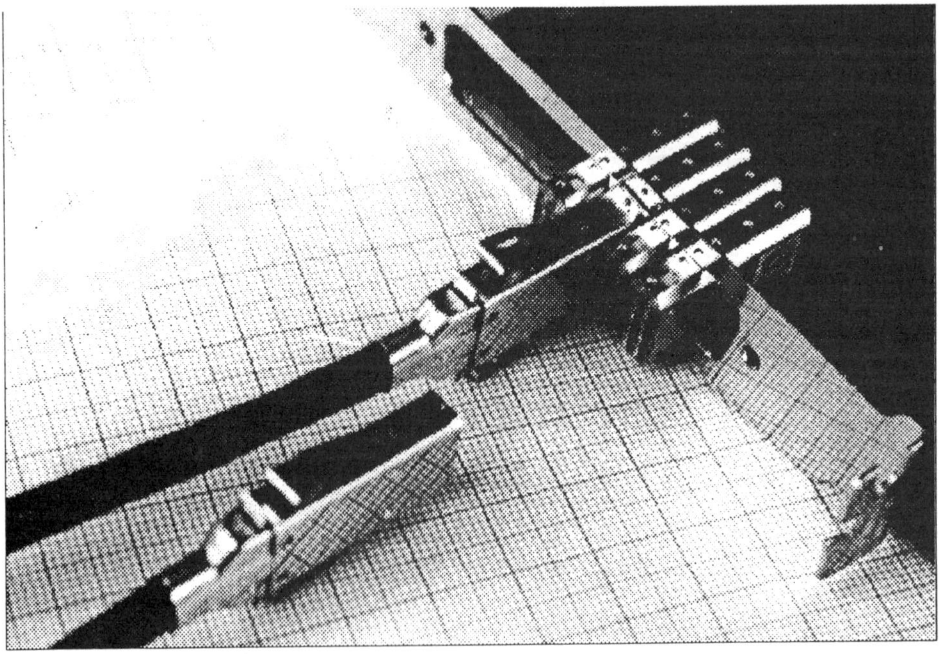

Figure A.1 The link new connector

Appendix B Link waveforms

A few example 'scope traces are shown of the waveforms seen with different lengths of connection and with different forms of buffering. The waveforms on this page are from simulated link signals: figure B.1 shows isolated 5ns pulses, with less than 1.5ns distortion resulting from the driver, receiver, and 10m of 30 AWG cable; figure B.2 shows waveforms from simulated link signals before and after transmission through 41 series buffers, the circuitry described in HP's Application Bulletin 78, and 100m of fibre (waveforms are identical when using Honeywell optical components).

The figures B.3 and B.4 on the next page show actual link waveforms, which were correctly received through the 41 series driver and receiver and 30m of cable.

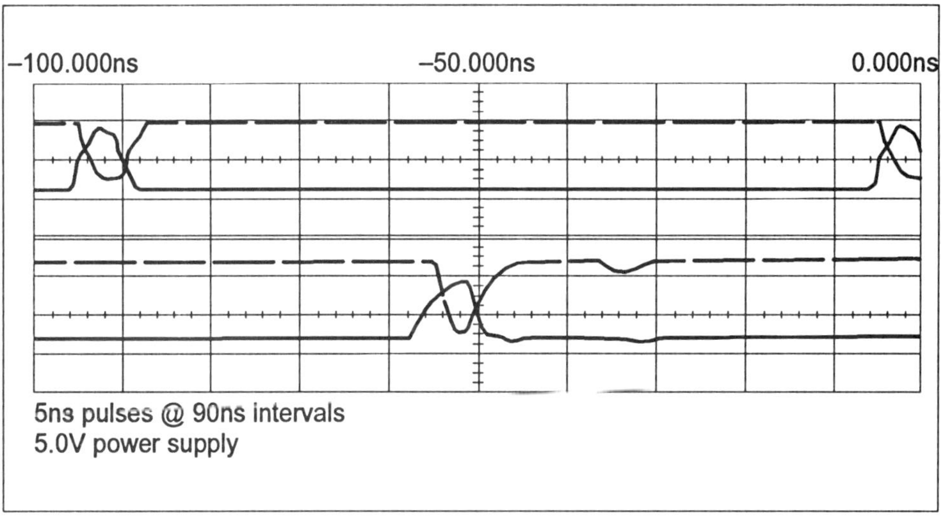

Figure B.1 Isolated 5ns pulses, AT & T 41M series, 10m×30AWG

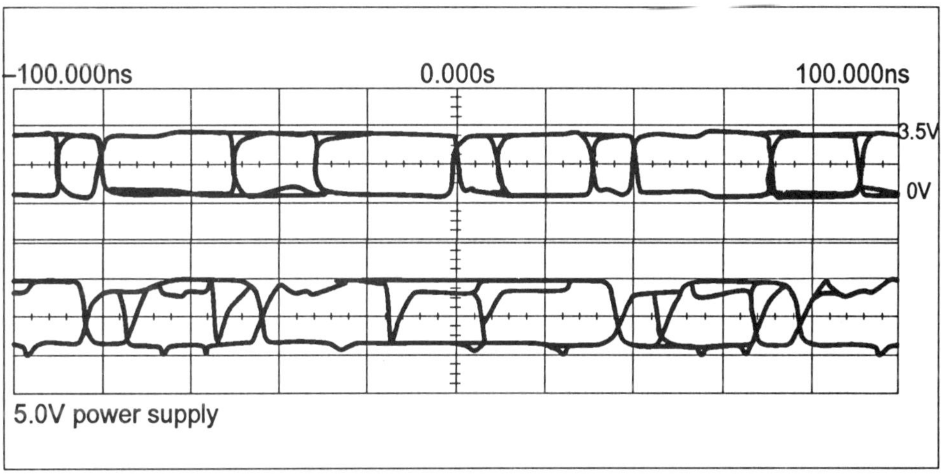

Figure B.2 HP1414 LED, 2416 receiver, 100m of 62.5μ fibre

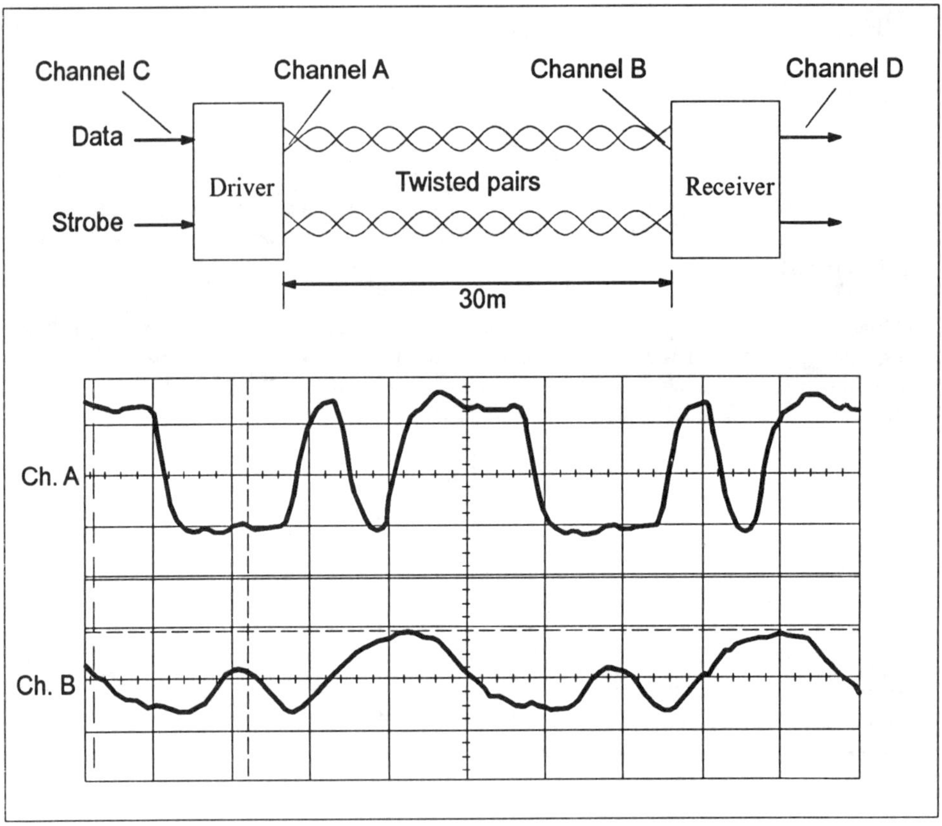

Figure B.3 DS-Link idle pattern, AT & T 41 series buffers, showing attenuation of differential pseudo ECL signal

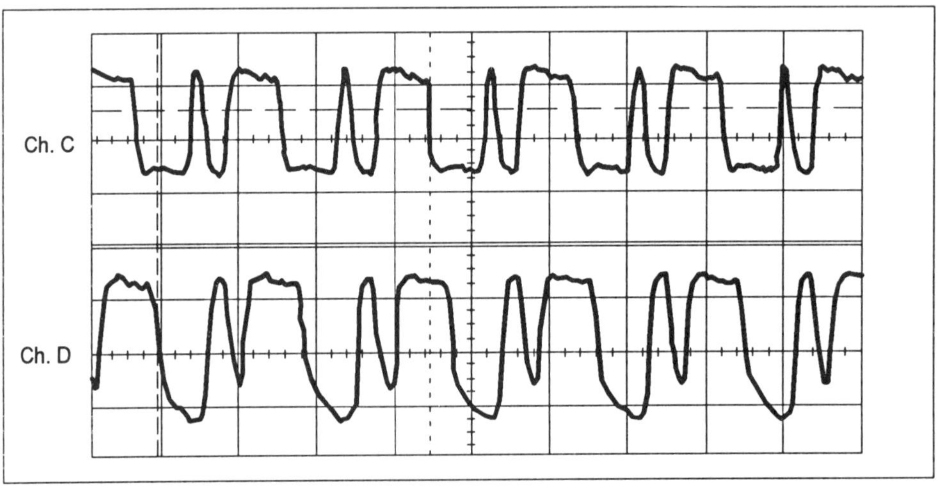

Figure B.4 TTL signals corresponding to figure B.3

Appendix C DS–Link Electrical specification

The DS–Link is designed for point to point communication which may be on a single pcb, board to board or box to box. Since this implies that transmission line problems will be present, the electrical level has been designed as a transmission line system. In order to reduce the power required for each link (enabling the use of many links) source only termination is used. The choice of impedance level (nom. 100 Ω)was made such that it is straight–forward to make these transmission lines with standard pcb materials.

The DS–Link connection at the electrical level usually comprises three parts: Link output driver, transmission line and link input pad (see figure 1). These parts are duplicated to provide the Data and Strobe wires for the DS–Link. The return connection is made from a similar pair of connections, thus there are four wires in all, two in each direction. The output driver has a controlled output impedance to reduce reflection problems. The transmission line is provided by pcb, coax or other suitable controlled impedance interconnect. The input pad is designed as a standard TTL input and has no internal termination.

Link Output pad

Since this system is effectively a driver driving an open circuit transmission line, careful consideration must be made to damp reflections from the load. This is catered for by providing an output driver which is designed such that reflections from it do not adversely affect the voltage received at the receiving end of the transmission line. To achieve this the driver has a controlled output impedance even when switching. Due to processing variations an exactly terminated line is not possible and nominal termination values other than 100 ohms have been used to ensure the receiving input does not receive spurious data or glitches. Since TTL thresholds are not balanced with respect to the power supplies, the pulling high output impedance is in fact different from the pulling low output impedance.

Output driver parameters

The following list of parameters covers the full range of processing, temperature and supply voltage encountered by a DS Link. Vdd may have the range 4.5 to 5.5V , Tj (junction temperature) in the range 0 to 100 degrees C. **Note that they apply to the implementation of the DS–Link current when this book went to press; for information relating to a specific product, the appropriate datasheet should be consulted.**

Parameter	Min	Max	units	Notes
fmax maximum operating data rate (as part of a DS Link)	100		Mbits/s	**1**
tr output rise time	2.5	6	ns	**1,2,4,6**
tf output fall time	2.5	6	ns	**1,2,4,6**
tph output high time for a nominal 20ns bit period (1.5v threshold)	15.8	24.2	ns	**1,2,4,5,6**
tpl output low time for a nominal 20ns bit period (1.5v threshold)	15.8	24.2	ns	**1,2,4,5,6**
Voh Io= 1ma	Vdd–0.4	Vdd	Volts	**3**
Vol Io=–1ma	0	0.4	Volts	**3**
Rl Output impedance, output driving low Vo=1volt	63	104	Ohms	**3**
Rh Output impedance, output driving high Vo=Vdd–1volt	110	247	Ohms	**3**

Note 1. Using the test circuit shown in figure C.1
Note 2. Measured at point **B** on the test circuit (figure C.1)
Note 3. Measured directly (without test circuit)
Note 4. Sample tested and/or characterised only
Note 5. Allowance made for a ground difference of up to 0.4 Volt between transmitting and receiving devices.
Note 6. See figure C.2

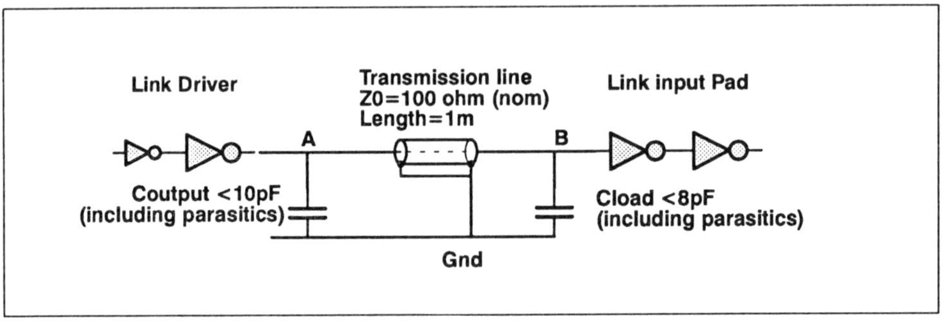

Figure C.1 Test Circuit

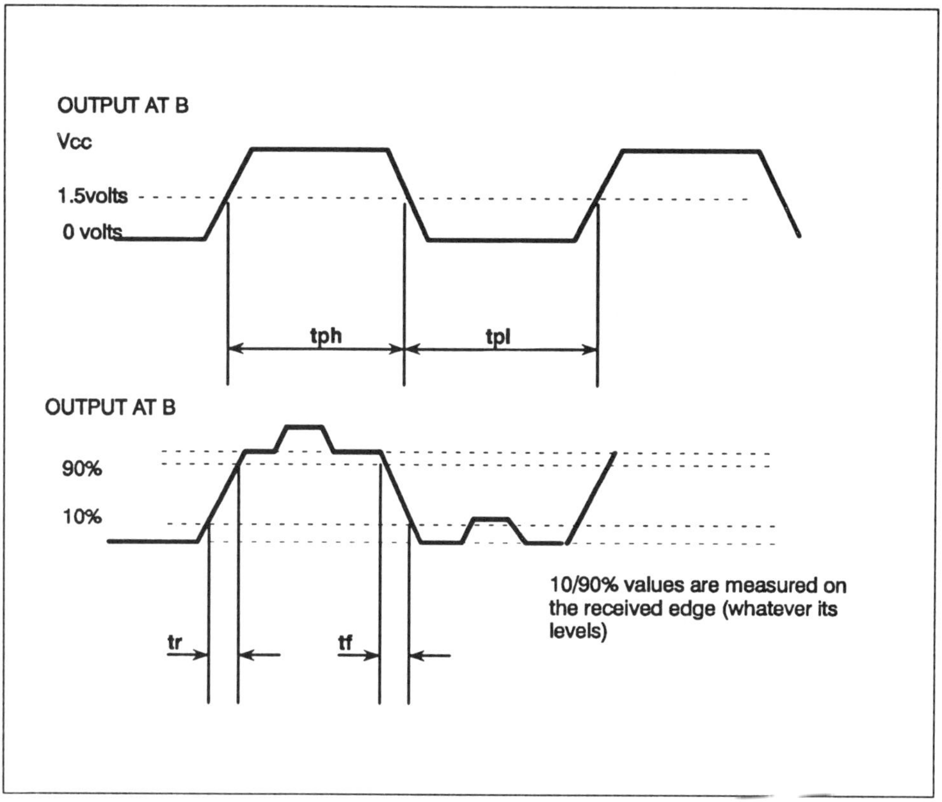

Figure C.2 DS–Link Timing

Transmission line requirements

Careful consideration must be made when connecting link output drivers to their corresponding receivers. For distances of greater than 20cm the link line must be considered as a transmission line. Discontinuities or variations in characteristics impedance should be kept to a minimum. The transmission line may be made on pcbs but care must be taken to provide a good ground or power plane beneath the link track and crosstalk should be minimised with other tracks (including between data and strobe lines of the same link). This can be helped by placing grounded tracks either side of the link track, as described earlier. The longest length of line achievable will depend on the materials used for interconnect and the grounding arrangements. **Note that they apply to the implementation of the DS–Link current when this book went to press; for information relating to a specific product, the appropriate datasheet should be consulted.**

Recommendation	Min	Max	units
Zo Characteristic impedance	90	110	ohms
tskew difference in transmission line propagation delay between data and strobe lines for DS–Link operating at 100 MBit/s	–4	4	ns

Link Input Pad

The link input pad is a standard TTL compatible CMOS input pad. Care should be taken not to introduce too much capacitance on the link line near the receiving input buffer. **Note that they apply to the implementation of the DS–Link current when this book went to press; for information relating to a specific product, the appropriate datasheet should be consulted.**

Parameter	Min	Max	units	Notes
fmax maximum operating data rate (as part of a DS Link)	100		Mbits/s	
Vih Input high voltage	2.0	Vdd+0.5	Volts	
Vil Input low voltage	–2	0.8	Volts	1
Iih input leakage current, Vin=2.0volts	–10	10	uA	
Iil input leakage current, Vin= 0 to Vdd volts	–10	10	uA	
Cin Input capacitance measured at 1MHz		7	pF	2

Note 1. Input voltages of less than –0.5 volts should only be transient in nature.
Note 2. Sample tested

Appendix D An Equivalent circuit for DS–Link Output Pads

The following preliminary equivalent circuit may be used to simulate the output from DS–Link pad drivers found on the IMS T9000, C100, and C104 devices. It has been done in such a manner that any circuit simulator (provided it can model inductors) will be capable of modelling the link pad driver, with no reliance on any specific device models.

The circuit (figure D.1) should be constructed from idealised components with the parameters listed below. For simulation time reasons it may be preferable to add a small capacitance (e.g. 100f) between the MOS device drains and their respective supply. In addition it is more realistic to add a supply–to–supply capacitance for the IC which will depend on which chip the DS–Link is on. This can be 1uF for a T9000 to only a few 100pF for a C100. The waveforms (figure D.2) can be straight line representations (e.g. SPICE Piecewise Linear), bearing in mind 10/90% times are quoted.

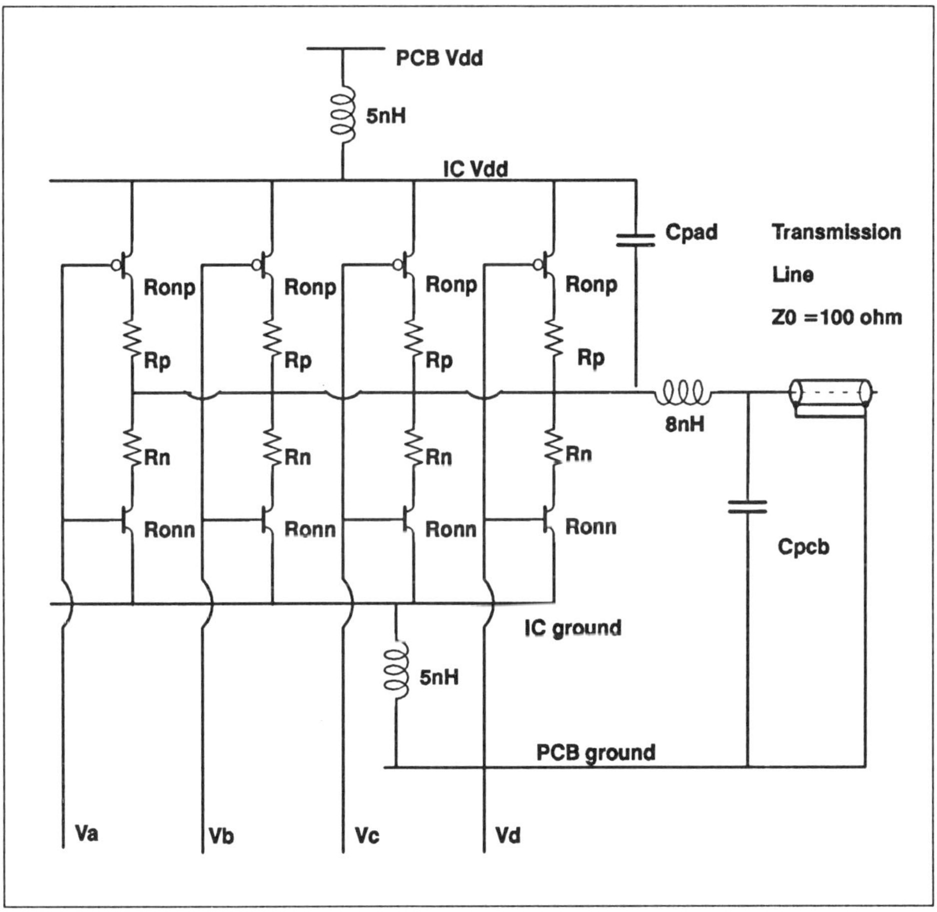

Figure D.1 Equivalent Circuit

Key parameters

The following list of parameters covers the full range of processing, temperature and supply voltage encountered by a DS–Link. Vdd may have the range 4.5 to 5.5V. **Note that these parameters apply to the first implementation of the DS–Link and may change subsequently.**

Parameter	Min	Max	units
Ronp, Vds=–1Volt	106	481	Ohms
Ronn, Vds=1Volt	25	82	Ohms
Rp	332	508	Ohms
Rn	227	333	Ohms
tpd, rising and falling transitions	0.66	2.0	ns
tf, 10/90% of Vdd Va,Vb,Vc,Vd	1.2	2.3	ns
tr, 10/90% of Vdd, Va,Vb,Vc,Vd	1.5	2.8	ns
Cpad	0.5	0.5	pF
Cpcb, any interconnect before transmission line.	2.0	As board layout dictates	pF

In SPICE simulations the following model may be used for the transistors:

.model n nmos Level=1 vt0=0.7 kp=50u tox=40n
.model p pmos Level=1 vt0=0.7 kp=20u tox=40n

This leads to the following transistor sizes (at 27°C only):

Ronn(max) w=55u,l=1u
Ronn(min) w=175u, l=1u
Ronp(max) w=23u, l=1u
Ronp(min) w=102u, l=1u

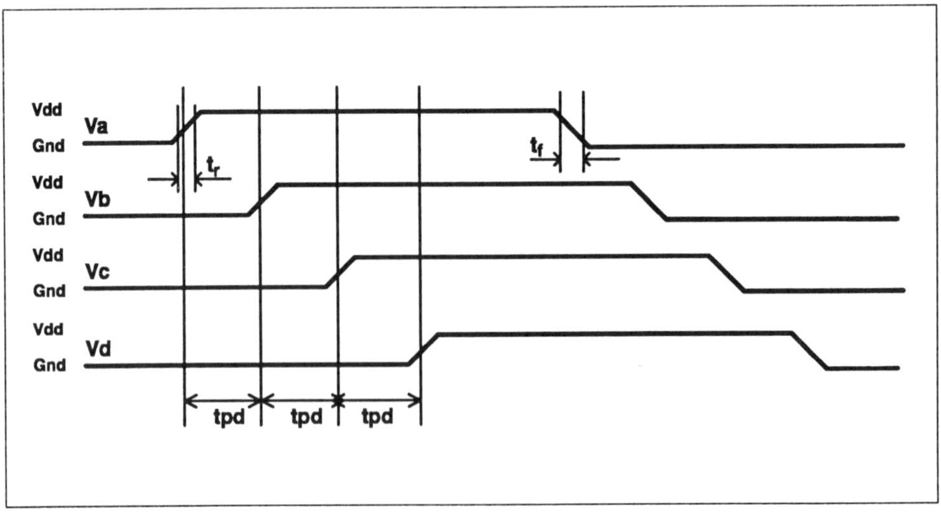

Figure D.2 Output Pad Timing